THE FATHERS
OF THE CHURCH

A NEW TRANSLATION

VOLUME 123

THE FATHERS
OF THE CHURCH

A NEW TRANSLATION

ANDREW OF CAESAREA

COMMENTARY ON THE APOCALYPSE

Translated by

EUGENIA SCARVELIS CONSTANTINOU

THE CATHOLIC UNIVERSITY OF AMERICA PRESS
Washington, D.C.

Copyright @ 2011
THE CATHOLIC UNIVERSITY OF AMERICA PRESS
All rights reserved

Printed in the United States of America

The paper used in this publication meets the minimum
requirements of the American National Standards for
Information Science—Permanence of Paper for Printed
Library Materials, ANSI z39.48-1984.

∞

Library of Congress Cataloging-in-Publication Data
Andrew, Archbishop of Caesarea.
[Hermeneia eis ten Apokalypsin. English]
Commentary on the Apocalypse / Andrew of Caesarea ;
translated by Eugenia Scarvelis Constantinou.
p. cm. — (The fathers of the church : a new translation ;
v. 123)
Includes bibliographical references and index.
ISBN 978-0-8132-0123-8 (cloth : alk. paper)   1. Bible.
N.T. Revelation—Commentaries.   I. Constantinou,
Eugenia Scarvelis.   II. Title.   III. Series.
BS2825.53.A5313 2012
228'.077—dc22
2011013228

This book is dedicated to the One Who Is
and Who Was and Who is to Come,

and to my beloved husband Constantine the Presbyter,
without whose love and support it would not
have been possible.

I know your works and toil and your patient endurance.

—Revelation 2.2

CONTENTS

Acknowledgments ix

Abbreviations xi

Select Bibliography xiii

INTRODUCTION

1. The Apocalypse Commentary of Andrew of Caesarea 3
2. Who was Andrew of Caesarea? 4
3. The Apocalypse in the Canon of the Ancient Church of the East 5
4. Andrew's Commentary Within the Trajectory of Apocalypse Commentaries 6
5. Who was Oikoumenios? 8
6. Andrew's Commentary as a Response to Oikoumenios 9
7. The Historical Milieu 11
8. The End is Not Near 12
9. Dating the Commentary 15
10. The Recipient of the Commentary 16
11. Structure and Style of the Commentary 18
12. Andrew's Orientation: Pastoral, Liturgical, and Sacramental 21
13. Training 24
14. Methodology 25
15. Technique 28
16. Sources 31
17. History and Prophecy 32
18. Andrew's Theology 34
19. Andrew's Eschatology 37
20. Translations of the Commentary and Its Influence on the New Testament Canon for the East 39
21. Andrew and the Apocalypse Text 41
22. The Lasting Legacy of Andrew's Commentary 42

COMMENTARY ON THE APOCALYPSE

Table of the Chapters 45

Prologue 51

Section One 55

Section Two   66
Section Three   73
Section Four   81
Section Five   90
Section Six   94
Section Seven   102
Section Eight   115
Section Nine   119
Section Ten   127
Section Eleven   134
Section Twelve   142
Section Thirteen   151
Section Fourteen   157
Section Fifteen   161
Section Sixteen   168
Section Seventeen   172
Section Eighteen   178
Section Nineteen   190
Section Twenty   200
Section Twenty-One   208
Section Twenty-Two   216
Section Twenty-Three   223
Section Twenty-Four   238
Epilogue   246

INDICES

General Index   249
Index of Holy Scripture   262

ACKNOWLEDGMENTS

The present translation originally formed a component of my doctoral dissertation at Université Laval, Quebec City, Canada, which I successfully defended in August of 2007. When I first proposed Andrew of Caesarea and his commentary on the Apocalypse as a dissertation topic many years ago, my director at Laval, Dr. Paul-Hubert Poirier, remarked that such a translation would make a suitable volume in the Fathers of the Church series. I wish to thank Prof. Poirier for his encouragement during the long process of my dissertation and for inspiring me with the thought that one day my translation might also stand as a volume within this distinguished series, a series which I myself have employed frequently over the years with great appreciation for the availability of high-quality patristic translations.

I also thank Dr. Thomas Schmidt of Université Laval, who reviewed the translation prior to my dissertation defense, for his helpful comments. Thank you to Dr. John Fendrick for his invaluable expertise and time-saving assistance with German texts. Many thanks also to the Catholic University of America Press for publishing this important commentary and especially to editor Carole Monica Burnett for her enthusiastic support, encouragement, expertise, and countless helpful suggestions, which improved the translation tremendously.

Finally, I wish to acknowledge and thank my family and friends for their support over the years, especially my son Christopher. The greatest appreciation is reserved for my husband and best friend, Rev. Dr. Costas Constantinou, for his love, encouragement, advice, and patience, not to mention his expertise and insights, which made the arduous process of translation considerably more bearable and successful.

ABBREVIATIONS

Cel. Hier.	Pseudo-Dionysios, *Celestial Hierarchy*
Chp.	Indicates chapter numbers as designated by Andrew of Caesarea
Chr. and Ant.	Hippolytus, *On Christ and Antichrist*
E.H.	Eusebius of Caesarea, *Ecclesiastical History*
Eccl. Hier.	Pseudo-Dionysios, *Ecclesiastical Hierarchy*
FOTC	Fathers of the Church Series, Catholic University of America Press
Heres.	Irenaeus, *Against Heresies*
LXX	Septuagint
NRSV	New Revised Standard Version
Oik.	Oikoumenios
Or.	Gregory the Theologian of Nazianzus, *Theological Oration*
Symp.	Methodios of Olympos, *Symposium*
Text	Indicates the page number in Josef Schmid's critical edition of Andrew of Caesarea's commentary
[27]	Square brackets enclosing a number indicate page numbers in Schmid's critical edition.
[ ]	Square brackets around text enclose those words bracketed in the critical text by Schmid to indicate questionable text from a critical or textual perspective.
< >	Angle brackets indicate words supplied by the translator for clarity.
( )	Parentheses indicate the Septuagint number of a Psalm.

SELECT BIBLIOGRAPHY

Castagno, Adele Monaci. "I Commenti de Ecumenio e di Andrea di Cesarea: Due letture divergenti dell'Apocalisse." *Memorie della Accademia delle scienze di Torino II, Classe di scienze, morali, storiche e filologiche* V. Fascicolo IV (1981): 303–424.

———. "Il Problema della datazione dei commenti al' Apocalisse di Ecumenio e di Andrea di Cesarea." *Atti della Accademia delle scienze di Torino II, Classe de scienze, morali, storiche e filologiche* 114 (1980): 224–46.

Chrestou, Panagiotis K. *Hellēnikē Patrologia.* 5 vols. Thessalonica: Kyromanos, 1992.

———. *Pateres kai Theologoi tou Christianismou.* 2 vols. Thessalonica: Tehnika Studio, 1971.

Constantinou, Eugenia Scarvelis. 2008. "Andrew of Caesarea and the Apocalypse in the Ancient Church of the East: Studies and Translation." Ph.D. diss., Université Laval.

Foss, Clive. "The Persians in Asia Minor at the End of Antiquity." *The English Historical Review* 96 (1975): 721–43.

Haldon, J. F. *Byzantium in the Seventh Century.* Rev. ed. Cambridge: Cambridge University Press, 1997.

Hill, Charles. *The Johannine Corpus in the Early Church.* New York: Oxford University Press, 2004.

Metzger, Bruce. *The Canon of the New Testament: Its Origin, Development and Significance.* Oxford: Clarendon Press, 1987.

———. *Textual Commentary on the Greek New Testament.* 3d ed. Stuttgart: Biblio-Druck, 1975.

Oikoumenios. *Oecumenii Commentarius in Apocalypsin.* Edited by Marc De Groote. Traditio Exegetica Graeca 8. Louvain: Peeters, 1999.

———. *The Complete Commentary of Oecumenius on the Apocalypse.* Edited by H[erman] C[harles] Hoskier. University of Michigan Humanistic Studies XXII. Ann Arbor: University of Michigan, 1928.

———. *Oecumenius. Commentary on the Apocalypse.* Translated by John N. Suggit. Fathers of the Church 112. Washington, DC: The Catholic University of America Press, 2006.

Schmid, Josef. *Studien Zur Geschichte des griechischen Apokalypse-Textes,* 3 parts. Part 1, *Der Apokalypse-Kommentar des Andreas von Kaisareia.* Part 2, *Die alten Stämme.* Part 3, *Historische Abteilung Ergänzungsband, Einleitung.* Munich: Karl Zink Verlag, 1955–56.

————. "Die griechischen Apokalypse-Kommentare." *Biblische Zeitschrift* 19 (1931): 228–54.

Stonehouse, Ned Bernard. *The Apocalypse in the Ancient Church.* Goes, Holland: Oosterbaan and Le Cointre, 1929.

Stratos, Andreas. *Byzantium in the Seventh Century.* 5 vols. Translated by Marc Ogilvie-Grant. Amsterdam: Adolf M. Hakkert, 1968.

Treadgold, Warren. *A History of Byzantine State and Society.* Palo Alto, CA: Stanford University Press, 1997.

INTRODUCTION

INTRODUCTION

1. The Apocalypse Commentary of Andrew of Caesarea

In the early seventh century, the most important Greek patristic commentary on the Book of Revelation (the Apocalypse) was produced by Andrew, Archbishop of Caesarea, Cappadocia.[1] Its impact on the use and understanding of the Apocalypse in Eastern Christianity would be enduring and unparalleled. Andrew's work not only became the standard Greek patristic commentary and significantly influenced nearly all subsequent Eastern Christian commentaries, but it directly led to the ultimate reception of Revelation into the New Testament canon of the Orthodox Church.

Immediately after its composition, Revelation was overwhelmingly accepted throughout the Church as genuine and apostolic, but it gradually fell under suspicion in the East due to questions that were raised about its apostolic authorship, as well as its strange imagery, and because of reactions against chiliasm and the Montanist movement. Support for Revelation had never seriously wavered in the Christian West. On the other hand, Eastern attitudes toward it had become largely nega-

---

1. The critical text and basis for the present translation was published by Josef Schmid, *Der Apokalypse-Kommentar des Andreas von Kaisareia*, vol. 1 of *Studien zur Geschichte des griechischen Apokalypse-Textes*, 3 parts (Munich: Karl Zink Verlag, 1955–56). The sections consist of the following: (1) *Der Apokalypse-Kommentar des Andreas von Kaisareia. Text* (1955), which I will refer to as "*Text,*" is the Greek critical text of the commentary; (2) *Die alten Stämme* (1955) is a study of the textual tradition of the Apocalypse itself and the relationship of the Andreas commentary to the textual transmission of the Apocalypse; and (3) *Historische Abteilung Ergänzungsband, Einleitung* (1956) is a review of the manuscript tradition of the commentary and the subsequent history and reception of the Andreas commentary.

tive by the fourth century. Revelation was never incorporated into the lectionary of the Christian East, and in many respects it remains peripheral in the East to this day. Eastern interest in Revelation was slowly renewed after the Moslem conquest and occupation of Byzantine territory, especially the fall of Constantinople in 1453. In particular, the Greek experience of four hundred years of persecution and martyrdom under Islamic rulers revived the early fascination with the Apocalypse and its message of patient endurance under persecution. The existence of an ancient, patristic commentary composed by Andrew, the respected Archbishop of Caesarea and a knowledgeable orthodox interpreter of the Scriptures, eventually resolved lingering doubts long held in the East regarding Revelation's apostolic authorship and canonical status.

2. *Who was Andrew of Caesarea?*

Nothing is known for certain of the life of Andrew except that he served as the Archbishop of Caesarea in the early seventh century and that he was a known expert in biblical interpretation. The episcopal see of Caesarea was under the jurisdiction of Constantinople, and yet Caesarea was so prominent and prestigious that it held a rank in ecclesiastical hierarchy which was second only to the see of Constantinople itself. Evidence from within the commentary indicates that Andrew was a skilled, trained, and well-educated interpreter of the Scriptures. The fact that he responded to exegetical questions and wrote his Apocalypse commentary after many individuals had requested it confirms that Andrew was a respected and well-known exegete. Unfortunately, except for his *Commentary on the Apocalypse* only a few fragments consisting of questions and answers[2] have survived.

2. These fragments were published by F. Diekamp in *Analecta Patristica* (Rome, 1938) 161–72, and came from a work entitled *Therapeutikē*. Andrew produced at least one other commentary, *Commentary On Daniel*, which is attributed to him in a catalogue of the Patriarchal Library of Constantinople, printed at Strasbourg in 1578, but that commentary is otherwise entirely unknown as no manuscript of it has been found. *Bibliotheca Sive Antiquitates Urbis Constantinopolitanae* (Argentorati, 1578), 22. See *Clavis Patrum Graecorum* 7478.

INTRODUCTION

3. The Apocalypse in the Canon of the
Ancient Church of the East

Interpreting the Apocalypse was a challenging task for Andrew since Revelation had been largely rejected in the East. Little exegetical tradition for the Apocalypse existed because of its questionable canonical status. Since most rejected it from the canon, no readings from Revelation were included in Greek lectionaries, and consequently Greek patristic sermons were not composed for it. Largely ignored, the book had not been systematically interpreted by anyone in the East until a commentary was produced by one of Andrew's contemporaries, Oikoumenios.[3]

The manner in which the Apocalypse of John eventually found a place in the New Testament canon is unusual. Generally speaking, those books which were universally accepted by the Church as genuine and apostolic from the beginning, such as the four Gospels and thirteen Epistles of Paul, never faced any serious challenges. Their place in the New Testament was secure. Other compositions of more uncertain apostolic authorship[4] remained under suspicion until they slowly received widespread approval. Only the Book of Revelation contrasted with this pattern. It was universally accepted as genuine and apostolic from the early second century and then slowly lost ground, first becoming somewhat suspect, then disputed, and finally overwhelmingly rejected by Eastern Christians because of its use by fringe groups and schismatic movements, such as chiliasts, Montanists, and monks who insisted on a literal interpretation of the book. Other Christians, such as the Alogoi, who opposed all writings attributed to John, included the Apocalypse in their fight against such movements and opinions. The two characteristics that had always been the hallmarks of Revelation, apostolicity and prophecy, were attacked

---

3. Oecumenius, *Commentary on the Apocalypse,* trans. John N. Suggit, Fathers of the Church 112 (Washington, DC: The Catholic University of America Press, 2006). The present work will employ the traditional Greek spelling, "Oikoumenios."

4. E.g., James, 2 Peter, 2 and 3 John, and Hebrews.

and undermined to such an extent that it nearly lost its place in the Orthodox canon of the New Testament forever. Interest in Revelation among Eastern Christians was revitalized during the crisis of the fall of Constantinople in 1453 and the subsequent subjugation of Greek Christians under Ottoman Turkish occupation. The number of Apocalypse manuscripts increased dramatically during this period, yet the renewed interest alone would not have resulted in the acceptance of Revelation into the New Testament canon of the East. The existence of an entirely orthodox and ancient patristic explanation that could illuminate its obscure meaning was essential to Revelation's unequivocal acceptance. The commentary of Andrew of Caesarea preserved the place of the Apocalypse in the canon of Eastern Christianity.

4. Andrew's Commentary Within the Trajectory of Apocalypse Commentaries

Among the major patristic figures, East or West, not a single one wrote a commentary on Revelation. Certainly, the difficulty in interpreting such a complex and highly symbolic text contributed to the challenge, along with the fact that Revelation was less useful for doctrinal purposes or catechesis than other New Testament books. Since it was never read as part of the lectionary in the East, it was rarely the subject of a sermon. Revelation was cited more frequently by writers in the earlier centuries of Christianity, primarily for the encouragement of Christians facing martyrdom, for use in treatises about the devil, to support chiliasm, and also to correct misuse or misinterpretations of the book.

Around the time that actual commentaries on Revelation began to appear in the West, the book was just beginning to fall out of favor in the East. The first Latin commentary was composed by Victorinus of Pettau, around the year 300. This commentary became very popular. Jerome extensively revised it later, removing the chiliastic portions (which by then had become discredited in the Church) and improving Victorinus's Latin. The revised version became one of two extremely influ-

ential Latin commentaries on Revelation. The other was a composition by a Donatist writer, Tyconius, whose interpretation,
even though he was considered a schismatic, was also widely
read and followed in the Catholic West. Tyconius's commentary
has not survived. It was quoted, however, by subsequent Latin
writers so extensively that his entire work has been recovered.[5]
The two commentaries of Tyconius and Victorinus formed the
basis for virtually every Latin commentary on Revelation into
the second millennium. Yet Tyconius and Victorinus had abso-
lutely no influence on the Eastern interpretation of Revelation
since few people in the eastern parts of the Empire read Latin.

After the appearance of Victorinus's first Latin commentary,
another 300 years would pass before the East would produce
a commentary of its own in the Greek language. At the end
of the sixth century a commentary was composed by Oikoumenios, a non-Chalcedonian with a philosophical inclination.
His commentary was quickly followed by Andrew of Caesarea's
commentary, which became the standard patristic interpretation of the Apocalypse in the East.

Among the books of the New Testament, Revelation is
unique not only in its early acceptance followed by a rapid
decline in the East but also in the history of its manuscript
transmission. Only the Apocalypse was copied and preserved
in both ecclesiastical and non-ecclesiastical contexts and com-
pilations. Not only is a dual stream of transmission evidenced
in the manuscript tradition, but also a Greek/Latin duality of
interpretation. The two interpretive traditions developed and
co-existed independently of each other. The points of com-
monality between the Greek and Latin interpreters primarily
reflect oral traditions and written sources reaching back into
the centuries before any written commentary existed, although
agreements might also result from a common canon of Scripture and shared exegetical techniques. Educated men in the
West were expected to know Greek; however, the converse was
not the case. Greek ecclesiastical writers show no knowledge of

5. Kenneth B Steinhauser, *The Apocalypse Commentary of Tyconius: A History of
Its Reception and Influence* (Frankfurt am Main: Peter Lang, 1986), 2.

Latin nor felt any need to learn it because the great centers of theological learning were in the East. Latin Fathers such as Victorinus, Ambrose, and Jerome knew Greek, but no Greek commentary existed to influence Victorinus. Since he and subsequent western interpreters such as Tyconius wrote in Latin, they exercised no influence on the Greek interpretive tradition whatsoever. The result was two divergent streams of interpretation of the Apocalypse. Even though Andrew of Caesarea and Oikoumenios wrote much later than the earliest Latin commentators, they looked only to the Greek tradition to interpret the Apocalypse. They had no knowledge of the interpretations offered by the Latin exegetes who had preceded them. Oikoumenios's commentary, although it was first, was entirely eclipsed in importance and influence by Andrew of Caesarea, who shaped and preserved the Eastern ecclesiastical tradition of Apocalypse interpretation.

5. Who was Oikoumenios?

Virtually nothing is known about the author of the first Greek commentary on Revelation, Oikoumenios. His unusual name has led to a frequent misidentification of him as a sixth-century Bishop of Trikki, in Thessaly. In fact, another Oikoumenios, also an exegete, served as the Bishop of Trikki, but he lived in the tenth century. Oikoumenios, author of the Revelation commentary, has also been incorrectly co-identified with a man by the same name who was a philosopher and correspondent with Severus, the Miaphysite Bishop of Antioch, in the first quarter of the sixth century. The Oikoumenios who penned the first Greek Apocalypse commentary, however, tells us that he is writing more than five hundred years after John witnessed the Apocalypse.[6] This clearly places him at the end

---

6. "But what does he mean by adding *what must soon take place* since those things which were going to happen have not yet been fulfilled, although a very long time, more than five hundred years, has elapsed since this was said?" Oikoumenios 1.3.6, *Commentary on the Apocalypse*, trans. John N. Suggit, Fathers of the Church 112 (Washington, DC: The Catholic University of America Press, 2006), 22.

of the sixth century, far too late to have been the friend and correspondent of Severus, who died in 538.

Oikoumenios's commentary frames the theological context in which Andrew composed his commentary. It was also one of Andrew's most important motivating factors. Andrew's assessment that Oikoumenios had committed many theological errors and arrived at unacceptable exegetical conclusions led Andrew to compose his commentary in response to the growing influence of Oikoumenios as the author of the only Revelation commentary available in the Greek language.

For centuries, Andrew had been credited with composing the first Greek Apocalypse commentary because his commentary so surpassed Oikoumenios's in popularity and influence that the Oikoumenios commentary was almost entirely lost to history. The Oikoumenios commentary exists in its entirety in only one manuscript, which was discovered by F. Diekamp in 1901.[7] The discovery was extremely important. Andrew had cited Oikoumenios's opinions, but without naming him. After the discovery of the Oikoumenios commentary many of the existing interpretations mentioned by Andrew could at last be identified, and thus it was conclusively established that Oikoumenios's commentary had preceded that of Andrew. Secondly, since Oikoumenios remarked that he was writing more than five hundred years after John witnessed his vision, the Oikoumenios commentary provides the first parameter for dating Andrew's commentary.[8]

6. Andrew's Commentary as a Response to Oikoumenios

Three primary factors seem to have motivated the creation of Andrew's commentary. First, Andrew provided an orthodox, Chalcedonian commentary so that Greek readers would

7. F. Diekamp, "Mitteilungen über den neuaufgefundenen Kommentar des Oekumenius zur Apokalypse," *Sitzungberichte der Königlichen Preussischen Akademie der Wissenschaften* 43 (1901): 1046–56.

8. We also know that Oikoumenios believed that John wrote his Apocalypse during the reign of the Emperor Domitian. Oikoumenios, 1.21.1, 2.13.9, and 12.20.6; see FOTC 112:28, 47–48, and 203.

not be forced to resort to Oikoumenios's slightly Origenistic, non-Chalcedonian, and philosophically influenced interpretation. Secondly, Andrew wished to allay fears that the end of the world had arrived, while at the same time encouraging a proper attitude of spiritual vigilance. Finally, Andrew composed his commentary after it had been commissioned by someone known to us only as "Makarios."

An analysis of the Oikoumenios commentary reveals that its author was a non-Chalcedonian Christian who had some theological background, including a good working knowledge of the Bible, but no exegetical training. Oikoumenios evinces, rather, a philosophical and literary background. It is certainly peculiar that this first Greek commentary on Revelation was scarcely utilized and not frequently copied, especially compared to Andrew's commentary, which, though only a few years subsequent in time, so surpassed Oikoumenios in influence and popularity that Oikoumenios's work nearly disappeared entirely. Literary works that were perceived as useful and valuable were frequently copied while little-used works were less likely to be copied. Oikoumenios's commentary was very peculiar in style and methodology, and he arrived at some highly unorthodox conclusions. Subsequent Greek-speaking Christians must have viewed Oikoumenios's commentary as unacceptable, unsuitable, or at least less effective or less useful than Andrew's, since Oikoumenios's commentary only survived in one complete copy along with a few partial copies. The manuscript evidence conclusively demonstrates that Oikoumenios's commentary was considered less desirable.

Those characteristics in the Oikoumenios commentary which over the course of time may have led readers to regard the commentary as less desirable, were also likely to be among the factors which prompted Andrew's composition. Undoubtedly, Oikoumenios's conclusions certainly influenced the content of Andrew's commentary. Among the features which Andrew responds to are Oikoumenios's non-Chalcedonian and Origenistic theological statements as well as his philosophical and Hellenistic tone.

7. *The Historical Milieu*

Dramatic and tragic circumstances provide the historical backdrop for Andrew's important commentary. The early seventh century marks the close of Late Antiquity and the inception of the dark ages for Byzantium. Serious trouble commenced in the mid-sixth century when bubonic plague erupted during the reign of Justinian. Between the initial occurrence in 541 and the outbreak in 610, just prior to the composition of this commentary, the plague ravaged the Empire seven times. One-third of the population succumbed to its effects.

The plague significantly diminished the Empire's strength, wealth, and stability because of loss of manpower, loss of revenue, and the disruption of agricultural production and trade. This led to famine, which was aggravated by very severe winters in the early seventh century that hampered grain shipments. In 609 the sea at Constantinople even froze. Famine was exacerbated even further when the Persians mounted a fierce invasion of the eastern Roman Empire during the early seventh century. Rural folk abandoned their planting and harvesting and packed into the walled cities of the eastern Empire for protection, straining the already limited food supply. Adding to everyone's distress, a number of large earthquakes in Antioch, Constantinople, and other parts of the Empire destroyed buildings and took many lives in the late sixth and early seventh centuries. Earthquakes were always interpreted as a sign of God's disfavor.

The most unsettling and destructive development was the murder of the Emperor Maurice in 602 by an army officer, Phocas, who seized the throne and ruled for several years as a violent tyrant. Anarchy and upheaval spread to every city in the Empire, and civil war erupted between Phocas's supporters and those who opposed him. Eight years passed before another army officer, Heraclius, raised an army and recaptured Constantinople, defeating and killing Phocas. In the meantime, a large variety of nations and tribes, such as the Huns, Visigoths, Lombards, Avars, Bulgars, and Slavs, continued to threaten the Empire with assaults on the northern and western areas. But the greatest threat had historically come from Persia, a large and wealthy empire to the east with a significant and well organized army. Earlier Persian forays into eastern Roman territory had been in the form of quick raids, during which Persian forces caused some destruction, stole property, and occasionally captured and briefly held border cities in the area of the eastern Roman Empire east of the Euphrates River.

But in the early seventh century, the Persians took advantage of the political upheaval and civil war in the eastern Roman Empire to mount a total invasion, sparking a war that would last more than twenty years until 628. The Persians invaded on a huge scale with two armies that moved progressively westward and penetrated deep into the Empire. Areas that had not seen war in three centuries experienced complete devastation. In the eastern regions, all of the leading cities were besieged, conquered, plundered, and often entirely destroyed, including Antioch, Alexandria, Chalcedon, and Jerusalem as well as countless smaller cities such as Ephesus, Sardis, Pergamum, and Magnesia. Thousands of inhabitants who survived were captured and taken back to Persia as slaves. At one point, the Persians actually reached the other side of the Bosporus and were within sight of Constantinople before Heraclius put them to flight, chasing them back across the Euphrates and eventually completely defeating the Persians in 628.

8. The End is Not Near

Plague, famine, extreme weather, earthquakes, a violent civil war, and barbarian invasions had convinced many people that the end of the world was at hand and undoubtedly led to a renewed interest in apocalyptic writings. Andrew believed that the plagues and destruction described in the Apocalypse are events that will occur in the end times, but despite the unusual confluence of different calamities in his time, including the capture of his own city of Caesarea, Cappadocia, he remarkably came to the conclusion that the end was *not* near. Andrew's opinion is expressed in the prologue of the commentary: "How could anyone who is deprived of the prophetic spirit not appear bold by attempting <to explain> these things whose end is not in sight?"[9] He based his sober assessment entirely on his careful interpretation of Revelation.

A lesser exegete would have read the events of his own times into the pages of Revelation, but Andrew is systematic and objective in his analysis of the book. To read the events of one's time into the Scripture, rather than allowing the Scripture to speak for itself, is irresponsible and leads to erroneous conclusions. Furthermore, predictions or speculation about when the end of the world will arrive is not allowed for Christians, since, as Andrew remarked, it is something that we are "forbidden to seek."[10] Such a pursuit is useless since Christ confirmed that the time of the end cannot be known by us[11] and is not even known by the angels.[12]

In the prologue of the commentary, Andrew writes that all divine Scripture has three levels. The first is the literal or the historical level. Since Revelation is prophecy and Scripture always has a historical basis, the destruction described in Revelation must be actual and not an allegory. Therefore, in spite of the horrific tragedies experienced by the populace in Andrew's time, they do not compare with the global and catastrophic destruction described in Revelation after the opening of the sixth seal. Andrew believes that the earthquake described at the opening of the sixth seal (Rv 6.12) is a symbol of the shift between the current era and the beginning of the end-times. The end has clearly not arrived because after the sixth seal, Revelation describes the afflictions, destruction, and misery of "such a sort as we have never known."[13]

Andrew is remarkably calm and objective in his assessment of Revelation. The end of time is not near, but the end is al-

9. *Prologue, Text* 8, page 51. For the method of citing Andrew's text in this volume, see p. 53, n. 14.

10. *Prologue, Text* 10, page 53. This is in reference to certain statements by Christ, such as, "It is not for you to know" (Acts 1.7), and, "But of that day and hour no one knows, not even the angels of heaven, nor the Son, but the Father only" (Mt 24.36). Andrew's stance is in keeping with the ancient tradition.

11. "The hour" will not be known. (Mt 24.42, 44; 24.50.) It will come like a "thief in the night" (Mt 24.43; 1 Thes 5.2; 2 Pt 3.10).

12. *Chp.* 21, *Text* 86, page 112.

13. *Chp.* 18, *Text* 69, page 98.

ways near for each of us since we do not know the time of our death. The catastrophes that his generation had witnessed can be utilized for a spiritual purpose. Andrew avoids promoting anxiety and instead uses Revelation appropriately to encourage his congregation to persevere, reminding them that their hardships will not be long-lasting since earthly life is brief: "For this reason, death must be despised, since in a little while it grants 'the unfading crown of life.'"[14]

Commenting on the beatitude of Rv 1.3 ("Blessed is the one who reads and the ones who hear the words of the prophecy and the ones keeping the things which have been written in it. For the time is near"), Andrew remarks:

He blesses those who read and hear through the actions, "for the" present "time is near," through which it is possible to acquire the blessing, and to all the work is laid open. As the Lord says, "Work while it is day."[15] And elsewhere, "the time is near,"[16] the time of the distribution of prizes, on account of the brevity of the present life in comparison to the future.[17]

The end of one's own life is the end for which we ought to be concerned and prepared constantly. Andrew's conviction that the end of the world is not near lends a dispassionate quality to his analysis. His explanation calms fears and gives reassurance while affirming traditional Christian themes and values: for example, repentance, the need for reliance on God, detachment from worldly goods, and pursuit of virtue. Andrew's commentary also balanced a danger that he perceived might result from Oikoumenios's interpretation: spiritual laziness and indifference. Oikoumenios's commentary had allegorized Revelation's prophecies and largely explained them as metaphors for events in the life of Christ. If Revelation is describing past events, then its impact as prophecy of a genuine historical expectation and its usefulness to encourage spiritual vigilance are lost.

14. *Chp.* 4, *Text* 28, page 67.
15. Jn 9.4; i.e., show vigilance and perseverance.
16. Rv 1.3.
17. *Chp.* 1, *Text* 12–13, page 56.

9. Dating the Commentary

Most previous scholars have maintained that Andrew wrote prior to the sack of his own city of Caesarea in 609 since he makes no direct reference to it. But Andrew did witness the Persian invasion, and his commentary alludes to the traumatic events that he and countless others had experienced. Three references in the commentary to the "barbarians"[18] as well as other clues establish that Andrew had in fact witnessed the conquest of Caesarea. Another comment also hints that Andrew had experienced a series of traumatic historical events and disasters that place his commentary firmly in the early seventh century.[19] Internal evidence supports the conclusion that the commentary was composed in the context of the dramatic events of the first few years of the seventh century, including the Persian invasions and the sack of Andrew's own city.

The first parameter for dating Andrew's commentary was the date of Oikoumenios's composition, more than five hundred years after the vision of the Apocalypse was recorded, and the second parameter is the sack of Jerusalem by the Persians in 614. Andrew presents Jerusalem as under the control of "pious"

18. Twice Andrew refers to bloodshed by "barbarian" hands (*Chp.* 22, *Text* 90, page 115; *Chp.* 27 *Text* 103, page 125), and later Andrew refers to "the unspeakable misfortunes encircling us by barbarian hands" (*Chp.* 49, *Text* 169, page 172). An interesting and easily overlooked clue can also be found in Andrew's comments about the swiftness of the fall of Babylon in Rv 18.8. The biblical text reads: "So shall her plagues come in a single day, pestilence and mourning and famine, and she shall be burned with fire; for mighty is the Lord God who judges her." Andrew mentions how quickly evils and deaths of various kinds can take place after "enemies" take the city. But there are no "enemies" in the scenario presented in the text of Revelation: *God* destroys Babylon. Andrew's comments reflect his own recent experience: "<It is> in the course of the day itself in which these things prophesied will prevail over her. For after the enemies have taken control of the city, even one day is sufficient for all of the evils to be brought upon the defeated ones and various manners of death…" (*Chp.* 55, *Text* 196, page 192).

19. *Chp.* 16, *Text* 65–66, pages 94–95. Andrew quotes from a section of Eusebius's *Ecclesiastical History* 9.8, which describes famine, plague, an Armenian revolt, and casualties so numerous that there were not enough people to bury the dead. Andrew then remarks, "In our own generation we have known each of these happenings."

kings.[20] Arriving at a precise date for the composition of Andrew's commentary requires careful analysis of Andrew's comments and of the events surrounding the capture of his city. Caesarea, Cappadocia, was in fact taken twice by the Persians. It was first captured but not destroyed in 609/610. The Jewish population of the city opened the city gates and welcomed in the Persians. This act actually spared the city from destruction at that time. Most of the Christians had fled the city in advance of the Persian army. It was more likely that the bishop of a city would remain in his see than that he would flee, although we have examples of both in the history of this period.[21] That Andrew stayed behind in Caesarea is witnessed by his allusion to "bloodshed by barbarians" and being "encircled" by barbarians. The Persians remained for a while, probably leaving a few officers behind to hold the city, but the majority left to continue their progress westward. Later, while chased by the eastern Roman forces, the invaders, who were led by the Persian general Shahin, returned to Caesarea and held it for one year while the Roman army surrounded and besieged the city. Eventually the Persians escaped from Caesarea in 612, but they set it on fire before departing. The city was entirely destroyed. It is most likely that Andrew wrote his commentary in 611, during the interval between the first capture of the city and its final and complete destruction.

10. The Recipient of the Commentary

Although many others had asked Andrew to write a commentary on Revelation, it was most likely a request by the new Patriarch of Constantinople, Sergius I (who may be the indi-

---

20. *Chp.* 52, *Text* 178, page 179.

21. When the Persian general Shahrbaraz was marching toward Egypt in 616, John, the Patriarch of Alexandria, left for Constantinople; see Andreas Stratos, *Byzantium in the Seventh Century*, vol. 1 (of 5 vols.), trans. Marc Ogilvie-Grant (Amsterdam: Adolf M. Hakkert, 1968), 113. On the other hand, the Patriarch of Jerusalem, Zacharias, could have fled the Persian army but remained in the city. He was captured and taken to Persia as a slave; see *Chronicon Paschale*, trans. Michael Whitby and Mary Whitby, Translated Texts for Historians series, vol. 7 (Liverpool: Liverpool University Press, 1989), 156.

vidual addressed as *Makarie*—"O blessed one"—in the opening lines of the composition), that finally prompted Andrew to interpret the book.[22] Andrew concludes that the end of the world is *not* near, despite the desperate situation of the Empire. As a bishop, he was concerned about the spiritual and emotional state of his flock. A sense of despair and hopelessness had set in, which needed to be replaced by Christian hope and vigilance. Although no hint of concern for earthly matters or for the survival of the Empire is seen in Andrew's commentary, it was certainly a pressing concern for the Patriarch of Constantinople, Sergius I, who possibly commissioned the commentary. Over the course of his many years of tenure as Patriarch, Sergius I would emerge not only as a religious figure but also as a charismatic leader who motivated the populace to resist the various barbarian invasions bravely. Sergius not only bolstered the confidence of the Emperor Heraclius and repeatedly raised his morale in times of despair, but also made the entire Church treasury available to Heraclius for the funds needed to finance the military defense of the Empire.

Heraclius was absent from Constantinople for long periods of time during his campaigns against the Persians, leaving Sergius in charge in Constantinople to rally the people and to serve as regent for Heraclius's young son. Sergius was up to the task. With Heraclius and most of the army absent fighting the Persians in the East, the Avars and Slavs seized the opportunity to attack the capital, surrounding Constantinople and besieging it in 626. Sergius refused to allow the people to become demoralized, despite the fact that the Emperor and most of the army were far away. Sergius called upon divine protection and rallied the people with church services and spirited religious processions which he personally led, marching along the tops of the walls, singing hymns, carrying icons, and bearing relics of the Mother of God. Sergius was convinced that the end was

---

22. *Prologue, Text* 8, page 52. It is possible that Makarios, which is a proper name in Greek, could be the actual name of the individual who requested the commentary; however, since the word is in the vocative case, it is impossible to determine whether *Makarie* is being used as an actual name or as a title, "blessed one," or "Beatitude."

not near and succeeded in renewing the fighting spirit of the people in the Empire and inspiring their resistance.

Was Andrew's commentary responsible for Sergius's conviction that the end was not near, or did Sergius commission the commentary because he already held that opinion? We will never know, but, without a doubt, Andrew of Caesarea's commentary on the Apocalypse played a significant role in quelling apocalyptic expectations. The commentary offered the hope, reassurance, and encouragement for which people had hungered by providing a thoughtful, traditional, and spiritual analysis of Revelation. The commentary endured and continued to influence Eastern Christian eschatological attitudes long after the crisis facing the Empire had subsided. The commentary's effectiveness and usefulness are confirmed by the existence of numerous manuscript copies.

11. Structure and Style of the Commentary

The commentary opens with a prologue in which Andrew addresses the recipient of the commentary. He refers to the "task" which had been "assigned" to him by the recipient and briefly addresses some preliminary matters such as the structure of the commentary and some basic principles of exegesis. He cites a well established principle of patristic exegesis, namely, that Scripture contains three levels which correspond to the three parts of a human being: the literal or historical sense, which corresponds to the body; the moral sense, which corresponds to the soul; and the spiritual level, which corresponds to the spirit.[23] As a conclusion to the commentary, he offers an overview in the form of a summary of his conclusions.[24] Following this is an epilogue that was added by someone who may have been the final compiler of the commentary since the epilogue's author refers to creating a compilation from the rough drafts of the commentary.

The commentary is divided into twenty-four sections, for the twenty-four elders around the throne of God, and then fur-

23. Andrew of Caesarea *Prologue, Text* 8, page 52.
24. *Chp.* 72, *Text* 263–67, pages 242–45.

ther divided into three chapters per section, for the three parts of each elder: body, soul, and spirit. This creates seventy-two chapters, which are numbered sequentially.[25] Each chapter was also given a heading to inform the reader of the contents of that section.

Andrew's presentation is thoughtful, succinct, straightforward, and disciplined. He does not stray from his purpose or from the text under consideration to digress by making comments on unrelated matters, whether historical asides, doctrinal elaborations, or denunciations of heretics. His commentary manifests a very traditional patristic style and methodology, which certainly contributed to the commentary's popularity over the centuries.

Andrew deals with the text of Revelation in an extremely orderly manner, usually quoting one or two verses at a time, and then offering as many interpretations as he knows, as well as his own. He reports on and quotes, extensively at times, the opinions of known Church Fathers, such as Methodios, Irenaeus, and Pseudo-Dionysios (whom he calls "Dionysios the Great"), but he also reports anonymous oral traditions and the opinions of Oikoumenios, albeit without naming him. Because of his extensive use of all available sources, the commentary has been criticized as a mere "catena."[26] Andrew, however, offers too much of his own analysis and insights for the commentary to be so disparaged. Furthermore, insufficient exegetical tradition existed in the East to create a complete commentary that would be nothing more than a catena.

Andrew's habit of reporting a variety of interpretations, especially when a verse is controversial, is what led some to the notion that the commentary is basically a catena. But Andrew's inclusive style and flexibility is also consistent with his expressed view that Revelation contains more than one level of meaning. Andrew unhesitatingly presents more than one pos-

---

25. Andrew of Caesarea, *Prologue, Text* 10, page 53.

26. Adele Monaci Castagno, "I Commenti di Ecumenio e di Andrea di Cesarea: Due letture divergenti dell'Apocalisse," *Memorie dell'Accademia delle scienze di Torino II, Classe di scienze morali, storiche e filologiche* V, Fascicolo IV (1981): 303–424, 423.

sible interpretation for numerous passages in Revelation and does not feel compelled to choose one as the "correct" interpretation. He rarely rejects an opinion outright but reports it and allows it to stand.

Andrew's custom of offering the widest possible variety of existing opinions was not only generous but also invaluable since he succeeded in preserving what is probably the entire Greek exegetical tradition for the Apocalypse. His openness to other opinions is the mark of an interpreter with a broadminded attitude who lacks egoism and is confident enough in his own abilities and in the intelligence of the reader that he willingly conveys the alternatives. For example, five possible interpretations are provided for the four living beings of Rv 4.6–8,[27] four possibilities for the image of the sky rolled up like a scroll in Rv 6.14,[28] and five options for the symbolism of the feet of Christ in Rv 1.15.[29]

It is not always immediately evident which interpretation Andrew prefers, if he has a preference at all. He hints at his preferred interpretation with subtle signals such as, "This may be understood differently...,"[30] "either this or perhaps...,"[31] "more suitably...,"[32] "more correctly...,"[33] or "much more...."[34] Such a statement is followed by a presentation of his opinion with an explanation to show why his view is more suitable, although he never states in an overt or egotistical manner why his opinion is superior. Andrew generally presents his preference last, if indeed he prefers one opinion over another. For this reason, it is necessary to read all of the possible explanations that he presents before one can ascertain which opinion was Andrew's. A hasty reading of the commentary will result in a misunderstanding of his true opinion. This fact is best illustrated by an interpretation very early in the commentary when he comments upon Rv 1.4 ("Grace to you and peace from the One who is, and who was, and who is to come, and from the seven spirits which are before his throne"). Andrew is usually cited

27. *Chp.* 10, *Text* 51–52, pages 83–84.
28. *Chp.* 18, *Text* 70–71, page 99.
29. *Chp.* 2, *Text* 21, pages 61–62.
30. *Chp.* 1, *Text* 14, page 57.
31. *Chp.* 10, *Text* 49, page 82.
32. *Chp.* 10, *Text* 49, page 82.
33. *Chp.* 19, *Text* 78, page 106.
34. *Chp.* 19, *Text* 73, page 102.

as interpreting this statement to refer to the Trinity: the Father as the one who is and said to Moses "I am"; the Son as the Logos, who was in the beginning; and the Holy Spirit as the seven spirits. That, however, was the opinion of *Oikoumenios,* which Andrew reports first. In *Andrew's* opinion, this statement in that context refers to the Father *alone,* not to the entire Trinity, and he supports his interpretation with an extensive explanation.[35]

12. Andrew's Orientation: Pastoral, Liturgical, and Sacramental

Andrew's role as a pastor dominates his interpretation of Revelation. He decides to undertake the task of the commentary since doing so will serve as "a form of contempt for the present things, since they are transitory, and <for the purpose of> coveting the future things, since these remain."[36] But everyone can benefit from reading the Apocalypse, because it contributes "not a little to compunction."[37] It teaches that "death must be despised."[38] "The book is also worthy for reading by the faithful.... It guides those who read it to true life."[39] It is "holy and God-inspired," and "guides those who read it to a blessed end."[40]

The enigmatic quality of the book itself is beneficial and can serve to sharpen the intellect as "training for the quick-wittedness of the mind."[41] Andrew makes this observation in

35. This mistake is found in the two books that have included excerpts in English from Andrew's commentary: *Revelation,* ed. and trans. William Weinrich, Ancient Christian Commentary 12, ed. Thomas C. Oden (Downers Grove, IL: InterVarsity Press, 2005), 3; and Archbishop Averky Taushev, *Apocalypse,* trans. Seraphim Rose (Platina, CA: Valaam Society of America, 1985), 44. In fact, in that statement Andrew is reporting the opinion of Oikoumenios, with whom he disagrees. Andrew believes the particular statement can be applied *theologically* to each member of the Trinity individually, but in its specific context the statement in Rv 1.4 is made with respect to the Father alone. See *Chp.* 1, *Text* 13–16, pages 56–59, especially *Chp.* 1, *Text* 15, page 58, where he points to the subsequent reference "and to Jesus Christ" as proving that the earlier statement was made about the Father.

36. *Prologue, Text* 9, page 53.   37. *Prologue, Text* 11, page 54.
38. *Chp.* 4, *Text* 28, page 67.
39. *Chp.* 71, *Text* 258, pages 238–39.
40. *Chp.* 72, *Text* 263, page 242.   41. *Prologue, Text* 9, page 53.

the prologue and also when he interprets the names of the twelve tribes, which he explains are included "for the exercise of the mind by those who are quick-witted."[42] The precious gems describing the heavenly Jerusalem of Rv 21 likewise are symbols which "serve as training for those pondering enigmas of truth."[43] Such remarks indicate that Andrew expected the reader of the commentary to be actively engaged by contemplating the symbols and discovering the meaning of the text, rather than passively adopting Andrew's insights. Having presented two interpretations for the twenty-four elders around the throne of God (Rv 4.4), which he believes are less satisfactory than the explanation that he is about to offer, he pauses to allow the reader to ponder those explanations, stating simply: "Let the reader be tested."[44]

The commentary abundantly demonstrates Andrew's strong pastoral purpose and orientation. His tone is consistently affirming and encouraging, degenerating neither into threats of "hellfire and brimstone" nor into scolding or rebuke, even when the text of Revelation mentions the sufferings of sinners. He does not elaborate on future punishment nor tries to use the text in an inflammatory or manipulative manner. But with a subdued and gentle pastoral style, Andrew encourages repentance and personal reformation for all, including himself. Andrew indeed seeks to motivate the reader, but not by fear. Displaying a typical Eastern Christian attitude, he frequently emphasizes individual free will and self-determination: the ability to choose one's final destination in the next world by one's behavior in this life. Motivation for change should come as our response to the love of God, whom Andrew repeatedly describes as *philanthropos*, the One who Loves Humankind. Used as both a noun and an adjective, the term is employed no fewer than fourteen times and is the commentary's most dominant description of God. It is also used twice to refer to the loving attention of angels who imitate God in their care for hu-

---

42. *Chp.* 19, *Text* 81, page 109.
43. *Chp.* 67, *Text* 247, page 230.
44. *Chp.* 10, *Text* 49, page 82.

manity. Because God loves all, he desires that "all be saved and come to knowledge of the truth."[45]

A liturgical orientation is also noticeable in the commentary which contains many allusions and references designed to evoke in the reader a recollection of a well-known hymn, prayer, or ritual action. The Apocalypse already contains many liturgical references: an altar, prayers, hymns, incense, angels, and worship. Andrew's interpretation of such details is influenced by and arises out of their expression and manifestation in his daily life and ministerial capacity. Just as the biblical text shapes Church doctrine, prayers, hymns, and sacraments, as far as Andrew is concerned, only the Church itself can provide the proper context for interpreting the biblical text. Andrew is not a detached interpreter but a pastor whose liturgical life and experience contextualizes Revelation in a unique manner. Andrew concludes each of the commentary's twenty-four main sections with a Trinitarian doxology that is specifically liturgical in style and tone. Christ is mentioned first, ordinarily with a description that relates to the exhortation in the conclusion of that section, usually followed by "together with the Father" and a reference to the "Holy" or "All-holy" or "Life-giving" Spirit, always concluding in typical Eastern Christian fashion with, "now and ever and unto the ages of ages. Amen."

Andrew's sacramental orientation is most visible in contrast to the interpretation of Oikoumenios, who associates some images in Revelation with sacraments, but far fewer of them than Andrew does, and with less precision. For example, Andrew interprets the promise of "hidden manna" made to the church of Pergamum (Rv 2.17) as the Eucharist and connects it to the Bread of Life statements in John 6. "The 'Bread of Life' is 'the hidden manna,' the One who descended from heaven for us and has become edible."[46] By contrast, Oikoumenios simply states that the "hidden manna" signifies "spiritual and future blessings."[47] For Andrew, the woman wrapped in the sun

---

45. 1 Tm 2.4. *Chp.* 59, *Text* 211, page 203; *Chp.* 72, *Text* 267, page 245.
46. *Chp.* 5, *Text* 31, page 69.
47. Oik. 2.7.5, FOTC 112:41.

with the moon under her feet (Rv 12.1) represents the Church, which has baptism as its foundation. The moon had long been associated with water because of its effects upon the tides, and Andrew's interpretation of this entire section of Revelation repeatedly evokes baptismal connections.[48] Oikoumenios, on the other hand, associates the moon with the Law of Moses, which he believes is waning.[49] Andrew consistently links water images with the Holy Spirit and baptism, for example, in the description of Christ's voice "like the sound of many waters" (Rv 1.15b), the Lamb guiding the faithful "to springs of waters of life" (Rv 7.17),[50] and the river "flowing from the throne of God and of the Lamb" (Rv 22.1).[51]

Not unexpectedly, Andrew associates the seal on the foreheads of the faithful (Rv 7.3) with the sacrament of Chrismation (or "Confirmation" in the West), a sacramental connection, which, again, Oikoumenios does not make. Later, locusts are instructed not to harm those who are sealed (Rv 9.1–4), whom Andrew identifies as those who had been "sealed with the divine seal on their foreheads and shine round about with the enlightenment of the Life-giving Cross through the Holy Spirit."[52]

13. Training

Andrew's commentary abounds with clues to his theological and exegetical training. Despite his self-expressed doubts and early protestations of inadequacy, Andrew does not disappoint. He knows and uses traditional exegetical techniques and technical terminology, and, most importantly, he applies them correctly. He is familiar with the Eastern tradition of Apocalypse interpretation, such as it was. For example, he articulates the long-standing belief that the seven churches of Asia represent all churches everywhere,[53] that the twenty-four elders (Rv 4) represent all the godly people of the Old and the New Testaments, and that the four living beings (Rv 4) symbolize the four evangelists. But he also indicates an awareness of traditional

---

48. *Chp.* 33, *Text* 121–23, pages 137–38.   49. Oik. 6.19.3, FOTC 112:108.
50. *Chp.* 20, *Text* 85, page 111.   51. *Chp.* 68, *Text* 250, page 232.
52. *Chp.* 26, *Text* 97, page 121.   53. *Chp.* 1, *Text* 13, page 56.

patristic interpretations of problematic scriptural passages in other parts of the New Testament, such as how differences between the genealogies in Matthew and Luke were explained in the patristic tradition.[54] His reference to Jn 7.38 demonstrates that he knew the problem related to this passage and that it was solved in antiquity by proper punctuation.[55] He also knows the traditional interpretations of place names and personal names, and the etymology of certain Hebrew words, such as "Satan"[56] and "amen."[57]

Andrew is familiar with textual variations, such as Rv 3.7, "These things says the Holy One, the True One, who has the key of David." A common variant is "key of Hades."[58] Angels are described as dressed in pure "linen" in Rv 15.6, but some manuscripts read "stone."[59] In each case, Andrew offers interpretations for both possible readings. Andrew has an extensive familiarity with Scripture and uses it effectively. Biblical quotations are precise and purposeful, not copiously strung together in a proof-text manner. His Old Testament quotations number approximately 180, and New Testament quotations appear approximately 325 times.[60] The commentary also includes countless allusions to biblical persons, events, and concepts.

14. Methodology

Andrew is conscious of his methodology and reveals his good training by commencing the commentary with an explanation of his underlying presumption that Scripture has three levels. "Since there are three parts to a human being, all divinely inspired Scripture has been endowed with three parts by divine grace."[61] As Andrew continues his exposition, it is evi-

---

54. *Chp.* 10, *Text* 51, pages 83–84.
55. See *Chp.* 20, *Text* 85, page 111.
56. *Chp.* 34, *Text* 130, page 143.
57. *Chp.* 1, *Text* 17, page 59.
58. *Chp.* 8, *Text* 38, page 75.
59. *Chp.* 45, *Text* 162, page 166.
60. This is a conservative estimate. It is difficult to decide what constitutes a true "quotation," since frequently Andrew only quotes a word or two, while making an obvious allusion to a scriptural text. These have not been counted as quotations.
61. *Prologue, Text* 8–9, page 52.

dent that he considers it the reader's responsibility to discover these levels of meaning and assumes that one's ability to do so directly correlates with one's level of spirituality.

The lowest level of meaning is *historia,* or the literal sense. This is represented by the body and can be an actual historical event or simply the text understood in a literal fashion, "like the letter and like history established according to sense perception."[62] The literal sense by itself is insufficient even as a recollection of history. Furthermore, since it corresponds to the body, to confine one's understanding to the lowest level is to remain on the level of the flesh and to ignore the moral and spiritual message of the Scripture. Nonetheless, Andrew does not reject the literal sense but often insists upon its reality in opposition to Oikoumenios's allegorization of Revelation's prophecies. Although the spiritual sense is the highest level, for the prophecies of Revelation to be true and genuine, the literal sense is essential as well. Andrew recognizes that Revelation had an original, historical context. Certain events had already taken place in fulfillment of John's prophecy, other events may have taken place since the time of John, and still others have yet to occur. He notes that "some of the predictions...are to come to pass immediately thereafter,"[63] and that part of his task is to "adapt the prophecies to the time after this vision."[64]

Andrew is well aware that parts of Revelation lend themselves to a literal interpretation (such as the letters to the churches in Rv 2–3 and the destruction occurring after the seven trumpets in Rv 8.7–9.21), and that other passages require a spiritual interpretation of the symbols (such as the opening vision of Christ in Rv 1, the vision of heaven with the twenty-four elders in Rv 4, and the woman wrapped in the sun in Rv 12). In connection with the literal-historical sense, Andrew refers to typology as a "foreshadowing that anticipates the truth."[65] His intentional linking of typology with history indicates that Andrew does not regard typology as pure allegory, but as rooted in a historical event which has a future fulfillment. He recognizes typology in Daniel, who "prophesied about Antiochus as being

62. *Prologue, Text* 8, page 52.   63. *Chp.* 1, *Text* 11, page 55.
64. *Prologue, Text* 7, page 51.   65. *Prologue, Text* 9, page 52.

a type of the coming of the Antichrist."[66] Since, however, typology was usually employed in connection with Old Testament interpretation, its use in Andrew's exposition of the Apocalypse is limited.

The second level of meaning is *tropology,* also known as the "figurative" or "moral" sense, and it is perceived by readers who function above the lowest level of understanding, those "governed by grace,"[67] presumably those who are active in the Christian life. These readers can extract the moral lesson from the passage. This level corresponds to the soul and leads the reader "from that which can be perceived by the senses to that which can be perceived by the intellect."[68] This is likewise an important level of understanding for Andrew since he frequently identifies moral lessons in Revelation, such as the need to perform good deeds, despise death, and pursue virtue. Tropology is sometimes called the "figurative sense," because one meaning of the word *tropos* is "a figure of speech." For this reason tropology is sometimes misunderstood or applied in a manner synonymous with allegory. But *tropos* also means "behavior," as in one's manner of life. Hence, it is more properly understood as the "moral sense," which is precisely what Andrew is indicating by his use of the term. He understands that *tropology* relates to proverbs as figures of speech, but not in an allegorical sense. Rather, proverbs are figurative expressions which provide moral lessons. Thus, the tropological interpretation is applied to Scriptures which contain "proverbial advice and other such pedagogical uses."[69] Andrew's good training allows him to resist a tendency found among many ancient interpreters who, upon finding difficulty with the literal or historical sense, simply disregarded it and dismissed it with the conclusion that the words must have a "figurative meaning," essentially allegorizing the passage. Andrew does not confuse allegory with tropology.

The third and most exalted part of the human person, the spirit, corresponds to the highest level of meaning for the Scriptures: the spiritual sense. This spiritual level of understanding

66. *Chp. 33, Text* 126, page 140.
68. *Prologue, Text* 8, page 52.
67. *Prologue, Text* 9, page 52.
69. *Prologue, Text* 9, page 52.

is the most difficult to acquire and is attained by very few, only those individuals in whose life "the Spirit governs."[70]

Andrew associates this level with "the future and higher things,"[71] which he identifies as the anagogical sense (*anagoge*) and contemplation (*theoria*). Andrew's accurate utilization of two different terms for the "spiritual sense" is significant because it indicates his training and methodology. *Anagoge* (literally, "to raise up") did not simply signal spiritual interpretation in general. When used with precision, it was a term that referred to an interpretation related to life in the Kingdom of God, hence, "the future things" in the next life. *Theoria* concerns "the higher things," and likewise does not indicate simply *any* spiritual interpretation, but a specific type associated with the Antiochene exegetical approach, which refrained from using allegory to arrive at a spiritual interpretation. It is very noteworthy that Andrew never uses the term "allegory" in his commentary and inveighs against fanciful and imaginative interpretations, which were often the hallmark of allegory. He recognizes the symbolic use of language and explains symbolic numbers such as 666 or 7; however, he interprets them not as pure allegory, but according to their symbolic use elsewhere in the Bible or according to a traditional ecclesiastical interpretation.

15. Technique

Andrew's exacting bifurcation of the spiritual sense into two parts, as well as his accurate use of terminology, indicates his advanced exegetical education and training. Elsewhere his training is indicated by his application of precise techniques, even when he does not employ the terminology. Among the techniques applied are his attention to the *skopos* (goal or purpose) of the biblical writer, his awareness of the context in which a statement is made, his sensitivity to sequence, and his use of word-association.

All writers, including biblical authors, have a goal, aim, or purpose for writing, which in the Greek tradition was called

70. *Prologue, Text* 9, page 52.
71. *Prologue, Text* 8, page 52.

the *skopos*. Patristic interpreters, especially those who employed the Antiochene method, consciously considered the author's purpose for the book when reaching exegetical conclusions. A conclusion that conflicted with the stated or implied *skopos* of the biblical author would be unmistakably erroneous. Specific passages or details within a passage also had a *skopos* and would prompt the interpreter to consider the author's intent or purpose for including that passage, statement, or detail. Andrew is aware of the historical *skopos* of Revelation to encourage patience and hope in times of tribulation, and he believes that this remained as the essential goal and can also serve the readers of his commentary. But he also finds an even deeper, spiritual purpose underlying Revelation, which he expresses at the end of the commentary: that the visions would inspire readers to pursue virtue, which would result in pure prayer, revealing a pure and uncorrupted mind.

Starting from these things by the vision and the enjoyment we might, by ardent yearning through keeping the divine commandments, acquire these in long suffering and meekness and humility and purity of heart. From which <heart> unsullied prayer is born free of distraction, and offers to God, the Overseer of all hidden things, a mind devoid of every material thought uncorrupted by demonic deception and attacks.[72]

Andrew's careful attention to context as an exegetical consideration is impressively displayed early in the commentary with his explanation of Rv 1.4, "the One who is, was, and is to come" (Rv 1.4). Interpreting that statement to refer to the Trinity would be natural, but it is not correct. Oikoumenios believes the phrase represents the Trinity: the One "who is" is the Father (who said "I am" to Moses); the "One who was" is the Son (the Logos "who was in the beginning"; see Jn 1.1); and the One who "is to come" refers to the Paraclete.[73] Andrew proceeds to explain that the statement *does* apply to all three Persons *theologically;* however, in that *specific context* it refers to the Father alone because the statement is followed by "and from Jesus Christ."

72. *Chp.* 72, *Text* 266, page 244.
73. Oik. 1.7.1–3, FOTC 112:23.

For here the addition of "and from Jesus Christ" appears to confirm the understanding we have presented. For it would be unnecessary if he were talking about the only Logos of God and the person of the Son to add immediately "and from Jesus Christ" in order to show him as distinct from the other one....[74]

Later, the same statement would be made of Christ alone (Rv 1.8), which Andrew also notes, but he is very adamant that "is, was, and is to come" in verse 4 applies to the Father only. Although Andrew does not use the word "context" to make his point, the thrust of his argument is entirely contextual.

Andrew displays his regard for context in the different interpretations he gives for the "white garment" imagery found in various passages in Revelation. Rather than always interpreting the symbol as "purity," Andrew's interpretation depends on the context in which the image appears. The white robes of the twenty-four elders around the throne of God (Rv 4.4) "are symbols of the brilliant life and the unending feast and gladness,"[75] probably recalling Christ's parables comparing the Kingdom of Heaven to a banquet.[76] The white robes worn by the crowd in Rv 7.9 indicate martyrdom for Andrew because a few verses later the text states that they have come out of "great tribulation" and "washed their robes in the blood of the Lamb" (7.14).

Sequence is also an important interpretive consideration and was applied by noticing and conforming one's interpretation to the biblical author's train of thought, the order in which statements were made, or the order in which pericopes appeared. Andrew respects the sequence and engages in a consistent and logical progression through the book. Sequence can be challenging in the Apocalypse, and it was particularly problematic for Oikoumenios. When his interpretation did not fit the context, Oikoumenios found it easier to ignore the sequence and interpret each scene as it struck him. Andrew directly challenges Oikoumenios's conclusions, which violate the sequence of events, by pointing out that they are illogical and often contradict the plain meaning of the text.[77]

One of the most common techniques of early interpreters

74. *Chp.* 1, *Text* 15, page 58.   75. *Chp.* 10, *Text* 49, page 82.
76. Mt 22.1–10; 25.1–13.   77. *Chp.* 17, *Text* 66, page 96.

was word-association: identifying a key word in a passage and searching for the same word elsewhere in the Bible. The meaning or use in the secondary location is used to interpret or explain the word in the verse under consideration, the two passages having been linked together by the common word. An appropriate use of word-association can be highly effective, but its inappropriate use can result in a muddling or distortion of the true meaning. Andrew uses word-association to understand the symbolic use of words in Revelation, such as an earthquake, the sky being rolled up like a scroll, the darkening of the sun, and the moon turning blood red (Rv 6.12–13). Andrew relates the descriptions to the same language found in apocalyptic passages in the Old Testament.[78] Another example is Andrew's proper use of word-association to explain the promise made to the church of Thyatira, "And I will give him the morning star" (Rv 2.28). A passage in Is 14.12, describing the fall of the "morning star," had traditionally been interpreted as the fall of Satan. Andrew, however, interprets the "morning star" as Christ, an interpretation that better suits the context since the rewards promised to the churches are always Christ and because Christ is described as the "bright morning star" later in Rv 22.16.

16. Sources

Yet another indication of Andrew's exegetical training is his reference to traditional interpretations by numerous unnamed sources that were not preserved elsewhere in the Greek tradition. For example, regarding the warning made to the church of Ephesus that its lampstand would be removed if the church did not repent, Andrew remarks, "Some understood the removal of the lampstand <to refer to> the throne of the archpriest of Ephesus, because it was moved to the seat of the king."[79] Among the interpretations reported for the four living beings surrounding the throne of God in Rv 4.6 is that they represented mastery over things in heaven and on earth and in

78. *Chp.* 18, *Text* 68–69, pages 97–98.
79. *Chp.* 3, *Text* 25, page 64.

the sea.[80] Andrew also preserves an interpretation of the millennium which is otherwise unknown. The one thousand years "some… explain…as the three-and-a-half years from the baptism of Christ until his ascension into heaven."[81]

With respect to recognized authorities, Andrew made every effort to utilize and align himself with known and respected Church Fathers. This practice begins in the prologue, in which Andrew cites Gregory the Theologian, Cyril of Alexandria, Papias, Irenaeus, Methodios, and Hippolytus as witnesses of the "trustworthiness" of the Apocalypse,[82] meaning that it is a genuine apostolic book. He continues in the course of the commentary to cite and quote various additional Fathers, including Pseudo-Dionysios (whom he calls Dionysios "the Great"), Basil, Justin Martyr, Epiphanios, and Antipater of Bostra. After explaining why the "One who is, was, and is to come" is a description of the Father only in Rv 1.4, but that the Trisagion Hymn[83] refers to the entire Trinity, he states, "<We say> these things to show that our own understanding does not contradict the patristic voices."[84] Andrew carefully and deliberately positions himself firmly in the ecclesiastical and patristic tradition. Andrew remarked in the prologue that he would take "many starting points" from the Fathers he listed,[85] a comment that indicates that Andrew knew that he could not fully rely on the Greek interpretive tradition to explain the entire Apocalypse. The best he could hope for were some "starting points," but for most of the book, he would need to rely on his own training and education. Eusebius of Caesarea, a fourth-century Church writer, and the first-century Jewish historian Flavius Josephus are also employed by Andrew, but only as historical sources.

17. History and Prophecy

Andrew's initial disagreement with Oikoumenios, his predecessor in the interpretive effort, concerns their differing views of prophecy. Oikoumenios began his exposition by explaining

---

80. *Chp.* 10. *Text* 51, page 83.   81. *Chp.* 63, *Text* 221, page 211.

82. *Prologue, Text* 10, pages 53–54.

83. "Holy God, Holy Mighty, Holy Immortal, have mercy on us."

84. *Chp.* 1, *Text* 16, page 58.   85. *Prologue, Text* 11, page 54.

that prophecy encompassed the past, present, and future.[86] But for Andrew, prophecy can only refer to the present and the future in relation to the time in which the prophet himself lived. Therefore, the images and prophecies of the Apocalypse cannot refer to any time prior to the moment when John received his Revelation.

And <this is> clear from what he says: "those things which are and those which must come to pass" (Rv 1.2). These are descriptions both of the present time and of the future.[87]

Andrew is primarily future-oriented in his reading of Revelation. Oikoumenios's opinion that prophecy also encompasses the past allows him to interpret images of Revelation as allegorical scenes representing events in the life of Christ. This creates tremendous problems for Oikoumenios in managing the sequence of events described, which Andrew deftly avoids.

Some Fathers had come to the conclusion that the earth would last for only 6,000 years, or six "days" corresponding to the six days of creation, with the seventh "day" being eternal rest, corresponding to the Sabbath rest. But others, including Andrew, believed that they were living in the "seventh day" [88] and saw world history as divided into seven periods of time represented by a succession of dominant kingdoms. This is clear in his interpretation of Rv 17.10: "They are also seven kings, five of whom have fallen; one is, the other has not yet come, and when he comes he must remain only a little while."

When John experienced his Revelation, five kingdoms had fallen: the Assyrians, the Medes, the Babylonians, the Persians, and the Macedonians (that is, the Greeks). The reigning kingdom at the time of John's Apocalypse was the sixth (the one that "is"), the pagan Roman empire. Andrew lived during the

86. Oik. 1.1.2, FOTC 112:19.
87. *Chp.* 1, *Text* 12, page 56.
88. Jean Daniélou, *The Theology of Jewish Christianity,* trans. and ed. John A. Baker, vol. 1 of *The Development of Christian Doctrine Before the Council of Nicea* (Chicago: Henry Regnery Co, 1964), 396–98. Andrew never mentions the "eighth day," but it is clear that he considers the future life in the Kingdom to represent the eighth day since the present life on this earth is described as the seventh day.

following era, the seventh period, the one that had "not yet come" at the time when John composed the Apocalypse, the New Christian Roman Empire, represented by Constantine the Great. Since that Empire, the seventh kingdom, was still in existence at the time of Andrew, and it was the final kingdom in the succession of kingdoms, Andrew shared the typical Eastern Christian belief that the Antichrist would come as "king of the Romans."[89]

18. Andrew's Theology

While the commentary was not written primarily to promote Chalcedonian orthodoxy, occasional statements refuting the interpretation of his Miaphysite[90] predecessor, Oikoumenios, subtly reveal Andrew's Chalcedonian beliefs. For example, Oikoumenios uses the description of Christ as the "holy one" in Rv 3.7 to promote the Miaphysite argument that the Trisagion Hymn of the Divine Liturgy is directed toward Christ.[91] The Chalcedonians considered it to be Trinitarian, and the differing interpretations of the hymn had come to symbolize the opposing camps. Andrew gives his interpretation of the hymn twice. The first time is early in the commentary when explaining how "the One who is, was, and is to come" (Rv 1.4) theologically applies to all three Persons of the Trinity even if, in that instance, it refers to the Father alone.[92] Later, commenting directly on the "holy, holy, holy" hymn of the living beings in

89. *Chp.* 36, *Text* 137, page 148.

90. An alternative term is "Monophysite." Those who belong to the "Oriental" Orthodox Churches object to this term as misleading, since they in fact do believe that Christ is both fully human and fully divine. The term is employed simply because it has historically been the term used to describe those Christians who rejected Nestorianism but who also did not accept the Ecumenical Council at Chalcedon. The term is accurate to the extent that it describes the reason why Monophysites/Miaphysites were so labeled: they insisted on using the terminology of "one nature" to describe the person of Christ after the Incarnation of the Logos.

91. "The holy one is the Son of God, so also he receives witness from the seraphim, who combine the three acclamations of 'holy' in the one lordship." Oikoumenios 2.13.1, FOTC 112:46.

92. *Chp.* 1, *Text* 13–15, pages 56–58.

Rv 4.8, he writes, "These holy powers do not rest, never ceasing the divine hymnody and offering the threefold blessing to the Tri-hypostatic Divinity."[93] Although he affirms Chalcedon, Andrew's presentation overall is more pastoral than theological. His occasional theological comments, however, indicate that he is educated, knowledgeable about theology, and entirely orthodox.

Andrew's orthodoxy extends to his views on salvation, understandably a frequent topic in the commentary. Human beings are expected to cooperate with God for their salvation. Andrew's commentary maintains the typical Eastern paradox between the affirmations that God alone saves and that salvation can never be earned, and the belief that humans are entirely responsible for their individual salvation. Andrew denies both predestination and any concept of merit. While acknowledging the reality of the sufferings that will face people at the end-times, Andrew's most frequent description of God is *philanthropos,* the One who loves humankind. God does not simply desire the salvation of all, but he "thirsts for our salvation."[94]

Salvation is a gift, but it is a gift given to those who accept it and who prove worthy of it by their deeds.

For thirst is necessary for the drink of life, for the firm possession of the one who has acquired it, especially because it is also granted as a gift, not to those who did not toil at all, but to those who offered not things worthy of the greatness of the gift, but only a genuine and fiery resolve instead of gold and silver and pains of the body.[95]

Yet salvation also requires great effort, and Andrew frequently brings out the moral lessons of Revelation and encourages his readers to pursue lives of virtue, to maintain an attitude of vigilance, and always to be prepared for the end, which could come for us at any time. He most commonly uses metaphors from the arenas of work (such as "wages" and "labor"), warfare (such as "weapons," "enemies," and "drafted"), and athletics (such as "crowns," "contest," and "arena") to describe the necessary efforts and the promised rewards. God respects human

93. *Chp.* 10, *Text* 52, page 84.
95. *Chp.* 72, *Text* 261, page 241.

94. *Chp.* 66, *Text* 236, page 222.

freedom and does not force anyone to have a relationship with him. The purpose of end-time torments is not the same as eternal punishment. The sufferings of the end-times described in Revelation are God's philanthropic attempt to lead sinners to repentance and salvation, which Andrew compares to the bit and bridle of a horse that lead it in the right direction. "God, who loves humanity, compels 'the jaws of those who do not approach him' in order that they might know repentance."[96]

Therefore, it is still possible to reject God's salvation, and those who do so will face eternal punishment, which is also the result of their free choice. "Each one..." will "receive the wages befitting the labors done."[97] The punishment of sinners by God is not the result of spite or rejection by God himself, but rather of sinners' choosing their own end by their lifestyle, each "human being receiving through his deeds that which he desired, either the Kingdom or punishment."[98]

On the one hand, the aforementioned will of God...is that "people be saved and come to knowledge of the truth"[99] and that they "return and live,"[100] and on the other hand, secondly <the will of God> is the punishment of those who pursue their own punishment.[101]

The punishment of sinners is also inevitable, since God is not only *philanthropos*, but he is also just. Andrew rejects Origenism and the suggestion by Oikoumenios that in the end all will be saved.

Wherefore, those who set the goodness, foreknowledge, and power of God as an impediment to eternal punishment, let them also attach righteousness to these <qualities>, as being distributive to each of them according to what is due, and in no way will they see an overturning of the divine sentence.[102]

Therefore, the purpose of afflictions in this life, both those sent by God for our repentance, as well as the ordinary trials and difficulties of life, is to acquire eternal life. "For to be born or not to be born is not up to us, but to struggle and to be

---

96. Ps 32(31).9; *Chp.* 49, *Text* 169, page 172.
97. *Chp.* 36, *Text* 139, page 149.
98. *Chp.* 59, *Text* 212, page 203.
99. 1 Tm 2.4; 2 Tm 2.25, 3.7.
100. Ezek 18.23, 32.
101. *Chp.* 59, *Text* 211, page 203.
102. *Chp.* 50, *Text* 172, page 174.

victorious <against> the evil demons and to gain the eternal blessings is for us."[103] If one has a heavenly mentality, he will recognize that difficulties in this life are an opportunity to acquire the Kingdom of Heaven. "For those who have 'citizenship in heaven'[104] difficulties become the starting point of unfading crowns and trophies."[105]

19. Andrew's Eschatology

Millennialism, also known as chiliasm, the belief that Christ would return to reign over an earthly kingdom for 1,000 years, was a popular belief among many in the early Church. By Andrew's time, however, a literal interpretation of Rv 20 had become almost universally rejected in favor of a spiritual understanding of the 1,000 years during which Satan is bound. Andrew offers a traditional patristic interpretation in which the 1,000 years is the period from the Incarnation of Christ until the coming of the Antichrist. The devil was bound during the earthly ministry of Christ, resulting in "the restraint of his evil activity."[106] Andrew also considers the number to be symbolic and not a literal period of years.

By the number "one thousand years" by no means is it reasonable to understand so many <years>. For neither…are we able to count out these things as ten times one hundred; rather <they are to mean> many <generations>. Here also, we infer the number one thousand to indicate either a great many or perfection. For these things require many years for the purpose of preaching the Gospel everywhere in the entire world and for the seeds of piety to take root in it…. The "one thousand years," therefore, is the time from <the year of> the Incarnation of the Lord until the coming of the Antichrist.[107]

Andrew did not apply the symbols of Revelation to the events of his time, nor did he believe that one could predict the end. He believed, however, that Revelation might accurately describe the events and occurrences of the end. He was convinced that the end was not near since there was no sign of

---

103. *Chp.* 50, *Text* 172, page 174.
105. *Chp.* 25, *Text* 95, page 120.
107. *Chp.* 60, *Text* 216, pages 206–7.

104. Phil 3.20.
106. *Chp.* 60, *Text* 216, page 206.

catastrophes on the order of those described after the opening of the sixth seal. Yet, in line with a traditional patristic interpretation that identified the "kings" of Rv 17.9 as successive worldwide kingdoms (Assyria, Media, Babylonia, Persia, Macedonia, pagan Rome, and New Rome), he also believed that he was living in the seventh and final age, the era of the final kingdom, which is described as remaining "a little while."[108] The Antichrist would arise from the empire to which Andrew belonged, and he would come as "king of the Romans."[109] Yet Andrew was uncertain about the length of time the final period might last and mused that "a little while" might simply indicate the brevity of this life in comparison with eternal life. "After all, every chronological number is short compared to the future everlasting kingdom of the saints."[110]

Along those same lines, Andrew concludes that the harlot of Babylon is the last of seven ruling kingdoms, "seven places standing out from the rest in worldly prominence and power, these upon which we know were established in due season the <ruling> kingdoms of the world," the hills symbolizing not actual locations but signifying "ranks of glory."[111] Since the red beast upon which the harlot rides is the devil, [112] and the harlot is drunk with the blood of the saints,[113] Babylon must represent a ruling power that persecutes the saints. The Babylon of the future cannot be ancient Rome since "ancient Rome from long ago lost the power of its kingdom…. for the Apocalypse says, 'The woman whom you see is the great city having dominion over the kings of the earth.'"[114] It also cannot represent the current capital of New Rome, Constantinople, since it neither has world-wide dominion nor the moral corruption which the Apocalypse indicates. Nonetheless, Babylon might represent a city in the Roman Empire, if one considers both as "one unit" since New Rome is a continuation of the former Roman Em-

108. Rv 17.10.
109. *Chp.* 54, *Text* 189, page 187.
110. *Chp.* 54, *Text* 188–89, page 187.
111. *Chp.* 54, *Text* 186–87, pages 185–86.
112. Rv 17.3. *Chp.* 53, *Text* 182, page 182.
113. Rv 17.6.
114. *Chp.* 53, *Text* 181, page 181.

pire. But no city in the Empire during his time exercised universal dominion, contributing to Andrew's opinion that the end-times were not near.

Wherefore, as it is said, someone who would truly take this to mean this <Roman> kingdom originally in one unit that has ruled until now, that poured out the blood of the apostles and prophets and martyrs, would not be led astray from what is appropriate. For just as also this is said about one chorus and one army and one city, even if they exchange each of those <individuals> constituting them, likewise in the same way the kingdom is one even though in many times and places it is divided. [115]

Andrew also presented a typical Eastern patristic eschatology that combined elements from Revelation, 1 John, and 2 Thessalonians. Andrew believed that just prior to the final destruction of all the forces of evil, represented by Gog and Magog, the Antichrist will sit in the temple and represent himself as God.[116] Andrew considered it unclear whether the "temple" would be the actual Jewish temple, which Jews still hoped to rebuild, or a church. This scenario is found in 2 Thes 2.4, and the term "antichrist" is found only in 1 Jn 2.18.

20. Translations of the Commentary and Its Influence on the New Testament Canon for the East

Andrew's commentary was previously translated into at least four ancient languages: Latin, Armenian, Old Slavonic, and Georgian. This publication marks its first translation into a modern language. The creation of the Armenian translation was described by Nerses of Lampron, the famous Armenian Archbishop of Tarsus (d. 1198). The Apocalypse had already existed in Armenian translation; however, it was not regarded as Scripture among the Armenians until Nerses acquired a Greek copy of Andrew's commentary, which he had translated into Armenian. His search for an explanation for the enigmatic book first took him to a Frankish monastery where, as Nerses describes it, he discovered the commentary "in the Lombard

---

115. *Chp.* 55, *Text* 202, page 196.
116. *Chp.* 63, *Text* 225–26, pages 213–14.

language, in the same script which the Franks use, composed by two authors."[117] It is unclear whether "the Lombard language" was Latin or an early form of Italian. The reception of the commentary by an Armenian synod held in Constantinople and its influence on the Armenian canon of the New Testament is recounted in a foreword by Nerses himself, quoting the statement made by the Armenian Catholikos Thetalios:

If we approach this Revelation with mistrust, then we despise the saints who cleansed the world of bad schisms, and they have borne testimony for <Revelation>. For if these are seen to be rejected by us, then also those who have accepted it would have to be rejected. Far be it to think this!... Therefore, I also, the poor Thetalios, and the holy synod that was with me, have accepted this Apocalypse into the catholic Church with honor as also a true revelation, but also the examination of the explanation which was composed by Andreas the Archbishop of Caesarea was accepted by this synod, for not out of himself but on the foundation of the Fathers did he make the construction of his words and whose gift of the Spirit he took as his guide and witness in his investigations. Therefore, this investigation, which the bishop of Caesarea has made concerning the Revelation, has been taken into our catholic Church on the resolution and testimony of the general synod.[118]

The Georgian Church had similarly excluded the Apocalypse from their New Testament canon until the text and Andrew's commentary were translated into the Georgian language by St. Euthymios (Ekwthime),[119] one of the founders of the Georgian monastery Iwiron on Mt. Athos (d. 1028). Andrew's commentary also influenced the acceptance of the Apocalypse in the Russian tradition, evidenced by the fact that the oldest extant manuscript of Revelation in Church Slavonic contains a condensed version of Andrew's commentary.[120]

117. Robert W. Thomson, *Nerses of Lambron Commentary on the Revelation of Saint John,* Hebrew University Armenian Studies series, vol. 9 (Leuven: Peeters, 2007), 17, fn. 80. Thomson explains that Nerses had found a copy of Arethas's revision of Andrew's commentary, presumably in early Italian or Latin. But the Greek copy that Nerses eventually found, translated, and adapted consisted of the commentary of Andrew alone.

118. Schmid, *Einleitung,* 103–4, translation by Dr. John Fendrick.

119. D. M. Lang, "Recent Work on the Georgian New Testament," *Bulletin of the School of Oriental and African Studies,* Vol. 19, No. 1 (1957): 82–93, 86.

120. *The Nikol'skij Apocalypse Codex,* dated mid-thirteenth century. To cre-

21. Andrew and the Apocalypse Text

The transmission of the text of the Apocalypse itself is unique among the books of the New Testament. Due to Revelation's uncertain status in the East, it never found a place in the lectionary, thus reducing the number of manuscript copies. Copies of Revelation were also frequently contained in collections of other non-canonical writings, such as sermons and lives of saints. Approximately seven times more manuscript copies exist of the Gospels than of Revelation, which exists in only about three hundred copies, one-third of which contains the commentary of Andrew of Caesarea. The existence of the commentary, therefore, is itself responsible for a large number of the copies of the book of Revelation and resulted in a unique text type known as the Andreas text type.

In the mid-twentieth century, Josef Schmid exhaustively studied all the manuscripts and text types of the Apocalypse and in connection with this monumental effort created a critical text of the Andreas commentary, from which the present volume has been translated. Schmid's primary interest in editing the commentary of Andrew of Caesarea was to determine one of the main text types for Revelation, the Andreas type, which he designated "*Av.*" Schmid found the Andreas type useful for unraveling the history of the Apocalypse manuscript transmission, and he determined that the original type found in the Andreas commentary predates the commentary itself and is closely related to the Sinaiticus corrector.

A complete copy of Andrew's commentary exists in eighty-three Greek manuscripts, not to mention the many Armenian, Georgian, and Slavonic copies. In addition, thirteen abbreviated Greek versions of the commentary survive, as well as fifteen

---

ate the abbreviated version, many of the patristic quotations were removed as well as the inspirational comments and doxologies at the end of each of Andrew's sections. The commentary and text of Revelation follow Andrew's divisions into twenty-four main sections and seventy-two smaller chapters. See Thomas Hilary Oller, "*The Nikol'skij Apocalypse Codex* and its Place in the Textual History of Medieval Slavic Apocalypse Manuscripts" (Ph.D. diss., Brown University, 1993).

manuscripts with scholia. The commentary was published in Migne's Patrologia Graeca,[121] which also contains a free Latin translation created by the Jesuit scholar Theodore Peltanus, a professor at the University of Ingolstadt, printed in 1584.

22. The Lasting Legacy of Andrew's Commentary

The commentary's large number of manuscript copies testifies to the enthusiastic reception which the commentary received in the Eastern Orthodox Church, the high esteem with which it was regarded, and the influence which it continues to exert. Throughout the centuries the commentary has been admired as useful, sensible, orderly, ecclesiastically and theologically sound, and orthodox in thought as well as in style. The commentary exudes a pastoral tone of love and care. Despite the popular association of Revelation with images of punishment and destruction, Andrew's commentary sounds a positive and affirming note that focuses on the brevity of one's earthly life, the ability to determine one's final destination in the next life by our choices and actions today, and the love of God, who desires to save all people. Andrew's commentary achieved a position of unparalleled influence in the history of biblical interpretation. No other commentary has so singularly impacted the interpretation of any book of the Bible or so influenced its reception into the canon of Scripture in either the East or the West. Andrew of Caesarea believed that reading the Apocalypse was spiritually beneficial for the faithful. His commentary was motivated by a desire to provide a useful, orthodox interpretation of this enigmatic book and to promote its acceptance among Eastern Christians. He could never have imagined the enduring success of his efforts.

121. PG 106:215–457.

COMMENTARY ON THE
APOCALYPSE

[1] [TABLE OF THE CHAPTERS OF THE INTERPRETATION OF THE APOCALYPSE OF SAINT JOHN THE APOSTLE

SECTION 1

Chapter 1   Apocalypse of Jesus Christ

Chapter 2   The vision in which he saw the Lord

Chapter 3   The things that had been written to the angel of the church of the Ephesians

SECTION 2

Chapter 4   The things declared to the angel of the church of the Smyrnaeans

Chapter 5   The things declared to the angel of the church in Pergamum

Chapter 6   The things declared to the angel of the church in Thyatira

SECTION 3

Chapter 7   The things declared to the angel of the church in Sardis

Chapter 8   The things declared to the angel of the church in Philadelphia

Chapter 9   The things declared to the angel of the church of the Laodiceans

SECTION 4

Chapter 10   About the door that was seen in heaven and the twenty-four elders and the things that follow

Chapter 11   About the small scroll sealed with seven seals which no one who has a created nature is able to open

Chapter 12   And I saw in the midst of the throne and of the four living beings

SECTION 5

Chapter 13   Loosening of the first seal
Chapter 14   About the second seal [2]
Chapter 15   Loosening of the third seal

SECTION 6

Chapter 16   Loosening of the fourth seal, showing the chastisements which befall the impious
Chapter 17   Loosening of the fifth seal, meaning the saints crying out to the Lord about the end of the world
Chapter 18   Loosening of the sixth seal, signifying the upcoming plagues at the end of time

SECTION 7

Chapter 19   About the 144,000 saved from the plague <inflicted> by the four angels
Chapter 20   About the innumerable crowd of those clothed in shining garments from the nations
Chapter 21   Loosening of the seventh seal, meaning the angelic powers bringing the prayers of the saints to God as incense

SECTION 8

Chapter 22   About the seven angels whose first blow of the trumpet brings hail, fire, and blood on the earth
Chapter 23   About the second angel and the destruction of living things in the sea
Chapter 24   About the third angel, and the river waters being made bitter

SECTION 9

Chapter 25   About the fourth angel and the darkening of the luminaries
Chapter 26   About the fifth angel and the mental locusts and the variety of their form

Chapter 27   About the sixth angel and the angels released upon the Euphrates

SECTION 10

Chapter 28   About the angel wrapped in a cloud and a rainbow, who is foretelling the end of the world

Chapter 29   How the Evangelist took the tiny scroll from the angel

Chapter 30   About Enoch and Elijah

SECTION 11

Chapter 31   How those who were destroyed by the Antichrist will be raised

Chapter 32   About the seventh trumpet and the saints praising God at the future judgment [3]

Chapter 33   About the prior persecutions of the Church and about those at <the time> of the Antichrist

SECTION 12

Chapter 34   About the war between the angels and the demons and the fall of Satan

Chapter 35   About how the dragon does not cease persecuting the Church

Chapter 36   About the beast with ten horns and seven heads

SECTION 13

Chapter 37   About the false prophet

Chapter 38   About the name of the Antichrist

Chapter 39   About the Lamb and the 144,000

SECTION 14

Chapter 40   About the angel proclaiming the imminence of the future judgment

Chapter 41   About the angel announcing the fall of Babylon

Chapter 42   About the angel warning the faithful not to accept the Antichrist

SECTION 15

Chapter 43	How the one sitting on the cloud destroys by means of the sickle the things growing on earth
Chapter 44	About the angel harvesting the vine of bitterness
Chapter 45	About the seven angels bringing the plagues upon people before the end of the world, and about the sea of glass

SECTION 16

Chapter 46	How, after the first bowl is poured out, sores come upon the apostates
Chapter 47	The second plague against those in the sea
Chapter 48	How the rivers are changed to blood from the third <bowl>

SECTION 17

Chapter 49	How the people are burnt by the fourth <bowl>
Chapter 50	How the kingdom of the beast is darkened through the fifth <bowl>
Chapter 51	How through the sixth <bowl> the way by the Euphrates is opened to the kings from the East

SECTION 18

Chapter 52	How through the seventh <bowl> hail and earthquake come against the people [4]
Chapter 53	About the one of the seven angels showing to the blessed John the destruction of the harlot's city, and about the seven heads and ten horns
Chapter 54	How the angel explained to him the mystery that was seen

SECTION 19

Chapter 55	About another angel declaring the fall of Babylon and the heavenly voice commanding flight from the city, and about the discarding of the delights which it had once possessed
Chapter 56	About the hymnody of the saints and the triple "Alleluia," which they chanted on the occasion of the destruction of Babylon

Chapter 57   About the mystical marriage and the supper of
                    the Lamb

                         SECTION 20

Chapter 58   How the Evangelist saw Christ on horseback with
                    angelic powers

Chapter 59   About the Antichrist and those cast with him into
                    Gehenna

Chapter 60   How Satan was bound from the crucifixion of
                    Christ until the end time, and about the one
                    thousand years

                         SECTION 21

Chapter 61   About the thrones prepared for those who
                    kept the undeniable confession of Christ

Chapter 62   What is the first resurrection and what is the
                    second death

Chapter 63   About Gog and Magog

                         SECTION 22

Chapter 64   About the one sitting on the throne and the
                    common resurrection and judgment

Chapter 65   About the new heaven and earth and the
                    heavenly Jerusalem

Chapter 66   About the things said by the one sitting on the
                    throne

                         SECTION 23

Chapter 67   About the angel showing him the city of the
                    saints and measuring its walls with its gates

Chapter 68   About the pure river appearing to flow from the
                    throne

Chapter 69   That Christ is the God of the prophets and
                    Master of the angels

[5]

SECTION 24

Chapter 70   About the credibility of the things seen by the
              apostle

Chapter 71   How he was commanded not to seal, but to preach
              the Apocalypse

Chapter 72   How the Church and the Spirit in it are invited to
              the glorious appearance of Christ, and about the
              curse by which those falsifying the book are
              thrown down]

[6] <blank>

INTERPRETATION OF ANDREW, ARCHBISHOP OF CAESAREA, CAPPADOCIA, ON THE APOCALYPSE OF JOHN THE THEOLOGIAN

\<PROLOGUE\>

To my lord brother and co-celebrant:

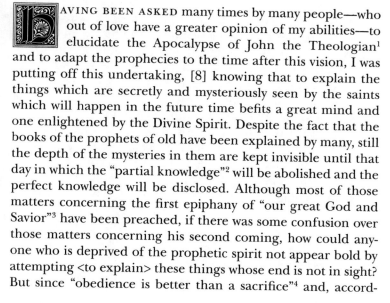AVING BEEN ASKED many times by many people—who out of love have a greater opinion of my abilities—to elucidate the Apocalypse of John the Theologian[1] and to adapt the prophecies to the time after this vision, I was putting off this undertaking, [8] knowing that to explain the things which are secretly and mysteriously seen by the saints which will happen in the future time befits a great mind and one enlightened by the Divine Spirit. Despite the fact that the books of the prophets of old have been explained by many, still the depth of the mysteries in them are kept invisible until that day in which the "partial knowledge"[2] will be abolished and the perfect knowledge will be disclosed. Although most of those matters concerning the first epiphany of "our great God and Savior"[3] have been preached, if there was some confusion over those matters concerning his second coming, how could anyone who is deprived of the prophetic spirit not appear bold by attempting \<to explain\> these things whose end is not in sight? But since "obedience is better than a sacrifice"[4] and, accord-

---

1. In the Eastern Christian tradition John "the Evangelist" is referred to as "John the Theologian." Elsewhere in this commentary, Andrew also refers to John as "the Apostle." Generally speaking, however, when an Eastern Father, including Andrew, refers simply to "the Apostle," with no other context provided and no indication of a specific apostle, it is a reference to St. Paul, as can be seen a few lines below in this paragraph.

2. 1 Cor 13.9.   3. Ti 2.13.

4. 1 Sm 15.22.

ing to the Apostle, "hope does not bring to shame,"[5] and, "love never fails,"[6] through which I am connected to your God-like soul, O blessed one,[7] I hope through this <treatise> for both the completion of the deficiencies and <to receive> the wages of obedience, which I have known is the fruit of love, and I will shortly fulfill this <task> that was assigned to me, with God who will enlighten me.

First, therefore, as you yourself well know, since there are three parts to a human being,[8] "all divinely inspired Scripture"[9] has been endowed with three parts by divine grace. And by this, the body is somewhat like the letter and like history established according to sense perception. In like manner, the soul is the figurative sense, guiding the reader from that which can be perceived by the senses to that which can be perceived by the intellect. Likewise, the spirit has appeared to be the anagogical sense and the contemplation of the future and higher things, so that the first level moreover [9] is appropriate to the ones "guided by the Law"[10] as pedagogue, the second to the ones who are governed by grace, and the third to those who exist in the blessed condition in which the Spirit governs, having subordinated to it all carnal thoughts and motions.

The first is suited to the histories of things which have already occurred, even though in many places this too has been adorned in no small degree by the foreshadowing that anticipates the truth. The second part suits proverbial advice and other such pedagogical uses, as for instance, "Thorns are sown

5. Rom 5.5.

6. 1 Cor 13.8.

7. The Greek word here, *Makarios,* could also be a proper name, but most likely it is employed as an expression of esteem or as a form of address similar to "O Beatitude."

8. St. Paul's comment that the human being consists of body, soul, and spirit (1 Thes 5.23) was paired by Origen with Prv 22.20, which advises one to hearken to the words of wisdom and to "record them threefold for yourself on the table of your heart for counsel and knowledge." These two verses inspired Origen to identify three levels of meaning in the Scriptures: literal, moral, and allegorical. (*On First Principles* 4.2.4). Origen exercised unparalleled influence upon Christian interpreters for centuries.

9. 2 Tm 3.16.

10. Gal 3.24.

in the hand of a drunkard,"[11] and "'Shame on you, Sidon,'"
it says, "said the sea,"[12] and things similar to these. The third
part, that is to say, the spiritual part, is found to be especially
abundant in the Apocalypse of the Theological Man; on the
one hand, lavishly seen with historical form and figurative
speech in the other prophets, whereas, on the other hand here,
<in the Apocalypse>, <the spiritual part> is especially seen in
abundance since it has been ordered by God to be proclaimed
to those who are more perfect in knowledge. Therefore, even
though we ourselves do not understand the entire depth of the
hidden spirit within it, we too will elucidate what was seen by
the blessed one. We neither dare to understand everything according to the letter, nor state that which we have conjectured.
But rather we will expound <these things> as if supplying a
training for the quick-wittedness of the mind and as a form of
contempt for the present things, since they are transitory, and
<for the purpose of> coveting the future things, since these
remain, [10] having relegated the exact knowledge of these
matters to divine wisdom, which also knows the times in which
these prophesied <events> will come to pass, which is forbidden
to seek <as we have learned> through the apostles.[13]

Out of obedience we have performed this <task>, and have
divided the present treatise into twenty-four sections, seventy-
two chapters for the three-part existence of body, soul, and
spirit of the twenty-four elders, through whom is symbolized
the full number of those who have pleased God from the beginning to the end of times, as will be explained in what follows.[14]
Concerning the divine inspiration of the book, we believe it
superfluous to lengthen the discussion, since its trustworthiness is witnessed by the Blessed Gregory the Theologian,[15] Cyr-

---

11. Prv 26.9.   12. Is 23.4.
13. Acts 1.7; 1 Thes 5.1.

14. Andrew's chapter divisions are indicated as *Chp*. The pagination from
Josef Schmid's critical text is indicated by brackets within the text and cited in
the footnotes as *Text*.

15. Gregory Nazianzus. In *Theological Oration* 29.17 Gregory quotes the
phrase from Rv 1.8, "he who is, was, and is to come," to support the full divinity of Christ. In *Or*. 42.9, Gregory seems to acknowledge apostolic authorship
of Revelation by his statement, "as John taught me through the Apocalypse,"

il,[16] in addition to the more ancient fathers, Papias,[17] Irenaeus,[18] Methodios[19] and Hippolytus.[20] From them we have also [11] taken many starting points leading into this, as well as reciting their sayings in certain places. And you, "O man of God,"[21] compensate our labor with your prayers, as I think it contributes not a little to compunction through remembrance of both the rewards that will be bestowed on the righteous and the retribution of the wicked and sinful.

---

which is the evidence to which Andrew refers here. Gregory, however, does *not* include the Apocalypse in his New Testament canon of Scripture, which he expounded in poetic verse (*Poem* 1.12.5ff), a fact of which Andrew may be aware, but has conveniently ignored.

16. Cyril of Alexandria, *The Adoration and Worship of God in Spirit and Truth* 6.

17. While Andrew cites Papias as an early witness, ironically Andrew himself becomes a witness to Papias's statements about the Apocalypse. The works of Papias, Bishop of Hierapolis, an early second-century Father, are no longer extant, with the exception of a few fragments. Andrew's commentary itself preserved one of these fragments that would have otherwise been lost (*Chp.* 33, *Text* 129, pages 142–43). Here, in this instance, Andrew cites Papias and by doing so indirectly provides the earliest written testimony to the tradition that the Apostle John was the author of the Apocalypse in Papias's work *Exposition of Dominical Oracles.* Despite the fact that this work is no longer extant, we know from Andrew's citation here that Papias provided important attestation to the early Church tradition of the apostolic authorship of Revelation.

18. Irenaeus frequently cited the Apocalypse, especially in his work *Against Heresies.* (See *Heres.* 1.26.3; 4.14.2; 4.17.6.; 4.18.6; 4.20.11; 4.11.3.) Irenaeus was a chiliast, as were Papias and Justin Martyr, all of whom relied on Rv 20 for their views.

19. Bishop of Olympus in Lycia, reportedly martyred in 311, according to Socrates' *Ecclesiastical History* 6.13. Methodios was one of the most important writers of his day. He frequently cited the Apocalypse, for example, in his works *On the Resurrection* 2.28 and *Symposium* 1.5; 5.8; 6.5; 8.4–13. Despite his early date and the tendencies of the times, Methodios was not a chiliast, preferring a spiritual interpretation of Revelation to the literal belief in an earthly kingdom.

20. Hippolytus wrote a treatise *On Christ and Antichrist* and also a *Commentary on Daniel,* the oldest extant and complete Scripture commentary. Hippolytus is also remembered for aggressively responding to the attacks by Gaius and the "Alogoi" against the writings traditionally attributed to the Apostle John.

21. 1 Tm 6.11.

CHAPTER 1

1.1. *Apocalypse of Jesus Christ, which God gave to him, to show to his servants that which must come to pass soon.*

N APOCALYPSE is the manifestation of hidden mysteries when the intellect is illuminated either through divine dreams or according to waking visions from divine enlightenment. To be *given to Christ,* it says, making this statement about him especially with respect to his human <nature>, since in the Gospel he <John> above all others dwelt on the sublime and things that befit God. And here, the magnitude of the divinity of Christ is shown through the attending angel, and through the name of the teaching servants, for "all things are his servants."[1] The *must come to pass soon* means that some of the predictions concerning them are to come to pass immediately thereafter, [12] and the things regarding the end are not to be delayed, because "one thousand years" to God is "like yesterday's day, which is reckoned as having <already> elapsed."[2]

1.1b–2. [1b]*And he made it known through the sending of his angel to his servant John,* [2]*who bore witness to the word of God and the witness of Jesus Christ, all that he saw, both those things which are and those which must come to pass afterward.*[3]

"Christ," he says, "declared these things to me through an angel, as a master to a household servant, as I had borne wit-

1. Ps 119(118).91. For convenience of reference, the number of a Psalm will follow the standard modern enumeration with the Septuagint number provided in parentheses.

2. Ps 90(89).4.

3. The phrase "both those things which are and those which must come to pass afterward," found here as part of verse 2, is absent from many Revelation

ness to my confession to him," of which, on the basis of the visions <he is> to bear witness and, in view of the return <to God> of those who hear, to preach both the things which are and which escape human understanding and the things which will occur in the future, for, prophetically, he had seen them both. And <this is> clear from what he says: *those things which are and those which must come to pass.* These are descriptions both of the present time and of the future.

1.3. *Blessed is the one who reads and the ones who hear the words of the prophecy and the ones keeping the things which have been written in it. For the time is near.*

He blesses those who read and hear through the actions, *for the* present *time is near,* through which it is possible to acquire the blessing, and to all the work is laid open. As the Lord says, "Work [13] while it is day."[4] And elsewhere, *the time is near,* the time of the distribution of prizes, on account of the brevity of the present life in comparison to the future.

1.4. *John, to the seven churches that are in Asia: Grace to you and peace from the One who is, and who was, and who is to come, and from the seven spirits which are before his throne.*

Due to the existence of many churches in many places, he sent <letters> to only seven, mystically meaning by this number the churches everywhere, also corresponding to the present-day life, in which the seventh period of days is taking place. For this reason also he mentions seven angels and seven churches, to whom he says, *Grace to you and peace from* the Tri-hypostatic Divin-

---

manuscripts. It represents, however, an example of the variations found in Andrew's copy of the Apocalypse. By its inclusion here, Josef Schmid indicates that it was part of Andrew's original commentary. Furthermore, Schmid's work on the text of Revelation confirmed that Andrew's version, now known as the Andreas text type, was not created by Andrew, as some maintained, but predated him. (See the Introduction to this volume, pages 41–42, and Georg Maldfeld, "Zur Geschichte des griechischen Apokalypse-Textes," *Theologische Zeitschrift* 14 (1958): 47–52, 49.) Its importance to the commentary as a whole lies in the fact that Andrew relies on this particular phrase to guide his interpretation of Revelation as prophecy. (See Introduction, page 33.)

4. Jn 9.4.

ity. For by the *who is* the Father is signified, who said to Moses, "I am He who is,"[5] and by the *who was* the Logos, "who was in the beginning with God,"[6] and by the *who is to come* the Paraclete, who always enlightens the children of the Church through holy Baptism, more completely and more strongly in the future.[7] It is possible to understand the seven spirits as the seven angels who were appointed to govern the churches, not [14] counting them equal to the most divine and royal Trinity, but mentioned along with it as servants, just as the divine Apostle said, "I call upon you in the presence of God and the chosen angels."[8] By the same token, this may be understood differently: *the One who is, and who was, and who is to come,* meaning the Father, who contains in himself the beginning, middle, and end of all that exists, and *the seven spirits* <meaning> the activities of the Life-giving Spirit, following Christ God, who became man for our sake. For in many places each divine Person is indifferently placed and arranged by the Apostle.[9] For this <reason> he says here:

1.5a. *And from Jesus Christ, the faithful witness, the firstborn of the dead, and the ruler of the kings of the earth.*

He is the one who witnessed to Pontius Pilate,[10] *faithful* to his words in all things, *the firstborn of the dead* as life and resurrection, for those whom he governs will no more see death, like those who were dead before and rose, but will live eternally.[11] *Ruler of the kings,* as "King of kings and Lord of lords,"[12] equal in power

---

5. Ex 3.14.   6. Jn 1.1.

7. At this point, Andrew is reporting the opinion of Oikoumenios, but does not agree with it. Because of the context, Andrew concludes that the One who is, was, and is to come refers to the Father alone in this verse. A careful reading of the statements that follow reveals his true interpretation as he supports his argument that only the Father is referenced here, while affirming that the statement is theologically appropriate to all three members of the Trinity.

8. 1 Tm 5.21.

9. The Trinity is represented here, but not in the usual order. Andrew accepts that all three members of the Trinity *give* the Revelation, but disagrees that all three Persons are expressed specifically here with the term "is, was, and is to come," primarily because Jesus Christ is introduced in the verse which follows.

10. Cf. Jn 19.37.   11. Cf. Jn 5.24, 8.51.
12. Rv 17.14.

with the Father and consubstantial. Elsewhere, *ruler of the kings of the earth* is also said <in reference to his mastery over> earthly desires. If, according to the Blessed [15] Gregory, this usage of *he who is, who was, and who is to come, the ruler of all* refers to Christ,[13] then it is not unreasonable that words similar to those which will be said shortly after refer to him,[14] to which also *the ruler of all* is attached and without the repetition or introduction of another person. For here the addition of *and from Jesus Christ* appears to confirm the understanding we have presented. For it would be unnecessary if he were talking about the only Logos of God and the person of the Son to add immediately *and from Jesus Christ* in order to show him as distinct from the other one, <since> the expressions that befit God equally honor and are appropriate to each of the divine Persons, and are common to the three, except for their distinctive properties, that is to say, the relationships <between them>, as said by Gregory the Theologian,[15] and except for the Incarnation of the Logos. <This is> also clear from the things from which we learn, that in the Gospel the thrice-holy hymn of the Seraphim[16] is said about the Son,[17] in the speech of Paul in the Acts about the Holy Spirit,[18] and then about the Father, in the offering of the awesome mysteries, to whom we are accustomed to say this prayer,[19] as the blessed Epiphanios [16] says in his homily *On the Holy Spirit*.[20] <We say> these things to show that our own understanding does not contradict the patristic voices, and also, with God's help, we continue.

1.5b–6. *To the One who loved us and freed us from our sins by his blood, ⁶and made us kings and priests to God and his Father. Glory and dominion to him to the ages of ages. Amen.*

The glory belongs to him, it says, who freed us through love from the bondage of death, and washed the stains of sin

---

13. *Or.* 29.17.　　　　　14. Rv 1.5.

15. *Or.* 30.19.　　　　　16. Is 6.3.

17. Mt 13.13–15; Mk 4.12. Andrew makes the link because Christ quotes Isaiah in these gospel passages.

18. Acts 28.25.

19. In Divine Liturgy of St. John Chrysostom.

20. This work by Epiphanios is no longer extant.

through the outpouring of his life-giving blood and water. And he has made us "a royal priesthood"[21] so that we may offer, instead of irrational sacrifices, "rational worship"[22] as a living sacrifice to the Father. [17]

1.7. *Behold, he comes with the clouds and every eye will see him, and the ones who pierced him, and all the tribes of the earth will mourn over him. Yes, Amen.*

Here, it says, he who has been slain as a lamb will come upon the clouds as a judge in the Fatherly glory.[23] Either the bodiless powers are implied by the clouds, or those which covered him on Mount Tabor with his holy disciples.[24] When he comes in glory every eye will see him. Those who pierced him and all the tribes of earth which persisted in their unbelief will mourn. *Yes, amen,* instead of "by all means." Thus he meant the same thing both in the Greek and Hebrew tongue, for *amen* is translated "let it be so."

1.8. *I am the Alpha and the Omega, the Beginning and the End, says the Lord God, the One who is, and who was, and who is to come, the Ruler of all.*

Christ is shown here both as God and as the Ruler of all things, both beginningless and at the same time endless, existing now and existing before and having no end, since he is [18] coeternal with the Father, and on account of this he will render to each one the wages of deeds done.[25]

1.9. *I, John, your brother and co-participant in the tribulation and in the kingdom and patience of Jesus Christ, was on the island called Patmos on account of the word of God and the witness of Jesus.*

"Inasmuch as <I am> *your brother,*" he says, "being also a *co-participant in the tribulations* on account of Christ, I naturally

21. 1 Pt 2.5, 9.   22. Rom 12.1.

23. See Mt 24.30–31, and also Lk 9.26, 21.27, Mt 16.27, Mk 13.26, and Mt 25.31 for similar references to Jesus coming in glory with the angels in an eschatological context.

24. Mt 16.27, 17.5; Mk 8.37, 9.7.

25. Cf. Ps 62(61).12; Prv 24.12; Wis 16.14; Rom 2.6; 1 Cor 5.10.

have acquired trustworthiness among you. Being condemned to live on the island of Patmos *on account of the witness of Jesus,* I will announce to you the mysteries seen by me on it."

CHAPTER 2

The Vision in Which He Saw the Lord in the Midst of the Seven Golden Lamps Clothed in a Long Robe

1.10–11. *I was in the Spirit on the Lord's day and I heard behind me a loud voice like a trumpet* [11] *saying, "I am the Alpha and the Omega, the First and the Last, and* [19] *write what you see in a book and send <it> to the seven churches in Ephesus and in Smyrna and in Pergamum and in Thyatira and in Sardis and in Philadelphia and in Laodicea.*

Having been possessed by the Holy Spirit and having a spiritual ear on the Lord's day, also <this day> would have been honored by him on account of the resurrection, he heard a voice that seemed like a trumpet because of the loud sound— "the sound of their voice went out to all the earth"[26]—declaring the beginninglessness and endlessness of God signified by the Alpha and Omega. By it he was commanded to send out his visions to the seven churches,[27] because of the aforementioned number seven applying to the Sabbath period of the future age. For this reason also the great Irenaeus had written that the seven heavens and seven angels leading the rest of them had been created by God first.[28]

1.12–13. *And I turned to see the voice that had spoken to me. And turning I saw seven gold lampstands,* [13] *and in the midst of the lampstands one like a son of man clothed in a long robe and around his breasts a golden belt.* [20]

That the voice <which he heard> was not sensory he signifies saying, *I turned,* not to hear it, but *to see the voice,* for spiritual hearing and seeing are the same. *I turned,* he says, *and I*

26. Ps 19(18).4; Rom 10.18b.
27. Rv 1.4.
28. *Proof of Apostolic Preaching* 9, which mentions seven heavens and various types of angels serving God.

saw seven lampstands—which he understood as representing the churches—and in their midst Christ, resembling a man[29]—because he is also God and not a mere man—clothed in a long garment as a high priest of the things above, "according to the order of Melchizedek."[30] A golden belt was wrapped around him, not on the hip as <worn by> other men in the era of hedonisms—the divine flesh is inaccessible to these <hedonisms>—but on the chest by the breasts <to show> also how the boundless and righteous divine anger is restrained by love for humankind. The truth is shown in the girding of the Master's breasts, that is, the two Testaments, through which the faithful are nourished. The belt is gold on account of honor, purity, and genuineness.

1.14. *His head and his hair were white as white wool, as snow, and his eyes as a flame of fire.*

For even though he is recent amidst us, nonetheless he is ancient; rather, he is before time. His white hair is a symbol of this. And *his eyes are as a flame of fire*, on the one hand, illuminating those who are holy and, on the other hand, burning the sacrilegious.

1.15a. *And his feet were like glowing brass, red-hot as in a furnace.* [21]

The divine Gregory[31] also understood that the feet meant the divine condescension through the flesh. For his feet by treading on the divinity achieved our salvation. The feet are also the foundations of the Church, *like glowing brass*, which physicians say is a sweet-smelling incense, which they call masculine incense.[32] Or otherwise: On the one hand, meaning the human nature by the glowing brass, and on the other hand the divine nature by the incense, through both of which is also shown the sweetness of the faith and the unconfused union <of

29. Cf. Dn 7.13. The entire description here in Revelation is influenced by Dn 7.9–10.

30. Ps 110(109).4.

31. This reference may be to Gregory the Theologian of Nazianzus, but the precise passage Andrew has in mind cannot be determined.

32. Dioscorides, *De materia medica* 1.68.

the two natures of Christ>. Or the fine brass signifies the beautiful melody of the gospel proclamation, and the incense is the return of the nations by which the bride is summoned.[33] And the feet of Christ are also the apostles,[34] who have been tested by fire in the furnace of trials in imitation of their Teacher.[35]

1.15b. *And his voice <was> like the sound of many waters.*

Naturally. His voice is in common with that of the Spirit, from which "rivers of living water flowed from the belly"[36] of the faithful, and it made a penetrating sound over all the earth.

1.16. *And he had in his right hand seven stars, and coming out from his mouth was a sharp, double-edged sword, and his appearance <was> as the sun shines in its power.* [22]

Further down he says that the seven stars are the seven angels of the churches. The *sharp, double-edged sword* means his decision against the wicked, "sharper than any two-edged sword,"[37] or the sword of the Spirit circumcising our inner man.[38] *Like the sun* his face shines, not in a splendor <appearing> to the senses, but to the intellect. For he is the "sun of righteousness,"[39] shining with his own power and authority, not like the sensory sun, which <shines> as a created object by God-given power and divine command.

1.17–18a. *And when I saw him, I fell down at his feet as dead. And he laid his right hand upon me saying, "Do not fear. I am the First and the Last, [18]and the living One. And I became dead, and behold, I am living unto the ages of ages. Amen.*

Christ revived the Apostle himself who had suffered through the weakness of human nature like Joshua son of Nun[40] and Daniel,[41] by saying to him, "*Do not fear,* for I have not come near to kill you, since I am beginningless and endless, having become dead for your sakes."

33. Song 4.8.
34. Rom 10.15; Is 52.7.
35. 1 Pt 4.12.
36. Jn 7.38.
37. Heb 4.12.
38. Eph 6.17.
39. Mal 3.20 LXX (4.2 RSV).
40. Jos 5.14.
41. Dn 8.17, 10.9–12.

1.18b. *And I have the keys of Hades and of death.* [23]

Instead <of being dead>, he has authority over bodily and spiritual death.

1.19 –20. [19]*Write, therefore, what you saw, the things that are and the things that are to come in the future after these things.* [20]*The mystery of the seven stars which you saw in my right hand, and of the seven golden lampstands: The seven stars are the angels of the seven churches, and the seven lampstands which you saw are the seven churches."*

Since Christ is the "true light,"[42] because of this, those abundant in his light are lamps as they shine in the night of this present life. Naturally, the churches are called *lampstands,* because, as the luminaries, they "have the word of life"[43] according to the Apostle. The lamps and lampstands are gold because of the honor and purity of the faith in them. An angel has stood guard for each of these, just as the Lord says,[44] and Gregory the Theologian had understood the present chapter: he figuratively called them "stars" because of the brightness and clarity of their nature.[45] [24]

CHAPTER 3

The Things that had been Written to the Angel of the Church of the Ephesians

2.1. *To the angel of the church in Ephesus write: "Thus says the one who holds the seven stars in his right hand, who walks among the seven golden lampstands.*

He discourses with the church through the angel just as if he were an educator <speaking> to the one being instructed. For the teacher develops a familiarity with those things that concern the student, either the grounds for complaint <against him> or his achievements, as he urges the student to imitate himself. By the seven stars, that is, the decoration lying in the right hand of Christ, is probably meant the angels, the seven

42. Jn 1.9.
44. Mt 18.10.

43. Phil 2.16.
45. *Or.* 42.9.

rational orders in heaven, <as> in the statements by the blessed Irenaeus[46] and Epiphanios,[47] in which "he is walking"[48] both "in the ends of the earth"[49] and *in the midst of the churches,* according to his familiar promise.

2.2–5a. [2]*I know your works and your toil and your patience, and that you cannot bear evil men, and you have tested those calling themselves apostles, and they are not, and you found them false.* [3]*And you have endurance and patience on account of my name and did not grow weary.* [4]*But I hold it against you that you have left your first love.* [5a]*Remember, therefore,* [25] *from where you fell, and repent and do the works <you did at> first.*

Accepting the church in two ways, he reprimands it in one way. He has put the one <reprimand> in the middle and the achievements on either side. He praised its hard work and patience for the faith and estrangement from the wicked ones, because, not believing every spirit,[50] <the church> tested the false apostles and, having determined them to be false, dismissed them, and, besides this, because he has hated the works of the shameful Nicolaitans. He complained that the love of neighbor and beneficence had grown lukewarm, and he called her to return to this <love> by those <words> which follow, on account of which he says, *do the works <you did at> first.*

2.5b– 6. [5b]*If not, I will come to you soon and I will move your lampstand from its place, if you do not repent.* [6]*But this you have: that you hate the works of the Nicolaitans, which I also hate.*

The movement of the church <means> to deprive them of divine grace, by which he brings down upon them swells and waves of evil spirits and evil men ministering to them. Some understood the removal of the lampstand <to refer to> the throne of the archpriest of Ephesus, because it was moved to the seat of the king.[51] [26] Anyone who comes upon the works of the Nicolaitans, which are hated by God, will know their detested heresy.

---

46. *Heres.* 1.5.2.   47. Epiphanios, *Panarion* 30.18.8.
48. Lv 26.12.   49. Ps 95(94).4.
50. Cf. 1 Jn 4.1.
51. The capital of the Empire. In 451, the Fourth Ecumenical Council

2.7. The one who has an ear, let him hear what the Spirit says to the churches. To him who conquers I will grant to eat of the Tree of Life, which is in the midst of the paradise of God."

Every person <has> a carnal ear, but only the spiritual person possesses a spiritual one, which was bestowed on Isaiah.[52] He promised to grant to such a victor in the war against the demons to *eat of the Tree of Life,* that is, to partake of the blessings of the future age, for, periphrastically, eternal life is meant by *the Tree.* Christ is each of these, as Solomon says and the present apostle elsewhere; the one, concerning wisdom, saying, "It is the Tree of Life,"[53] and likewise the other, concerning Christ, <says,> "He is God and eternal life."[54] Therefore, if we are allowed to attain them,[55] let us achieve victory over the passions, for the rewards will certainly follow the pains [27] by the grace and love for humankind of our Lord Jesus Christ, with whom glory belongs to the Father together with the Holy Spirit, unto the ages of ages. Amen.

---

issued the 28th canon of Chalcedon formalizing what had previously been a *de facto* situation in which the Bishop of Constantinople exercised authority over the Bishop of Ephesus, contrary to existing canonical regulations. The new canon gave explicit authority to the Bishop of Constantinople to ordain bishops in Pontus, Asia, and Thrace, as well as in "barbarian lands."

52. Is 50.5. 53. Prv 3.18.

54. 1 Jn 5.20.

55. The previously mentioned "blessings of the future age."

CHAPTER 4

The Things Declared to the Angel of the Church of the Smyrnaeans

2.8. And to the angel of the church in Smyrna write: "Thus says the First and the Last, who was dead and came to life.

HE FIRST AS GOD, and *the Last* as having become man in the latter times, and having opened eternal life to us through his three-day death.

2.9a. I know your works and the tribulation and the poverty, but you are rich.

"Affliction and poverty in the bodily things, which you suffer patiently for my sake, being afflicted by the unbelievers and deprived of your possessions, but in spiritual things *you are rich*, having 'the treasure hidden in the field'¹ of your heart." [28]

2.9b. And the blasphemy of those who say they themselves are Jews and are not, but a synagogue of Satan.

The *I know* used <previously is implied here as well>. And <as to> the *blasphemy* of *the synagogue of Satan*, he says, "I know that they are not that which they are called." "For the Jew is not the one who is manifest, but is hidden."² For "Judah" means "confession."³

1. Mt 13.44.
2. Rom 2.28.
3. Gn 29.35 indicates that "Judah" means "praise" or "give thanks," suggesting "to profess" or "to acknowledge"; hence the interpretation of "Judah" as "confession."

2.10. Do not fear what you are about to suffer. Behold, the devil is about to put some of you in prison that you might be tested, and you will have tribulation for ten days. Be faithful until death, and I will give you the crown of life.

He says, "Do not fear the tribulation from the enemies of God through afflictions and trials, for <it will last only> *ten days* and not <be> long-lived." For this reason, death must be despised, since in a little while it grants "the unfading crown of life."[4]

2.11. He who has an ear, let him hear what the Spirit says to the churches: The one who is victorious will not be harmed by the second death."

He says, he who hears spiritually and conquers the devil's evil suggestions, even though he receives the first death through the flesh, he will not be harmed by the *second death* of Gehenna.[5] [29]

CHAPTER 5
The Things Declared to the Angel of the Church in Pergamum

2.12–13a. [12]And to the angel of the church in Pergamum write: "Thus says the one who has the sharp two-edged sword: [13a]I know your works and where you dwell, where the throne of Satan is.

This city was full of idols, regarding which he says these things to them, accepting the faithful in it on account of their patience in temptations. The *two-edged sword* either means the word of the Gospel which he says circumcises the heart, separating the faithful and the unbelievers, or the sharp decision against the impious.

2.13b. And you keep my name. You did not deny my faith even in the days of Antipas, my faithful witness, that all-faithful martyr, who was killed among you, where Satan dwells.

Antipas, whose name had become known as the bravest martyr in Pergamum, whose martyrdom I have read,[6] the Evange-

---

4. 1 Pt 5.4.   5. Rv 20.6, 14, and 21.8.
6. Exactly which martyrdom Andrew had read is unclear. St. Antipas

list now mentioned to point to both their patience and the cruelty of those who had been led astray.

2.14–15. *¹⁴But I have a few things against you: that you have <some> there keeping the teaching of Balaam, who in Balaam taught [30] Balak to put a stumbling-block before the sons of Israel, to eat meat sacrificed to idols, and to practice fornication. ¹⁵Thus you also have those who keep the teaching of the Nicolaitans, which I likewise hate.*

So it seems this city had possessed two difficulties: First, the majority was Greek,[7] and second, among those who were called believers, the shameful Nicolaitans had sown evil "tares among the wheat."[8] For this reason he recalled Balaam, saying, *who in Balaam taught Balak,* through these words signifying that the *Balaam* of the mind, the devil, by means of the perceptible *Balak,* taught the stumbling block to the Israelites, fornication and idolatry. For by means of that pleasure <fornication> they were thrown down into performing this <idolatry> to Beelphegor.[9]

2.16. *Repent. If not, I will come to you soon, and I will war against them by the sword of my mouth.*

Love for humankind is also in the threat. For he does not say, "against you," but *I will war against them,* those who are incurably "diseased."[10]

2.17. *The one who has an ear, let him hear what the Spirit says to the churches: To the one who is victorious I will give to him to eat from the*

(whose feast day in the Orthodox Church is listed as April 11 in the *Acta Sanctorum* and the Greek *Menaion*) is said to have been the Bishop of Pergamum and a disciple of John the Theologian. The *Great Horologion* states that he was put into a hollow bronze bull, which was a Roman torture device. The individual to be executed was placed inside and the device was heated over a fire until red-hot and the person inside roasted to death. See *Bibliotheca Hagiographica Graeca,* 3d ed. (3 vols. in one), ed. François Halkin (Brussels: Société des Bollandistes, 1957), 1:48.

7. I.e., pagan.   8. Mt 13.24–30.

9. The Moabite fertility god, "the Baal of Peor." See Nm 25; also Dt 4.3–4 and Ps 106(105).28–30.

10. Nm 25.9.

hidden manna, [31] *and I will give to him a small white stone, and a new name written upon the stone, which no one knows except the one receiving it."*

The "Bread of Life"[11] is *the hidden manna,* the One who descended from heaven for us and has become edible.[12] Figuratively, the future good things are also called "manna," inasmuch as they are coming down from above, just as the heavenly Jerusalem.[13] He says those who are victorious against the devil will obtain <these things>. And they will receive both *the small white stone,* that is, the victorious being deemed worthy of the portion of the right hand,[14] and the new name which is unknown in the present life. For "eye has not seen and ear has not heard"[15] and mind has not grasped the good things of the future and the new name which the saints will inherit.

CHAPTER 6

*Things Declared to the Angel of the
Church in Thyatira*

2.18. And to the angel of the church in Thyatira write: "Thus says the Son of God, who has eyes like a flame of fire and whose feet are like glowing brass. [32]

It is said that the fiery <aspect> of the *eyes* signifies the enlightenment of the righteous and the burning of the sinners. The *feet* and the *glowing brass* mean the fragrance of the spiritual "myrrh of Christ in those who are saved"[16] and the indivisible and unconfused union of divinity and humanity.[17] For this union, ignited by means of the divine Spirit, cannot be grasped by human reasoning.

2.19–20. [19]I know your works and your love and faith and service and your patient endurance, and that your latter works exceed the first. [20]But I have this very much against you, that you allow the woman

---

11. Jn 6.35, 48.

12. Jn 6.50–51.

13. Gal 4.26; Rv 21.2.

14. Cf. Mt 25.33–34.

15. 1 Cor 2.9.

16. 2 Cor 2.15.

17. See Andrew's comments on Rv 1.14, page 61.

Jezebel, who calls herself a prophet, to teach and to lead my servants astray to practice immorality and to eat food sacrificed to idols.

"Even if I accept your piety by reason of faith, service to the needy, and endurance, yet I justly find fault with you. For you allow the heresy of Nicolaitans"—clearly identified as *Jezebel* on account of the impiety and licentiousness[18]—"to speak freely, thus placing a stumbling-block before my servants through their simplicity of thought and attracting them toward food sacrificed to idols, which they rightly renounced. You are obligated to silence her, also because, animated by an evil spirit, she pretends to be a prophet." [33]

2.21. *I gave her time to repent of her immorality.*

The evil \<is\> a choice, he says, since, having received time to repent rightly, she did not use it.

2.22–23a. [22]*Behold, I will throw her on a sickbed, and those who commit adultery with her I will throw into great tribulation, unless they repent of their deeds.* [23a]*And I will strike her children dead.*

He continues in that manner, and having likened the gathering of the heretics to an adulteress, he threatens to encompass her with illness and death, and also those perishing with her and those committing fornication against God, if they do not return to him through repentance.

2.23b–25. [23b]*And all the churches shall know that I am he who searches reins and hearts, and I will give to each of you according to your works.* [24]*And I say to the rest of you in Thyatira, who do not hold this teaching, any who have not learned the deep things of Satan, as they say: I do not lay upon you any other burden;* [25]*only hold fast to that which you have until I come.*

These things are \<addressed\> to the deceived heretics and those deceiving others. [34] To the more simple he says: "Since you, through your simple manner, are not able to endure the cunning and quick-witted men, inasmuch as you do not know *the deep things of Satan,* as you say, I do not request that you do

18. Cf. 1 Kgs 16.31–21.26.

battle through words but that you safeguard the teaching which you have received, until I will take you from there."

2.26 –28a. [26]*And he who conquers and who keeps my works until the end, I will give him authority over the nations, [27]and he shall rule them with a rod of iron; as earthen vessels they will be shattered, [28a]just as I myself have received <authority> from my Father.*

To him who does *my works,*" he says, *I will give authority* "over five or ten cities,"[19] as the Gospel said. Or, by this, he also hints at the judgment of the unbelievers, through which those who have been deceived, being judged by those who are believers in Christ, will be shattered as if they were ruled by *a rod <of iron>,* as the Lord said, "The men of Nineveh shall rise and condemn this generation."[20] And the *even as I received* <authority> *from my Father* <is said> in terms of his human nature which he has assumed through the flesh.

2.28b–29. [28b]*And I will give him the morning star. [29]He who has an ear, let him hear what the Spirit says to the churches.*"

Morning star, or, it says, the one about whom Isaiah was saying, "How did he fall from heaven, the bright rising morning star?"[21] whom he promised he will hand over to be "crushed under the feet of the saints."[22] Or <it is> the One who brings light, as has been said by the blessed Peter, [35] "dawning in the hearts"[23] of the faithful, the well-known illumination of Christ. Also John the Baptist and Elijah the Tishbite <are> designated light-bearers.[24] For the one, <John>[25] is discerned as the Forerunner[26] of the first rising of the "Sun of Righteousness,"[27] and the other is the Forerunner of the second.[28] With them, the victors over

19. Lk 19.17.
20. Mt 12.41; Lk 11.32.
21. Is 14.12–15.
22. Rom 16.20.
23. 2 Pt 1.19.
24. Cf. Jn 5.35; Mt 17.10–13.
25. It is the custom in the Christian East to refer to John not as "the Baptist" but as "John the Forerunner" since the role he served in relation to Christ was not primarily as Christ's baptizer, but as the one who prepared the way for the Messiah according to Mt 3.3, recalling the prophecy of Is 40.3: "Prepare the way of the Lord."
26. Cf. Is 9.2–7, 11.1–5; Lk 4.18–19.
27. Mal 3.20 LXX (4.2 RSV).
28. Elijah is here identified as the Forerunner of the *second* rising or ap-

the devil will have their part, we believe. It is not surprising that we have taken this as referring to two things totally contradictory to each other.[29] For we learn from the divine Scriptures that the lion of Judah <is> the Christ,[30] and <the lion> from Bashan <is> the Antichrist.[31] According to what is meant, it is this or the other. It <the morning star> also implies both the dawn of the future day, by which the darkness of the present life will be covered, and also its "messenger" bringing the good news of this <dawn>.[32]

For it <the dawn of the future day> goes before the "Sun of Righteousness,"[33] appearing to the saints and scattering the gloom of the present life, by whose rays may we also be illuminated by the good will of the Father with the All-Holy Spirit, to whom glory belongs unto the ages. Amen. [36]

---

pearance because of the widespread belief that he is to be one of the "two witnesses," along with Enoch, who will return in the end times prior to the Second Coming of Christ. See Rv 11.3–4, pages 131–32.

29. The contradiction is that the "morning star" could be either Lucifer or Christ.

30. Gn 49.9–10; Rv 5.5.

31. Dt 33.22.

32. Mal 3.1–2.

33. Mal 3.20 LXX (4.2 RSV).

SECTION THREE

CHAPTER 7
The Things Declared to the Angel of the Church in Sardis

3.1. *And to the angel of the church in Sardis write: "Thus says the one who holds the seven spirits of God and the seven stars: I know your works, that in name you live, and you are dead.*

HE SEVEN STARS, we said previously,[1] are the divine angels, and the seven spirits are either the angels themselves or the acts of the Life-giving Spirit, both of which are in the hand of Christ. On the one hand, <if the stars represent angels>, as the Master, he rules <them>; and on the other hand <if they represent the Spirit> he bestows the Spirit, being of the same essence. He also reprimands the church for having the mere name of living faith, having become dead with respect to good deeds.

3.2. *Wake up and strengthen those things which remain and which were about to die; for I have not found your works being fulfilled in the sight of God.*

"Shake off the sleep of laziness," he says, "and strengthen your members, who are about to die completely through unbelief." For it is not the beginning of good works that crowns the worker, but the completion.

3.3a. *Remember, therefore, what you received and heard, and keep [that], and repent.* [37]

"Keep the tradition which you received from the apostles,[2] and repent of laziness."

---

1. Referring to his comments on Rv 1.16, *Chp.* 2, *Text* 22, page 62.
2. Cf. 2 Thes 3.6 and 2 Thes 2.15. See also Phil 4.9 and 2 Tm 1.13–14.

3.3b. *If you do not wake up, I will come like a thief, and you will not know at what hour I will come upon you.*

Naturally. For both the death of each one and the common end are unknown to all. For those who are prepared <it will be> rest from pains, but for those who are unprepared, <it will be> like a thief[3] bringing death of the soul.

3.4. *You have a few people in Sardis who have not soiled their garments; and they will walk with me in white, for they are worthy.*

"You possess this good," he says, "that some people, those who have not soiled the garment of the flesh by filthy deeds, will be with me in the rebirth[4] brilliantly attired because they have kept 'the garment of incorruption'[5] spotless."

3.5–6. [5]*He who conquers shall be wrapped about in white garments, and I will not blot out his name from the Book of Life, and I will confess his name before my Father and before his angels.* [6]*He who has an ear, let him hear what the Spirit says to the churches."*

He who is victorious in the above-mentioned victory will shine like the sun in the clothing of his own virtues, and his name will remain indelible in the book of the living. [38] "He will be *confessed before my Father* and the holy powers,"[6] even as triumphant martyrs, just as he says in the Gospel, "the righteous will shine as the sun."[7]

---

3. Cf. Mt 24.42–43; Lk 12.39–40; 1 Thes 5.2.

4. Cf. Mt 19.28.

5. This expression is used several times in the prayers of the Orthodox baptismal service and in the prayer for catechumens during the Divine Liturgy of St. John Chrysostom.

6. Mt 10.32; Lk 12.8.

7. Mt 13.43.

CHAPTER 8

The Things Declared to the Angel of the Church in Philadelphia

3.7. And to the angel of the church in Philadelphia write: "Thus says the Holy One, the True One, who has the key of David, who opens and no one shuts, who shuts and no one opens.

His kingdom is called *the key of David,* for it is the symbol of authority. The key is also the Holy Spirit, <the key> of both the book of Psalms and every prophecy, through which the "treasures of knowledge"[8] are opened. On the one hand, he receives the first according to his humanity, and on the other hand he possesses the second according to the beginningless-ness of his divinity. Since in some manuscripts *Hades* is written instead of *David,* <this would mean that> through the key of Hades, the authority over life and death has been confirmed in Christ. He is holy and true, as absolute Holiness and self-existent Truth.

3.8. I know your works. Behold, I have set before you an open door, which no one is able to shut; <I know> that you have little [39] *power, and you kept my word and did not deny my name.*

From what has been written we learn that this city is small in size, but great in faith. Therefore, he says to it: *I know your works,* that is, "I accept," just as he says to Moses, "I know you above all."[9] "I opened before you a door of instructive preaching, which cannot be closed by temptations. I am satisfied with the attitude, and I do not demand things beyond strength."

3.9. Behold, I will give <you> those of the synagogue of Satan—who say that they are Jews and are not, but they lie. I will make them so that they come and bow down before your feet, and they will know that I have loved you.

"As a reward for the confession of my name," he says, "you will have the return and repentance of the Jews, who will kneel before your feet, asking to approach me for the illumination

8. Col 2.3.
9. Ex 33.12, 17.

which comes from me, remaining Judaizers secretly in their hearts, <though> not in appearance."[10]

3.10–11. [10] *Because you have kept the word of my patience, I will keep you from the hour of trial which is coming on the whole world, to try those who dwell upon the earth. I am coming soon.* [11] *Hold fast what you have, so that no one may seize your crown.* [40]

At the hour of trial has been said either <regarding> the persecution by the impious kings of Rome against the Christians which will come immediately at that particular time, from which he promises she <the church> is to be delivered; or <regarding> the worldwide movement at the end of the age against those who believe in the Antichrist, from which he promises to free her zealous ones who were arrested beforehand, through departure at that time, so that "they will not be tested beyond their strength."[11] He rightly says, *I come quickly,* for "after the affliction of those days immediately"[12] the Lord will come, as he says. For this reason he suddenly commands <them> to keep the treasure of the faith inviolate, so that no one loses the crown of patience.

3.12a. *He who conquers, I will make him a pillar in the temple of my God; he will never go out of it,*

Naturally. The victor over the opposing powers is established <as> a pillar and a foundation of the truth, having in it the immovable base according to the Apostle.[13]

12b. *And I will write on him the name of my God, and the name of the city of my God, the new Jerusalem, which descends out of heaven from my God, and my new name.* [41]

"Upon the heart of such a pillar," he says, "I will engrave the knowledge of the divine name and of the heavenly Jerusalem, so that he will see in her the beautiful things through the eyes of the Spirit, and also *my new name* which will be known by the saints in the future." He said *my God* in a human fashion about

10. Cf. Rv 2.9; Rom 2.28–29.
11. 1 Cor 10.13.
12. Mt 24.29; Mk 13.24.
13. Cf. 1 Tm 3.15.

the Father, since he became flesh for our sake, <remaining> unchanged <in his divinity>. The *Jerusalem descends* from above, <because> the knowledge of divinity first began from the angels, then <continued> until it finally came down upon us, united to one another through Christ our head.[14]

3.13. *He who has an ear, let him hear what the Spirit says to the churches."*

Let us pray that we ourselves possess such a little ear.

CHAPTER 9
Things Declared to the Angel of the Church of the Laodiceans

3.14a. *And to the angel of the church in Laodicea write: "Thus says The Amen, the faithful and true witness,*

Through faithfulness the truth of Christ is shown, or rather, that he is Truth in its essence. [42]

3.14b. *the beginning of God's creation:*

Beginning instead of "kingdom," and the beginning of all that is, as the Master over all created things. For the beginning of creation is the primary and uncreated cause.

3.15–16a. *[15]I know your works: you are neither cold nor hot. Would that you be cold or hot! [16a]Thus it is that you are lukewarm and neither hot nor cold,*

Gregory the Theologian says, "We must live exactly hot or exactly cold."[15] Naturally. For the one who is cold and has not tasted the living faith, will often be in hope of attaining it. But the one who has been warmed through baptism in the Spirit and has been cooled later through laziness, has cut off from himself the hopes of salvation, having condemned the chosen faith. For actions, the middle way is not refused, just as a legal

14. Cf. Eph 4.15.
15. If this is intended to be an exact quotation of Gregory, its source cannot be identified.

marriage is not rejected, being the middle way between virginity and fornication. But in faith, the middle way and the lukewarm are worthless. [43]

3.16b–17. *16bI intend to vomit you out of my mouth. 17For you say, 'I am rich, I have prospered, and I need nothing,' and you do not know that you are miserable and wretched and poor and blind and naked.*

"Just as lukewarm water causes people who receive it to vomit," he says, "hence I too, through a word of my mouth, will vomit you like detested food into eternal punishment, for you mingled the thorns of riches with the seed of the divine word[16] and you are unaware of your own poverty in spiritual matters and the blindness of your spiritual eyes and the nakedness of good deeds."

3.18. *I advise you to buy from me gold refined by fire, so that you will become rich, and that you may put on white garments, that the shame of your nakedness may not be revealed, and salve to anoint your eyes, that you may see.*

"If you would *be rich*," he says, "to acquire a burning resolve and a willing heart take *refined gold* from me, the Enricher, the instructive Word, illumined by the fire of trials, through which you will have the inviolable treasure in the heart and be clothed in the most brilliant garment [44] of virtues through which the nakedness attached to you from sin will be covered." *Eye salve* <is> also lack of possessions. For if gifts render seeing eyes blind, then by all means, a lack of property[17] will open them.

3.19. *If I love someone, I reproach and correct <him>. Therefore, be zealous and repent.*

Oh, the love for humanity! How much goodness the reproach holds!

---

16. Cf. Mt 13.7, 22; Mk 4.7, 18; Lk 8.7, 14.
17. Cf. Ex 23.8; Dt 16.19.

3.20. Behold, I stand at the door and I knock; if one will hear my voice and will open the door, I will come in to him, and I will dine with him, and he with me.

"My presence is not forced," he says. "I knock at the door of the heart and rejoice with those who open for their salvation. For I consider this as food and supper, being fed with these things with which they feed themselves and they escape the famine of hearing the Divine Word and the darkness[18] of error."

3.21. He who conquers, I will grant him to sit with me on my throne, as I myself have conquered and taken my seat with my Father on his throne. He who has an ear, let him hear what the Spirit says to the churches." [45]

The Kingdom and the repose of the future age are indicated by the *throne*. Therefore he says that "those who have conquered the enemy will be co-glorified"[19] with me and will "co-reign."[20] The *as I myself conquered* is said in human terms to refer to the assumption <of the flesh>. For God the Logos did not acquire the Kingdom as a reward for virtue, for this he possesses eternally as part of his essence. For if this were not the case, he would not have been able to share it <the Kingdom> with others; but according to the Theologian and "Son of Thunder,"[21] he has imparted this to all the saints from his own fullness.[22] Therefore he has promised to the holy apostles that they will "sit on twelve thrones to judge the twelve tribes of Israel"[23] of the future. Since he became human for our sake, being God and King before the ages, he had partaken of everything that is our own except sin,[24] and imparted all that is his to those victorious [46] over the devil, as much as it was possible for people to receive. Therefore, having made the cloud a vehicle for the rise heavenward in his Ascension,[25] he also says through the Apostle that the saints will be "caught up in the clouds to meet him,"[26] and he will come <as> Judge, as Creator and Mas-

18. Cf. Am 8.9–11.
20. 2 Tm 2.12.
22. Cf. Jn 1.16.
24. Cf. Heb 4.15.
26. 1 Thes 4.17.

19. Rom 8.17.
21. Mk 3.17.
23. Mt 19.28; Lk 22.30.
25. Acts 1.9.

ter of creation, handing over to the saints to judge those who opposed the truly divine and blessed slavery, as the Apostle says, "Do you not know that we will judge angels?"[27] that is, the "rulers of darkness."[28] Since we have such a lover of humanity as Judge, let us hurry to gain his favor, fulfilling endlessly Solomon's saying "At all times my garments have been white,"[29] not being stained by evil deeds. For this way, having decorated our beloved souls as for a wedding,[30] we will present them to the King for a union, and we will gain the eternal blessings in him, Christ our God, the Supplier of these, to whom is due glory, honor, and worship with the Father, together with the [All]-Holy Spirit, unto the ages of ages. Amen.

27. Eph 6.12.
28. Ibid.
29. Eccl 9.8.
30. Cf. Mt 22.11–12.

SECTION FOUR

CHAPTER 10
About the Door That Was Seen in Heaven and the Twenty-Four Elders and the Things that Follow

4.1. After these I saw, and behold, an open door in heaven! And the first voice that I heard was like a trumpet [47] speaking to me, saying, "Come up here, and I will show you the things which must happen after these."

HE REMOVAL OF the *door* of the secret mysteries of the spirit means the declaration, and the *trumpet* <means> the great voice of the one revealing, and the *come up here* <means> the complete removal of the mind of the one hearing it from the earthly <realm> and its coming-to-be in heaven.[1]

4.2–3. [2]And immediately I was in the Spirit. And behold, a throne stood in heaven, [3]and one sitting upon the throne who appeared like the stone jasper and carnelian, and a rainbow was around the throne that looked like an emerald.

After hearing the voice and being stamped by the Spirit, he says, he saw the sovereign throne, through which is meant the repose in the saints of God, for he is enthroned with these. After that he presents the Father seen here, not attributing bodily characteristics to him, just as in the previous vision of the Son, but he compares him to precious stones; first, jasper, meaning, as pale green, the evergreen at once both the life-bringer and bestower of the food of the divine nature, through which every seed brings forth young sprouts. [48] In addition to this <it in-

1. Cf. Col 3.2.

81

dicates that the Father is> fearsome to opponents—for they say that *jasper* is fearsome to wild beasts and phantoms[2]—and also after this <it means> the therapeutic spiritual healing of those who receive <him>. For the great Epiphanios says that when placed upon <someone> this stone heals illnesses and wounds made by iron.[3] And the *rainbow* like an emerald shows the variety and blooming virtues of the angelic orders.

4.4. *And around the throne <were> twenty-four thrones, and sitting on the thrones <were> twenty-four elders wrapped in white garments, and upon their heads <were> gold crowns.* [49]

Someone before us took these <to be> Abel, and twenty others of the Old <Testament> and three of the New <Testament>.[4] Either this, or perhaps we must understand it to be indicating those who have been adorned in deeds and speech by twenty-four primary elements. Let the reader be tested. To understand it quickly more suitably, by the twelve elders <is meant> those who excelled in the Old, and by the twelve others those who excelled in the New. For from those both the twelve leaders of the tribes, also those twelve apostles in the New, were pre-eminent, whom the Lord promised to seat on twelve thrones.[5] The white clothes are symbols of the brilliant life and the unending feast and gladness,[6] the crowns of victory which <belong> to those who behaved like men and were successful against the evil demons.

4.5a. *From out of the throne came flashes of lightning and sounds and peals of thunder.*

And from here is demonstrated the fearsome and astonishing <aspect> of God against those unworthy of his long-suffering. To those, however, who are worthy of salvation, both of these <the lightning and thunder> inspire enlightenment, the one to the eyes of the mind and the other to the spiritual ears upon which they have fallen. [50]

2. Epiphanios, *De gemmis*, PG 43:297D. See also Dioscurides, *De materia medica* 5.142.

3. Epiphanios, ibid.

4. Oik. 3.7.1.

5. Mt 19.28; Lk 22.30.

6. Cf. Mt 22.1–10 and 25.1–13.

4.5b–6a. [5b]*And seven torches of fire burn before the throne, which are the seven spirits of God;* [6a]*and before the throne <something> like a glass sea like crystal.*

We must understand these spirits <are> either, as Irenaeus says, the seven angels who surpass the others,[7] or the activities of the Life-giving Spirit, which Isaiah had recalled.[8] I think it is unlikely to be neither of the two. The *glass sea* designates the multitude of the holy powers, and also the clarity, spotlessness, and calmness of the future life. Perhaps what is indicated by this is the back of the sky which is covered with the water that is inaccessible to us, according to the Psalm.[9] If some had considered it to be the crystal-like nature of the sky, we must also consider whether the substance of the God-trodden surface is meant by this, having both the brightness and clarity. But the search into things beyond the apprehension of the mind is laughable.

4.6b. *And in the midst of the throne, and around the throne, <were> four living beings, full of eyes in front and behind:*

The *throne* is shown by this to be signifying the reign and resting-place of God, in which and around which he saw the seraphim, being taught through the multitude of their eyes their ability to see God with regard to the divine light, and also that those eyes behind and in front receive light and knowledge from God. [51]

4.7. *And the first living being <was> like a lion, the second living being <was> like a calf, the third living being had a face like a man, and the fourth living being <was> like an eagle flying.*

These living beings, we think, were also seen by Isaiah;[10] by the four individuals is meant either the four elements of both God's creation and maintenance, as some thought, or the mastery over the things in heaven and earth and in the sea; or the four virtues[11] and the four Gospels, as it had been well stated by

7. *Proof of Apostolic Preaching* 9.   8. Is 11.2.
9. Ps 104(103).3.   10. Is 6.2.
11. Possibly the four principal virtues in Stoic philosophy: courage, justice, self-control, and intellectual discernment.

others: the *lion* meaning bravery and the Gospel according to John, as Irenaeus says,[12] through this signifying the Kingdom from before the ages. For "in the beginning" is "the Word,"[13] he preached. The *calf*, inasmuch as it endures its own pains, signifies righteousness and the Gospel according to Luke, as the one providing the legal and priestly genealogy of Christ. The *eagle* is prudence, for this is witnessed by the living being and the Gospel according to Mark, as brief and having its origin in the prophetic spirit.[14] The *man* <signifies> the intellect as well as the Gospel according to Matthew, as they proclaimed the birth of Christ by nature and not by the law. Perhaps through these the Incarnation of Christ is also indicated, through [52] the *lion* as a king, through the *calf* as a priest, perhaps also a sacrifice, through the *man* as being made man for our sake, and through the *eagle* as the provider of the Life-giving Spirit, which came upon us from above.

4.8a. *And the four living beings, each of them having six wings, are full of eyes all around and within,*

This is what Dionysios the Great says. For this reason the two wings cover the face, the other two cover the feet, and <by means of> the middle they fly,[15] so that their reverence is shown concerning the higher and deeper things of their own apprehension, on account of which <reverence> they are lighted up towards the divine light by means of their divine middle pair <of wings>.

4.8b. *And they do not rest day and night, saying, "Holy, holy, holy, is the Lord God Almighty, who was and who is and who is to come!"*

These holy powers do not rest, never ceasing the divine hymnody and offering the threefold blessing to the Tri-hypostatic Divinity. And the *who is and who was and who is to come* we said means the Holy Trinity.[16]

12. *Heres.* 3.11.8.   13. Jn 1.1.
14. Mk 1.2–3, which quotes Mal 3.1 and Is 40.3.
15. This is Andrew's first reference to Dionysios, whom he entitles "the Great," also known as Dionysios "the Areopagite" and today most commonly referred to as "Pseudo-Dionysios." *Eccl. Hier.* 4.3.8. See Is 6.2.
16. Cf. Andrew's comments on Rv 1.4–5, *Chp.* 1, *Text* 13–15, pages 56–58.

4.9–10a. [9]*And whenever the living beings give glory and honor and thanksgiving* [53] *to him who is seated on the throne, who lives for ever and ever,* [10a]*the twenty-four elders fall down before him who is seated on the throne and worship him who lives for ever and ever.*

Through these is signified that the twenty-four elders are also understood by us participating in the hymnody of the heavenly powers, confessing that they have received from God the power of victory over spiritual enemies.

4.10b–11. [10b]*They cast their crowns before the throne, saying,* [11]*"You are worthy, Lord our God, to receive glory and honor and power, for You created all things, and by Your will they exist and were created."*

They say, "You, Master, are the cause and the provider of the crowns of victory, and thanksgiving is due to You from all things as creatures."

CHAPTER 11

About the Small Scroll Sealed With Seven Seals Which No One Who Has a Created Nature is Able to Open

5.1. *And I saw in the right <hand> of the One who was seated on the throne a small scroll covered in writing on the inside and outside, sealed with seven seals.*

We think *the small scroll* is the all-wise memory of God, in which, according to David, all things [54] are written[17] and <there is> the "abyss of the divine judgments."[18] The things written on the outside are easily understood according to the literal meaning, but the things inside <symbolizing> the spiritual meaning are very hard to comprehend.

The *seven seals*, which no one of created nature is able to loosen, <signify> either the fulfillment of the scroll, which is obscure and unknown to all, or the dispensation of the one "who searches the depths of the Spirit of God."[19] The scroll also means the prophecy which Christ himself said in the Gospel according to

17. Cf. Ps 139(138).16.   18. Ps 36(35).6.
19. 1 Cor 2.10.

Luke had been fulfilled,[20] which things occurring thereafter are to be fulfilled in the last days.

5.2–3. [2]*And I saw a strong angel proclaiming with a loud voice, "Who is worthy to open the scroll and loosen its seals?"* [3]*And no one in heaven, or on earth, or under the earth, was able to open the scroll or to look at it.*

By these is meant that neither angels nor human beings, those [55] existing in the flesh, nor the saints who had departed from the flesh <are able> to grasp the precise knowledge of the divine judgments, except the "Lamb of God,"[21] through his presence releasing the obscurity of the things prophesied about him.

5.4. *And I was weeping much because no one was found worthy to open and to read the small scroll nor to look at it.*

I was weeping, he says, perhaps since the most spotless order of the angelic substances fell into ignorance.

5.5. *And one of the elders said to me, "Do not weep; behold, the Lion of the tribe of Judah, the Root of David, has conquered; he will open the scroll and its seven seals."*

If *the small scroll* is incomprehensible even to the angels, he says, it is not, however, to God, who became incarnate for human beings, who is the Root of David, on the one hand as a Creator on account of his divinity, and on the other coming from the root on account of his humanity.

20. Cf. Lk 4.21.
21. Rv 5.6; Jn 1.29, 36.

CHAPTER 12

*Concerning the Vision in the Middle of the Throne and
the Four Living Beings*

5.6. *And I saw, in the midst of the throne and the four living beings
and in the middle of the elders, a Lamb standing, as one slain,* [56]
*having seven horns and seven eyes, which are the spirits of God sent
out into all the earth.*

The *seven eyes* and the *seven horns* of the Lamb signify the seven spirits of Christ, which Isaiah[22] and Zechariah[23] the prophet recalled. The *as one slain* means his life after the sacrifice, by which he displayed the signs of his passion, as the one who truly had been slain, after rising from the dead.

5.7–8. [7]*And he went and took <the scroll> from the right <hand> of the
one sitting on the throne.* [8]*And when he took the scroll, the four living
beings and the twenty-four elders fell down before the Lamb, each holding a harp and golden bowls full of incense, which are the prayers of
the saints.*

The *harps* signify the harmonious and beautiful-sounding divine doxology, and the *incenses* <signify> the sweet-smelling sacrifice of the faithful being offered through a life of purity, as the Apostle says, "We are a sweet fragrance of Christ."[24] The bowls symbolize the thoughts out of which come forth the fragrance of good works and pure prayer.

5.9–10. [9]*And they sang a new song, saying, "You are worthy to take the
scroll and to open its seals, for you were slain* [57] *and you purchased
us for God by your blood, from every tribe and tongue and people and
nation,* [10]*and you made them kings and priests to our God, and they
shall reign upon the earth."*

Through this the elders are shown to be the ones who have been well-pleasing to God in the Old and the New <Testaments>,[25] and the ones who offer thanksgiving on behalf of all the world to the *slain Lamb* of God who *purchased us*. The *song*

---

22. Is 11.1–5.
24. 2 Cor 2.15.

23. Zec 4.10.
25. Cf. *Chp.* 10, *Text* 49, page 82.

is *new* which the ones illuminated *from every tribe and tongue* had been taught to sing through the Spirit, having been released from the "former stroke"[26] <of condemnation>. These will *reign over* the new *earth,* it says, which the Lord promised to the meek.[27]

5.11–13. [11]*And I saw, and heard a voice of many angels around the throne and of the living beings and of the elders, and their number was myriads of myriads and thousands of thousands,* [12] *saying in a great voice, "Worthy is the Lamb who was slain, to receive power and wealth and wisdom and might and honor and glory!"* [13]*And I heard every creature that is in heaven and on earth and under the earth and on the sea, and all the things which are in them,* [58] *saying to the one who sits upon the throne and to the Lamb, "Blessing and honor and glory and might for ever and ever! Amen."*

For God, as the originator of all, is glorified by all things, those known by the intellect, those perceived by the senses, those which are living beings, and those which simply exist by the laws of nature. And his Only-begotten and Consubstantial Son <is glorified>, as the one who graciously bestows renewal on humankind[28] and on the creation brought into being by him, even though it has been written that he would receive authority as a man over those in heaven and on earth.[29]

5.14. *And the four living beings said, "Amen," and the elders fell down and worshiped.*

Through this it is shown <that> angels and human beings have become "one flock"[30] and one Church, through <the> Christ of God, who has joined together the things which were divided and has destroyed "the middle wall of separation."[31] For behold, as we have heard for ourselves, together with the four living beings, who are [59] superior to the rest of the angelic orders, those who characterize the fullness of people be-

26. Rom 7.6.
27. Mt 5.5.
28. Cf. Rom 6.4 and 7.5; 2 Cor 4.16 and 5.17; Gal 6.15; Col 3.10.
29. Mt 28.18.   30. Jn 10.16.
31. Eph 2.14.

ing saved are also worthy <to offer> the praise and worship of God. May we too be worthy of this in Christ himself, the Giver of peace[32] and our God, to whom, along with the Father, together with the Holy Spirit <are due> glory, power, unto the ages of ages. Amen.

32. Jn 14.27.

SECTION FIVE

CHAPTER 13
Loosening of the First Seal

6.1. *And I saw when the Lamb opened one of the seals, and I heard one of the four living beings saying, with a voice like thunder, "Come!"*

ND HERE THE good order of those in heaven is shown, from the first orders coming down to the second. Thus, from one of the fourfold-appearing living beings, that is, the lion, he heard originating from the first voice the command *"come"* <being spoken> to the angel forming the vision through an angel in a figurative fashion. The first living being, the lion, seems to me to show the princely spirit of the apostles against the demons, about whom it has been said: "Behold, the kings of the earth have been gathered together,"[1] and also, "You will appoint them as rulers upon all the earth."[2] [60]

6.2. *And I saw, and behold, a white horse, and the one sitting on it having a bow; and a crown was given to him, and he went out conquering and to conquer.*

The loosening of the present seal and of all those which follow, some have interpreted[3] as unfolding the dispensation in the flesh of the Logos of God: the first in the birth, the second in the baptism, the third in the divine signs subsequent to this <baptism>, the fourth in standing before Pilate, the fifth in the cross, the sixth in the placing in the tomb and the spoiling of Hades.[4] But we have agreed with Methodios, who said in the

1. Ps 48(47).4.   2. Ps 45(44).16.
3. This "some" definitely includes a reference to Oikoumenios (4.7–15), but others may also have made this interpretation.
4. Either Andrew misunderstands Oikoumenios's exposition, or he knows

text, thus verbatim, that it is not necessary to think "that Christ himself is the one who has been born. For long ago, before the Apocalypse, the mystery of the Incarnation of the Logos had been fulfilled. John is speaking with authority concerning the present and future things,"[5] and from there on he gave an explanation about how the fire-red dragon was subdued. Thus we explained the loosening of the first seal as meaning the generation of the apostles, [61] those who bend the gospel message like a bow against the demons, leading them to be fatally wounded by the saving arrows of Christ, having grasped a crown; through the truth <as a weapon> against them <the demons> they conquered the leader of deception in the hope of a second victory, confessing the name of the Master to the point of a violent death. Wherefore it is written, *he went out conquering and to conquer.* For the first victory is the return of the nations, and the second is the voluntary departure from the body by means of tortures on account of it.

CHAPTER 14
Loosening of the Second Seal

6.3. *And when he opened the second seal, I heard the second living being saying, "Come."*

I think the second living being, the calf, is said to characterize the priestly sacrifice of the holy martyrs, while the first <living being> describes the apostolic authority, as was said.

6.4. *And out came another horse, bright red, and the one sitting* [62] *upon it was permitted to take the peace from the earth, so that people should slay one another; and he was given a large sword.*

We suppose that this means the second succession of the apostles, which is completely fulfilled through martyrs and teachers,

---

of another similar interpretation. Andrew reports Oikoumenios's interpretation of the fifth seal as the cross, but that is not exactly correct. The fifth seal for Oikoumenios is the souls under the altar who were objecting to the treatment of Christ, presumably on the cross, but Oikoumenios specifically states that the *sixth* seal is the cross, death, resurrection, and ascension (4.15.2).

5. Methodios of Olympos, *Symp.* 8.7.

during which, while the remainder of the gospel message was spreading, the peace of the world was abolished, <human> nature having been divided against itself according to that which had been said by Christ, "I did not come to bring peace to the earth but a sword,"[6] through which the slain martyrs were lifted up to the heavenly altar. The fire-red horse <is> a symbol of either the shedding of blood or the flaming disposition of those suffering for Christ. What was written about *the one seated* on <the horse>, that *he was permitted to take the peace,* shows the all-wise allowance of God testing the faithful servants through trials.

CHAPTER 15
Loosening of the Third Seal

6.5. *And when he opened the third seal, I heard the third living being saying, "Come!"*

I think the third living being, the man, is said to signify the fall of people [63] and, because of that, torment, on account of the easy fall into sin through the power of free choice.

6.5b–6. [5b]*And I saw, and behold, a black horse, and the one sitting on it having a scale in his hand;* [6]*and I heard <something> like a voice in the midst of the four living beings saying, "A quart of wheat for a denarius, and three quarts of barley for a denarius; and do not harm oil and wine!"*

It is likely and sensible for a literal famine to occur then, just as it will also be announced by what follows. We think that by the *black horse* the mourning for those who have fallen from the faith in Christ on account of extreme torture is signified. The *scale* is the examiner of those who had fallen from the faith, both through an easily changing mind or vainglory, and on account of weakness of body. The *quart of wheat* worth as much as *a denarius* means figuratively those who "lawfully struggled"[7] and perfectly guarded the divine image which was

6. Mt 10.34.
7. 2 Tm 2.5.

given to them, and the *three quarts of barley* suits those who, in a manner befitting a beast, bowed down before their persecutors on account of cowardice, but accordingly [64] repented later, and washed clean the soiled image with tears. The command *do not harm wine and oil* means not to disregard the healing through returning to Christ, which healed the one who has "fallen among robbers,"[8] in order that those who through long-suffering were about to renew the fight would not be carried off by death. Therefore, so that we too will gain, for the disease of our souls, the Physician-God who loves humankind, let us hurry to be such for our fallen brothers, by offering to them the oil of sympathy mingled with the wine of exhortation, "in order that the maimed parts not worsen but be healed,"[9] according to the divine Apostle, so that becoming "co-workers with God,"[10] we will delight forever in his blessings, by the grace and love for humankind of our Lord Jesus Christ, with whom glory <is due> together with the Father, with the Holy Spirit unto the ages of ages. Amen.

8. Lk 10.30.
10. 1 Cor 3.9.

9. Heb 12.13.

SECTION SIX

CHAPTER 16
Loosening of the Fourth Seal, Showing the Chastisements Which Befall the Impious

6.7. *And when he opened the fourth seal, I heard the voice of the fourth living being saying, "Come!"* [65]

 HE FOURTH LIVING *being*, that is, the eagle, its high flight and keen eyesight coming down upon its prey from above, can signify the wounds from the divinely led wrath of God for the revenge of the pious and the punishment of the impious, unless being improved by these <wounds> they return.

6.8. *And I saw, and behold, a pale horse, and the name of the one sitting upon <it> was Death. And Hades follows him. And they were given authority over a fourth of the earth, to kill by sword and by famine and by death and by wild beasts of the earth.*

The series <of events> drawn out previously are connected to the present events. For as Eusebius says in the eighth chapter of the ninth book of his *Ecclesiastical History*,[1] in the zenith of the persecutions, during the reign of Maximin the Roman Emperor, innumerable crowds were killed by the coming of famine and plague among them, along with other calamities; and such that <the living> were not able to bury them, and yet the Christians then generously busied themselves with the burial <of the dead>, and many of those who had been deceived[2] were

---

1. Eusebius of Caesarea, *E. H.* 9.8.
2. The pagan unbelievers were deceived by the devil because they rejected Christ and persecuted the Christians.

94

led to [66] the knowledge of the truth by the philanthropy of the Christians. The Armenians revolted against the Romans, not a few taking up the sword, and, he says, the bodies of the dead were eaten by the dogs. Then those remaining who had survived, turned to killing the dogs, fearing lest they too <upon> dying would occupy those living tombs.[3] It is not unlikely that the wild beasts participated in this banquet with the dogs due to the abundance of food. In our own generation we have known each of these happenings.[4]

3. I.e., the dogs' stomachs.

4. This oblique reference by Andrew to his "own generation" witnessing each of these horrors in turn—an Armenian revolt, plague, famine, and the death of massive numbers of people by the sword—is the strongest evidence that this commentary was composed in the early seventh century. This period formed a critical turning-point for the history of the Roman Empire due to numerous and varied catastrophes. James Howard-Johnston notes that the first event in the *History* attributed to the Armenian historian Sebeos is the Armenian revolt of 572, which sparked the fourth Persian-Roman conflict of the sixth century. The conflict lasted until 591. See *The Armenian History Attributed to Sebeos*, trans. R. W. Thomson, notes by James Howard-Johnston, part 1 "Translation and Notes" (Liverpool: Liverpool University Press, 1999), xviii–xxi. The Eastern Roman Empire had experienced several waves of bubonic plague in the mid to late sixth century, which decimated the population, creating labor and revenue shortages that strained the Empire and weakened it considerably. Illness and decreased population also meant that fewer crops were planted and famine resulted. Severe winters in the years prior to the composition of this commentary also contributed to famine. Another blow to the Empire occurred when a usurper, Phocas, murdered the sitting Emperor Maurice, seizing the throne by force for the first time in the history of the Christian Roman Empire. This led to chaos, the breakdown of social order in most cities, and then to civil war when Heraclius took up arms against Phocas, defeating him in 610. Bubonic plague also broke out again in 608, not long before the composition of this commentary; see Warren Treadgold, *A History of Byzantine State and Society* (Palo Alto, CA: Stanford University Press, 1997), 239. The political and economic upheaval weakened the Empire such that it became vulnerable to invasion, especially by the Persians. Illness and depopulation caused by plague, civil war, and the Persian invasion of 609 exacerbated and prolonged the famine. Only these events, capped off by Persian invasion and death and destruction in his own city, Caesarea, Cappadocia, can correspond to Andrew's poignant reference to witnessing a catastrophe on such a scale that there were not enough survivors to bury the dead. The first capture and occupation of Caesarea occurred in 609. A second conquest and its complete destruction by the Persians happened in 611.

CHAPTER 17

Loosening of the Fifth Seal, Meaning the Saints Crying
Out to the Lord About the End of the World

6.9–10. ⁹*And when he opened the fifth seal, I saw under the altar the*
souls of people who had been slain on account of the word of God and
on account of the witness which they had <made>. They cried out with
a loud voice, saying, ¹⁰*"How long, O holy and true Master, before you*
judge and avenge our blood on those who dwell upon the earth?"

If anyone forces the loosening of the four seals to apply to
the foregoing acts of dispensation by Christ, he will naturally
adapt this to the previously fulfilled prophets and the remaining saints who cry out loud because of the divine forbearance,
after whom he <Christ> endured unto the cross, being insulted by the Jews.[5] [67] And if any take these things to mean a
foretelling of future events according to the teachers of the
Church, he will suppose that such a thing is fitting, that those
who were killed for Christ will cry out against their persecutors,
at which <time> the worthy will return to cut off the impiety
of the disobedient at the consummation of the world, so that
"the righteous will not stretch out their hands in lawlessness."[6]
For even though, already at that time, as it has been said, the
ungodly were tested by the divine wrath, nonetheless the relics

---

5. The interpretation to which Andrew is referring here is that of Oikoumenios, who believed that the seals represented events in the life of Christ
(4.13.3–5; see FOTC 112:72–73). Andrew strongly disagrees with this, first
because prophecy cannot refer to the past, but also because Oikoumenios's
interpretation often violates the context, sequence, and plain meaning of the
text. The opening of the fifth seal reveals the souls of (presumably Christian)
martyrs under the altar. But if the seals represent the life of Christ, then the
souls cannot be those of Christian martyrs since Christ himself has not even
been crucified yet. Oikoumenios is forced to conclude that these are the souls
of the righteous of the Old Covenant. Andrew states that this explanation is
strained or "forced," and he offers his interpretation in the sentence which
follows, pointing out that his understanding is in keeping with the tradition
of the Church. Much of Andrew's commentary is devoted to correcting Oikoumenios's interpretation, and many of Andrew's references to unnamed interpreters are pointing to Oikoumenios. (See Introduction, pages 9–10.)

6. Ps 125(124).3.

\<of the saints\> were asking for punishing or chastising afflictions.

6.11. *And he gave them each a white robe and told them to rest again a little longer, until their fellow servants and their brethren who were to be killed in the future, even as they \<had been\>, completed \<their number\>.*

And by these \<words\> the saints seem to be asking for the full consummation of the world. Wherefore, they are called upon to endure patiently until the completion of the \<number of\> brothers, so that they will not become *complete* without them, according to the Apostle.[7] The white robes show the blooming brightness of the virtues in which they are vested, even though they "have not yet received the promises."[8] [68] So at least in the hope of these things, to which they look forward spiritually, having ceased from all earthliness, they naturally delight in reposing in the bosom of Abraham. For this has been said by many of the saints, that each one will have as one's share a place worthy of each worker's virtue through which also their future glory is to be assigned.

CHAPTER 18
Loosening of the Sixth Seal, Signifying the Upcoming Plagues at the End of Time

6.12–13. [12]*And I saw, and when he opened the sixth seal, and a great earthquake occurred, and the sun became black as sackcloth, and the moon became like blood.* [13]*And the stars of the sky fell to the earth as the fig tree casts its winter fruit when shaken by a great wind;*

Some took all these things to mean the siege of Vespasian, having figuratively understood each of these things mentioned. It seems to us that here a shift has taken place beginning from the time of persecutions to [69] the time before the departure of the pseudo-Christ, during which so many afflictions were prophesied to come, and perhaps the people, being practiced

7. Heb 11.40.
8. Heb 11.39.

in these afflictions, did not renounce the punishments brought upon them by the Antichrist, of such a sort as we have never known. We often find in the Scriptures that an earthquake certainly <represents> a change in <the course of> events.[9] For "once more I will shake"[10] signifies the change of the things being shaken, as the Apostle says. And in the Old <Testament> it is said, concerning the journey of the Israelites out of Egypt, "the earth was shaken and the heavens dripped."[11] The darkening of *the sun,* and *the moon* without light and blood-like, shows those who are unenlightened overtaken by divine wrath—for thus many times the blessed Cyril also interpreted these things in this manner[12]—the *falling of the stars* as it already has been written about the ones deceived by Antiochus,[13] <means> also the falling of those who think they are "luminaries in the world,"[14] who bend the knee to created things; as the Lord says, "Even the chosen will be deceived, if possible, by the magnitude of the affliction."[15] For perhaps on account of this also the fig tree is taken as an example, like the unripe fruits which had not yet suffered [70] burning temptations and have not yet been sweetened by grace, in which <example>, shaken by diabolical winds, <it> is thrown down. For in two <ways> we have seen this

9. Jgs 5.4; 2 Sm 22.8; Ps 18(17).7; Ps 68(67).8; Ps 114(113).7; Acts 16.26.

10. Heb 12.26–27, quoting Hg 2.6.

11. Ps 68(67).8.

12. Cyril of Alexandria, *Glaphyra on Genesis* 5.33, *On Worship in Spirit and Truth* 9, and *Commentary on John* 6.17.

13. Antiochus IV, "Epiphanes," was a mid-second century BCE Greek king of the Seleucid dynasty, which at that time also encompassed Palestine. He attempted to Hellenize the Jews completely by forbidding Jewish religious practices. He also attempted to force Jews to participate in Greek religious ceremonies, including the worship of Greek gods. Led by a group of brothers nicknamed "the Maccabees," the Jews revolted in 165 BCE and won their freedom. Since the oppression of Antiochus IV occurred long before John received his vision, one might wonder whether Andrew is violating his premise that prophecy cannot refer to events prior to the composition of Revelation. (See Introduction, page 33.) The key, however, is in Andrew's words "as it is already written." Andrew probably has in mind a parallel passage from Is 34.4, which he likely believed was a prophecy given in the time of Isaiah and which was fulfilled during the Maccabean revolt in the time of Antiochus IV.

14. Dn 12.3.

15. Mt 24.24.

<fig tree>, taken in a good <way> and a bad <way> shown in Jeremiah's two baskets of useful figs and bad figs,[16] and also from the fig tree dried up by Christ[17] and the one referred to in the Canticle.[18] Whether these will happen perceptibly when Christ the Judge will come in glory, would be known by him who holds the "secret treasures of wisdom and knowledge."[19]

6.14a. *And the sky vanished like a scroll that is rolled up,*

The sky rolled up like a scroll hints at either the unknown <time> of the second coming of Christ—because silently and in a moment the scroll is opened—or also that the heavenly powers feel pain over those who fall from the faith as if they will suffer some kind of twisting on account of sympathy and sorrow. Through this something else is also meant, that the sky does not endure disappearance, but rather a sort of rolling movement and a change for the better, as Irenaeus said in the fifth discourse of his *Refutation of False Knowledge,*[20] thus verbatim: "Neither the subsistence nor the essence [71] of creation disappears—for he who formed it is truthful and certain—but 'the form of this world is passing away,'[21] that in which the transgression occurred, as the elders say."[22] And the great Irenaeus <said> these things. We think that we should use the Apostle for <an understanding of> the ancient custom. Because the Hebrews were using scrolls instead of our books, the unrolling of them did not bring about a disappearance but the complete disclosure of what is written, so that the opening of the heavenly body also shows the revelation of the blessings reserved for the saints. And this <verse> we have understood in four ways, as it has been given to us from God. And we continue with the following.

---

16. Jer 24.1–5.
17. Mt 21.19–22 and Mk 11.13–14, 20–24.
18. Song 2.13.
19. Col 2.3.
20. Today this work is ordinarily referred to as *Against Heresies.*
21. 1 Cor 7.31.
22. *Heres.* 5.36.1.

6.14b–17. [14b]*And every mountain and island was moved from its place.* [15]*And the kings of the earth and the great men and the rich and the commanders of thousands [and the strong], and every slave and every freeman, hid themselves in the caves and among the rocks of the mountains,* [16] *and they say to the mountains and to the rocks, "Fall on us and hide us from the face of him who is seated on the throne, and from the wrath of the Lamb;* [17]*for the great day of his wrath has come, and who can stand?"*

Our Lord foretold the future events to the apostles who were asking about the destruction of the Temple in Jerusalem and about the end of time, as much as they were able to receive.[23] These things already happened, in the siege of Vespasian [72] and Titus, to the Judeans who killed Christ, just as Josephus the Hebrew narrates.[24] The end of all things will come to the world with great flourish, so to speak, upon the sojourn of the Antichrist, just as he said, in which the men who exist as the leading men either of ecclesiastical administration or world-ly rule are figuratively called *mountains,* and the churches of "the faithful" are figuratively called *islands,* according to Isa-iah; "being consecrated before God to their place," they will flee,[25] passing from place to place on account of the pseudo-Christ, by which things we too had been tempted by sin before his <Christ's> coming, which was out of love for humanity. *The kings of the earth,* that is, "those who exercise authority"[26] over her and who possess nothing in the heavens, along with all the great men and rich men who are under slavery of things below and are free of the slavery of Christ, will pray to be covered by the caves and the rocks and the mountains, or to be tested by the divine wrath raining down upon them, or <will pray> ac-cording to <divine> will <for> the afflictions from famine and other plagues <to occur> in the coming of the Antichrist or at the time of the endless punishments expected after the <gen-eral> resurrection, and especially when the divine wrath justly will "burn as an oven"[27] those who built upon the "foundation

23. Mt 24.1–44; Mk 13.1–37; Lk 17.21–37.
24. Flavius Josephus, *The Jewish War* 6.4–5.
25. Is 41.1.   26. Mt 20.25; Mk 10.42.
27. Mal 4.1.

of faith <with> wood, grass, and reed <becoming> like food for the fire,"[28] <divine wrath> consuming them. From this <wrath>, God, who loves humankind, [73] redeems us, making us partakers of the eternal blessings which he has prepared for his saints, joining <us> to the total number of those who are saved, by the grace of his Only-begotten Son, who with the Father deserves glory and worship, together with the Holy Spirit unto the ages. Amen.

28. 1 Cor 3.12–13.

SECTION SEVEN

CHAPTER 19
About the 144,000 Saved from the Plague
<Inflicted> By the Four Angels

7.1. And after these I saw four angels standing at the four corners of the earth, holding the four winds of the earth, in order that no wind might blow on the earth nor on the sea nor on any tree.

F SOME[1] have interpreted these things as having happened to the Judeans under the Romans of old,[2] considering the four divine angels to be showing that to escape the wrath of those being put to trial either on the earth or on the sea is impossible, much more, they describe that which will occur at the coming of the Antichrist, not <only> in the Judean part of the earth, but in all *<of the earth>* of [74] which *the angels stand holding the four corners,* having undertaken to perform a service given to them by God, but which is unknown to us. The season of *the winds* clearly means the loosening of the good order of creation and the inescapability of the evils, for it is through the winds that earthly vegetation is fed and the sea is sailed.

---

1. Oik. 4.17.1.

2. "Of old" is a necessary detail since Andrew and his readers themselves were part of the Roman Empire. Modern historians may refer to the continuation of the Eastern Roman Empire as the "Byzantine Empire," but it is an artificial distinction, and such a characterization was never part of the consciousness of those who lived in those lands during those centuries. Even to the present time, Greeks from Constantinople still refer to themselves as *Romaioi,* which means "Romans."

7.2–3a. ²And I saw another angel ascending from the place of the rising of the sun, having the seal of the living God. And he cried out with a loud voice to the four angels to whom had been given <power> to harm the earth and the sea, ³ᵃsaying,

Just as it had been revealed to Ezekiel long ago[3] about the one dressed in fine linen who sealed the foreheads of those who groan so that the righteous would not be destroyed together with the unrighteous—because the hidden virtue of the saints is unknown even to angels—this <is> also shown here to the blessed one <John>, the superior holy power urging the punishing holy angels to do nothing to those who committed offenses, <to do nothing> before recognizing those distinguished by the sealing who serve the truth. If this has partially taken place a long time ago, it was to the ones who had believed in Christ who had escaped the sack of Jerusalem by the Romans,[4] reckoned as many tens of thousands, according to the great James, who had shown the blessed Paul [75] their great number.[5] But accordingly, it is said, this will definitely happen during the time of the coming of the Antichrist, the seal of the Life-giving Cross separating the faithful from the unfaithful, <the faithful> without shame and, having been emboldened, bearing the sign of Christ before the impious. Wherefore the angel says,

7.3b. "Do not harm the earth or the sea or the trees, until we have sealed the servants of our God upon their foreheads."

Creation, having come into being for us, partakes with us in the afflictions when we are chastised;[6] likewise, therefore, it will rejoice with the saints who are glorified. Through these we learn also before the bringing of trials the virtuous need to be strengthened through angelic assistance, through the "seal of the Spirit"[7] given to us and manifesting our own power according to the amount of work we have put to it. The rest will remain without help, for by their own will they will not be helped.

---

3. Ezek 9.2–11.
4. Oikoumenios's opinion. 4.17.4–7.
5. Acts 21.18–20.
6. Cf. Rom 8.19–23.
7. 2 Cor 1.21–22; Eph 1.13 and 4.30.

7.4. And I heard the number of the sealed, one hundred and forty-four thousand sealed out of every tribe of the sons of Israel. Twelve thousand sealed out of the tribe of Judah, [76]

Judah <means> "confession," through which are shown the ones being saved through confession to Christ, who is descended from the root of Judah.[8]

7.5. Twelve thousand sealed from the tribe of Reuben,

Reuben, "son of vision,"[9] through which are shown the ones who through cleanliness of heart possessed spiritual vision.[10]

7.5b. Twelve thousand from the tribe of Gad,

Gad, "trial,"[11] through which are meant those who are crowned through patience in trials, according to Job.[12]

7.6a. Twelve thousand from the tribe of Asher,

Asher, "blessed,"[13] through which are shown those who are worthy of the blessings of the Master through the way of life, those being judged worthy to stand at the right hand of Christ[14] and famous as "sons of light and of day."[15]

7.6b. Twelve thousand from the tribe of Naphtali,

Naphtali, "prayer,"[16] through which are designated those who are attached to God through unceasing prayer.[17]

---

8. Gn 29.35.

9. Gn 29.32.

10. Cf. Mt 5.8.

11. The meaning given for the name "Gad" differs greatly even in the Bible. Gn 30.11 explains that Gad means "good fortune," whereas in Gn 49.19 it means "raid."

12. Jb 42.

13. Gn 30.13.

14. Mt 25.33.

15. 1 Thes 5.5.

16. In Gn 30.8, it is said to mean "prevail."

17. 1 Thes 5.17. Paul's admonition to "pray without ceasing" is considered the Christian ideal and may be the reason why Andrew explains the name Naphtali as "prayer" when it actually means "prevail."

7.6c. *Twelve thousand from the tribe of Manasseh,* [77]

Manasseh, "forgetfulness,"[18] that is, the ones who forget "the <things> behind"[19] and their fathers' houses on account of divine love.[20]

7.7a. *Twelve thousand from the tribe of Simeon,*

Simeon, "obedience,"[21] clearly <signifies> the ones who are justified through obedience to divine commandments.

7.7b. *Twelve thousand from the tribe of Levi,*

Levi, "the one received in addition,"[22] through which are meant the ones who have been received in addition by Christ through their reverent way life. Levi is placed eighth because true priesthood became famous on the eighth day, the day of the Resurrection.

7.7c. *Twelve thousand from the tribe of Issachar,*

Issachar, "wages,"[23] that is, the ones living virtuously for the sake of the wages from God.

7.8a. *Twelve thousand from the tribe of Zebulun,*

Zebulun, "habitation of strength,"[24] or "sweet fragrance,"[25] through which are meant the ones who are strengthened against the passions by the in-dwelling of Christ[26] and have become his "sweet fragrance,"[27] as Paul says.

18. Gn 41.51.
19. Phil 3.13.
20. Cf. Gn 12.1 and Ps 45(44).10.
21. In Gn 29.33, it is said to mean "heard." The interpretation no doubt occurs to Andrew because he is using the Septuagint and in Greek the word "hear" is closely related to the word "obedience."
22. Gn 29.34, or "joined."
23. Gn 30.16.
24. Possibly inspired by Gn 49.13, in which Zebulun is compared to a safe harbor.
25. In the Hebrew of Gn 30.20 it is said to mean "honor." Andrew may take his interpretation from Hippolytus, who, commenting on Gn 49, states, "And Zabulun is, by interpretation, 'fragrance' and 'blessing.'" *On Genesis* 49.12–15.
26. Cf. 1 Cor 3.16 and 2 Cor 6.16.
27. 2 Cor 2.15.

7.8b. *Twelve thousand from the tribe of Joseph,* [78]

Joseph, "addition,"[28] that is, the ones who receive in addition to a portion of the kingdom of heaven, the things necessary for life, as the Lord said.[29]

7.8c. *Twelve thousand sealed from the tribe of Benjamin,*

Benjamin, "son of grief" or "son of day" or "son of the right <hand>,"[30] in other words, "those who have grief of heart,"[31] either the faithful from among the Hebrews who have escaped the captivity of the Romans[32] and who complete this number, or more correctly, those saved from among the Jews in the end of time, when, as the Apostle says, after "the complete number of Gentiles enters, all Israel will be saved."[33] Neither of these is unacceptable. The precise equality of each tribe seems to me to show the multiplication of the apostolic seed,[34] twelve times by twelve times more along with the perfect number of one thousand, and in this way amounting to the thousands previously stated. [79] For they were the disciples of the Kernel,[35] which fell upon the earth out of love for humankind, and, bursting forth, bore much fruit of the universal salvation. This should be noted, as the tribe of Dan, since the Antichrist would be born from it,[36] was not included with the rest but, instead of it, that of Levi, as the priestly <tribe> of old, which did not share in the division <of the land of Israel>.[37] And from the interpretation of the names it is possible to attach some idea to each of the tribes adduced in the things nearby. It placed Joseph <there> instead of Ephraim his son. This number that was mentioned is appro-

---

28. Gn 30.24.   29. Cf. Mt 6.33; Lk 12.31.

30. Gn 35.18. Rachel named him "son of my sorrow" (Ben-oni) because she realized she was dying due to a difficult childbirth. But the same verse in Genesis explains that Jacob named him Benjamin, "son of the right hand." Yet Philo of Alexandria interprets the name to mean "son of day." Philo, *Change of Names* 92.

31. Ps 94(93).19.   32. Oik. 4.17.7–8.

33. Rom 11.25–26.

34. Cf. Mt 13.8; Mk 4.8; Lk 8.8.

35. Jn 12.2.

36. Irenaeus, *Heres.* 5.30. 2, relying on Jer 8.16.

37. Dt 10.9, 12.12.

priate to them, as has been said, because of the twelve tribal leaders of the ancient Hebrews, and because of the sublime apostles who "became rulers over the entire earth"[38] instead of them, as has been written, through whom the Jews of the diaspora of the earth are saved in these last days.

[It is time to fulfill the promise <to interpret the names> since many times in the divine Scriptures we find <meaning> under the names of some people, either having been born, or having been named by parents, applied to children, as has been written about Leah during birth-giving, who said, "The Lord saw my humility"[39] and called her newborn Reuben, that is, "son of vision," and about the second one to be born she [80] had said, "The Lord listened because I am hated"[40] and called him Simeon, which means "listening,"[41] and about Rachel, who had a hard labor and who called the child from that event "son of grief,"[42] and other such appellations are known to those skilled in the divine sayings. On account of this, believing necessary the explanation of the names of the patriarchs, we say of the tribe of Judah, which is interpreted as "confession,"[43] that it alludes to those who are saved through repentance and love toward the Lord, who was descended from <the tribe of> Judah, who justified the publican,[44] the harlot,[45] and the robber.[46] The tribe of Reuben, meaning "the visionary son," or "the son of vision,"[47] alludes to those who are "pure in heart"[48] and those seeing in the Spirit; the tribe of Gad, which means "test" or "something which tests," to those who through afflictions and trials are "tested in the fire like gold"[49] and are crowned by the test of faith; the tribe of Asher, by which is meant "the blessing," to those who create the blessedness of eternal praises by keeping ceaselessly the God-taught beatitudes; that of Naphtali, interpreted as "intelligent" or "tree trunk,"[50] to those being support-

---

38. Ps 45(44).16.
39. Gn 29.32.
40. Gn 29.33.
41. Gn 29.32.
42. Gn 35.18.
43. Gn 29.35.
44. Lk 18.14 and 19.9.
45. Lk 7.47.
46. Lk 23.43.
47. Gn 29.32.
48. Mt 5.5.
49. 1 Pt 1.7.
50. A variation in the manuscripts of the commentary. In other manuscripts it is interpreted to mean "prayer." *Chp.* 19, *Text* 76, page 104.

ed with intelligence by the trunk of the Master's cross and with it smashing the demons; that of Manasseh, which is interpreted from "forgetfulness," to those "forgetting the father's house" on account of Christ, so that the king "will desire" their spiritual "beauty"[51] and make them worthy of the invitation to the mystical wedding.[52] The tribe of Simeon, which means "hearkening," alludes to those who hearken to the divine commandments through good deeds. [81] The tribe of Levi, which means "accepted,"[53] to those "elected and accepted by God," according to the saying of the Psalm, and "those who will dwell in the divine courtyards"[54] in the future as those who will become priests of the eighth week after the present age; for this reason it is placed eighth. For it is also the first, since all of it had not been gained by one continuous road; the tribe of Issachar, which is "wages," to those who are separated by virtue for the wage of the future prizes, and for this reason, those sincerely pursuing virtues for the good. The tribe of Zebulun, which is interpreted "flow accepted,"[55] to those who give up possession of the liquid wealth for the poor and who are "received by Christ"[56] and those who heal by the memory of the Gehenna of fire the flow of the output of the soul to which vainglory gives birth; the tribe of Joseph which is "the addition of Iaoth," the "Iaoth-" being the divine name,[57] mentions those who receive, in addition to a part of the Kingdom of heaven, also the necessities of life from the Master who never lies.[58] The tribe of Benjamin, which is interpreted "son of grief," or "son of day" <alludes> to those who succeed "through the multitude of the heart's griefs,"[59] according to the Psalmist, and in addition through the excess of bodily pain

51. Ps 45(44).10.
52. Cf. Mt 22.1–10 and 25.1–13.
53. Gn 29.33.
54. Ps 65(64).4.
55. Another manuscript variation. In other manuscripts, it is said to mean "habitation of strength," or "sweet fragrance." *Text* 77, *Comm.* 88, page 105.
56. Rom 15.7.
57. Referring to the Hebrew "Ya-", as in "Yahweh." Rendering the "Ya" as "Iaoth" in Greek is unusual, and Andrew most likely found this variation in Irenaeus (*Heres.* 2.35.3), who may have added the "th" from the title for God "Sabaoth."
58. Cf. Mt 6.33.
59. Ps 94(93).19.

shown to be <suffered> on account of Christ, are shown to be "sons of light and sons of the day."[60] And these things, <taken> from the interpretation of the names, are for the exercise of the mind by those who are quick-witted. We ponder Dan, not only because he was not mentioned on account of the Antichrist since he <the Antichrist> will be born from him, as it has been said,[61] but also because it is difficult to "judge another's house-servant."[62] Therefore, the Lord says, "Do not judge, that you not be judged,"[63] and as the great James says, "for One is the Law-giver and Judge."[64] For "Dan" is interpreted "judgment."[65][82]

CHAPTER 20

About the Innumerable Crowd of those Clothed in Shining Garments From the Nations

7.9 –10. [9]*After these I saw, and behold a great crowd which no one could number, from all nations, and tribes and people and tongues, standing before the throne and before the Lamb, clothed in white robes, with palm branches in their hands.* [10]*And crying out with a loud voice, saying, "Salvation <belongs> to our God, who sits upon the throne, and to the Lamb!"*

Those are the ones of whom David says, "If I should count them they will be more in number than the sand,"[66] both those who had formerly struggled as martyrs for Christ and those who contested as of late with the greatest bravery *from every tribe and tongue* who, by the pouring out of their own blood for Christ, made the garments white by their own deeds, and those destined to make them white; and who hold in their hands the victory-designating branches of the useful and upright and white-hearted palm trees and dance around the divine throne of the divinely derived repose, and as grateful servants proper-ly ascribe the victory against the demons to the Provider. [83]

60. 1 Thes 5.5.
61. See *Text* 79, *Comm.* 91, page 106.
62. Rom 14.4.   63. Mt 7.1; Lk 6.37.
64. Jas 4.12.   65. Gn 30.6.
66. Ps 139(138).18.

7.11–12. *¹¹And all the angels stood around the throne and around the elders and the four living beings, and they fell down on their faces before the throne and worshiped God, ¹²saying, "Amen! Blessing and glory and wisdom and thanksgiving and honor and power and might to our God for ever and ever! Amen."*

Behold one church of angels and humans! And the <angels> of old appeared amazing to men <who were> equal to the angels, just as we know through Daniel;[67] then they will become co-celebrants with men, either—according to some of the saints—appearing to them in their own bodies through an immediate impression—or, according to others—as not having the three dimensions, length, width, and depth, which is a characteristic of bodies—they do not appear in their own nature, but, according to the opinion, being made as figures and forms by God. Standing in a circle around the cherubim and elders they show through the placement the magnitude of honor by which those shown through the number of elders are glorified. Through all of these, thanksgiving is sent up to God for his divine dispensations in his creation for our sake.

7.13. *Then one of the elders responded, saying to me, "Who are these clothed in white robes, and from where have they come?" And I told him, "My lord, you know."* [84]

Through the question, the <elder> who has been seen arouses the blessed one <John> to <make> an inquiry about the things that were observed. And the one candidly making a show of ignorance is made wise by the seen one.

7.14–15 *¹⁴And he said to me, "These are they who have come out of the great tribulation, and they washed their robes and made them white in the blood of the Lamb. ¹⁵For this reason they are before the throne of God and worship him day and night in his temple; and he who sits on the throne will dwell among them.*

Blessed are those who through temporary pains bear fruit for eternal rest, who, through "co-suffering with Christ,"[68] co-reign

67. Dn 10.7–9.
68. Rom 8.17.

with him and worship him uninterruptedly. For *day and night* means here "unceasing." For there will be no night there, but a single day, illuminated not by a sensory sun, but by the "<Sun of> Righteousness."[69] And perhaps by *night* is to be understood the hidden and deep mysteries of knowledge, and by *day* the things which are clear and easy to understand. *His temple* <signifies> all of creation being "renewed by the Spirit,"[70] especially those who have kept the "pledge of the Spirit"[71] whole and unquenched, to whom it has been promised to *dwell*[72] and "walk."[73] [85]

7.16. They will no longer hunger or thirst.

Naturally. For they will have the "heavenly bread"[74] and the "water of life."[75]

7.16b. The sun will not fall upon them, nor any burning heat.

For they will no longer suffer under trials, which is what is meant by the sun and the burning heat, the time of struggles having passed.

7.17. For the Lamb in the midst of the throne will shepherd them, and he will guide them to springs of waters of life; and God will wipe away every tear from their eyes."

Those who are shepherded by Christ then, it says, will not be afraid of attacks by wolves, inasmuch as they <the wolves> will be sent to the "unquenched fire,"[76] but instead they <who have washed their robes> will be spiritually shepherded towards the clean and clear fountains of the divine thoughts, being meant by the waters, characterizing the already abundant flow of the Spirit, as the Lord has said about "him who sincerely believes" in him that "out of his belly will flow rivers of living water."[77] The saints, those watered by it abundantly, will live endlessly in great joy and gladness, the "partial knowledge"[78] [86] being

69. Mal 3.20 LXX (4.2 RSV). See also Rv 21.23 and 22.5.
70. Ti 3.5.
71. 2 Cor 1.22 and 5.5.
72. Cf. 1 Cor 3.16 and 6.19.
73. 2 Cor 6.16.
74. Jn 6.31.
75. Jn 4.10, 7.38; Rv 22.17.
76. Mk 9.43.
77. Jn 7.38.
78. 1 Cor 13.9.

abolished, and they will possess perfect <knowledge> and escape the change of corruption.

CHAPTER 21

Loosening of the Seventh Seal, Meaning the Angelic Powers
Bringing the Prayers of the Saints to God as Incense

8.1–2. ¹*And when he opened the seventh seal, there was silence in heaven for about half an hour.* ²*And I saw the seven angels who stood before God, and seven trumpets were given to them.*

Often the number seven is taken by this saint <John> as corresponding to this age and to "the Sabbath rest"[79] and the repose of the saints. Therefore, here by the loosening of *the seventh seal,* through which is meant the loosening of the earthly life, the seven angels ministering by chastisements against those people who are in need of education or punishment. The *silence* signifies both the angelic good order and piety, and also that which concerns the second coming of Christ is unknown even to the angels.[80] The *half an hour* shows the shortness of time in which, when the plagues are brought on and are completed on the earth, the kingdom of Christ will appear.

8.3a. *And another angel came and stood at the altar having a golden incense holder;* [87]

Even if the things seen by the saints take form in matter and colors, either the altar or the censer or anything else, yet they happen to be invisible and mental. Therefore, the *angel stood* at this <altar> and <held> the *incense holder,* that is, the censer containing incense, holding the prayers of the saints, offered them as incense to God, through which <prayers> they <the saints> were asking <Christ> for the universal end of the world with the punishing affliction of the impious and lawless, to lessen the future suffering, and by his own coming to distribute the wages among those who had labored. And this is shown by what follows.

79. Heb 4.9.
80. Mt 24.36; Mk 13.32.

8.3b. *And to him was given much incense, in order to offer the prayers of all the saints upon the golden altar before the throne;*

This *altar* is Christ, upon whom is established every ministering and holy power and to whom the sacrifices of martyrdom are carried, of whom the altar was the foreshadowing shown to Moses on the mountain together with the tabernacle.[81] The *incense* is *the prayers of the saints,* as sweet fragrances to God, as has been said. And *before the throne* meaning Christ, clearly the supreme [88] holy powers, as has been said, on account of the flow of fiery divine love in them and pure wisdom and knowledge. The interpretation of the names of the supreme powers who approach God shows precisely that.

8.4–5a. [4]*And the smoke of the incense rose with the prayers of the saints from the hand of the angel before God.* [5a]*And the angel took the censer and filled it with fire from the altar and threw it upon the earth;*

The *prayers of the saints,* served and brought forth through *the angel,* caused *the censer* to be filled with the punishing *fire* and to be poured upon *the earth,* as it was shown long ago to Ezekiel,[82] from one of the cherubim who took such fire and gave it to the angels sent to cut off the most impious inhabitants of Jerusalem. This angel is representative of each hierarch, as a "mediator between God and men,"[83] both raising up their entreaties and bringing down his propitiation, converting the sinners by either spoken word or strict discipline.

8.5b–6. [5b] *And there were sounds, and thunders and lightning, and an earthquake.* [6]*And the seven angels holding the seven trumpets made themselves ready to blow <them>.*

All of these things are describing the horrors preceding the end of the world, just as on Mount Sinai they were symbols which made known the Divine Presence,[84] [89] amazing all and leading the most prudent toward conversion. The angels serve these <people> as sympathetic doctors imitating Christ, healing those weak from the horrific sickness of sin by cauter-

---

81. Ex 25.8–22.
83. 1 Tm 2.5.

82. Ezek 10.6.
84. Ex 19.16–19.

ization and surgery, or the more moderate <sickness afflicting> the lazy, lightening the future punishments in whatever manner they thankfully receive it. We, who are sealed with the honorable name of Christ and desire the glory of the saints, pray that we escape the grievous future pains of chastisement here. May the Lord, who loves humankind, who educates us, not surrender us to the death of sin, as it was written, but "soothe for us the evil days" of eternal punishments when "the pit is dug"[85] for the inventor of sin, the dark and deepest place of Gehenna; so that in this place, "the dwelling place of all gladness,"[86] we will dwell together with the saints with him, the Savior Christ our God, to whom belongs every glorification, honor, and worship, together with the Father and the All-Holy Spirit, now and ever and to the ages of ages. Amen. [90]

85. Ps 94(93).13.
86. Ps 87(86).7.

SECTION EIGHT

CHAPTER 22

About the Seven Angels Whose First Blow of the Trumpet Brings Hail, Fire, and Blood on the Earth

8.7. The first angel blew his trumpet, and there were hail and fire mingled with blood. And it was thrown on the earth; and a third of the earth was burnt, and a third of the trees was burnt, and all of the green grass was burnt.

 OME THINK these things imply in an obscure way the variety of punishment of sinners in Gehenna, figuratively described through physical pains.[1] We, however, think it does not mean that, especially because not one-third is to be punished in the future out of all the people, but the majority—"for the road is wide that leads to destruction"[2]— but that these things mean rather the plagues prior to the final consummation of the world, and *hail* from heaven means those afflictions that will come according to the just judgment of God, the *fire mingled with blood* <indicating> the destruction by fire and the daily murders taking place at the hands of barbarians. From these, as we see, not less than one-third of all the creatures living on earth will be killed in a perceptible manner, destroying by wars not only people, but also [91] all the things that the earth brings forth. And the blessed Joel strengthens our own opinion regarding the things set forth, saying that "blood and fire and vapor of smoke" are to come "before the great day."[3]

1. Oik. 5.9.1–2. 2. Cf. Mt 7.13.
3. Jl 2.30.

CHAPTER 23

About the Second Angel and the Destruction of Living
Things in the Sea

8.8–9. *[8]The second angel blew his trumpet, and something like a great mountain burning with fire was thrown into the sea; [9]and a third of the sea became blood, a third of the living creatures in the sea died, and a third of the ships was destroyed.*

According to the opinion of some,[4] we should think that through these things is meant the *burning* of *the sea* together with all the things in it through the cleansing fire burning after the resurrection, if it were not that the mention of a third is shown to us to be incongruous with that. For those being punished are more than the saved, as was said. Nevertheless, according to the anagogical sense it is not unlikely that the present life, figuratively called "sea," supports these things and that the third of those in it were consumed by the plagues through the abyss of the divine judgments, which [92] on the one hand punishes quickly, but on the other hand is greatly patient for their return and repentance. We believe that the *great mountain* means the devil, as some of the teachers thought,[5] burning by the fire of his anger against us, to be kept for the Gehenna, and in the time of his allowance with his cooperation one-third of the islands in the sea, and of the ships and of the things that swim in the sea are destroyed, just as he had done to Job during the former time. For he is the enemy and the avenger against the divine righteous sentence. For "whoever is defeated by him becomes his slave."[6] And if those in the sea of life through words or deeds blaspheme the Trinity, spiritual death is brought upon them, <which is> neither a strange nor an unsuitable end.

4. Oik. 5.11.2.
5. No known Greek author provides this interpretation of the mountains prior to this reference in Andrew's commentary. Since Andrew uses the word "teachers," rather than "Fathers," this more likely indicates an oral tradition rather than a written authoritative source. If it was a written source, it has since been lost.
6. 2 Pt 2.19.

CHAPTER 24
About the Third Angel, and the River Waters Being Made Bitter

8.10–11. [10] *The third angel blew his trumpet, and a great star fell from heaven, burning like a torch, and it fell on a third of the rivers and on the springs of water.* [11]*The name of the star is Wormwood. And a third of the water became wormwood, and many people died from the waters, because they were made bitter.* [93]

Some say that *Wormwood* implies the bitter grief shown happening to the sinners being punished in Gehenna, those who because of their great number naturally are called *the waters.*[7] We think that the grievous pains are what are signified through these things, according to the time being described. Either the *star* means these things which come upon men from the heavens, or the devil is signified by this, concerning whom Isaiah says: "How did he fall from heaven, the morning star rising at dawn?"[8] For he, upset, agitated, and bitter, makes people drunk through pleasure and thus connives to bring chastising punishment on them here, not to everyone, but only the one third, on account of the long-suffering of God, and causes <people> not to believe in the future reward, bringing spiritual death down upon those who do not endure. For bitter things will happen to those who find themselves <living> before the end, which were seen previously, but which the Lord knew well, anticipating the beginning.[9] Therefore, if we do not wish to be judged we must examine ourselves, according to the divine Apostle—"for if we judged ourselves, we would not be judged"[10]—judging ourselves, corrected by the Lord, thankfully receiving the pains which are brought <upon us>, just as we see the grateful ones among the sick in body bearing with patience the surgery and cauterization by the doctors [94] because of their willingness to be healed; so that we, too, being spiritually healthy and not

7. Oik. 5.13.1–2.
8. Is 14.12.
9. Cf. Mt 24.16–22; Mk 13.14–20; Lk 21.20–24.
10. 1 Cor 11.31.

offering ourselves as fuel to feed the Gehenna of fire, might not be condemned together with the world, but rather so that we might "co-reign eternally with Christ,"[11] to whom is due glory, honor, and worship together with the Father and the Holy Spirit unto the ages. Amen.

11. 2 Tm 2.12.

SECTION NINE

CHAPTER 25
About the Fourth Angel and the Darkening
of the Luminaries

8.12. And the fourth angel blew his trumpet. And a third of the sun was struck, and a third of the moon, and a third of the stars, so that a third of them was darkened and a third of the day did not shine, and the night likewise.

E THINK that these things also fit the sayings by Joel about the sun and the moon,[1] which things were already drawn out according to the decision of the Master concerning the end.[2] We say that by the one *third of the* luminaries and *stars* and the one *third of the day and night* is shown an interval \<of time\>, so that we might know that, even then, God does not bring unmitigated suffering, but, allowing those who have been wounded to suffer the one-third interval of time, [95] \<he\> imperceptibly encourages the greater portion which remains \<to repent\>. For who will be able to bear the cup of the divine wrath unmixed?

8.13. And I saw, and I heard one angel flying in mid-heaven saying with a great voice, "Woe, woe, woe to those who dwell on the earth, and from the rest of the sounds of the trumpet which the three angels are about to blow!"

Through these is also shown the sympathy and love for humankind of the divine angels imitating God, pitying those sinners being punished, but even much more those who do not

---

1. Jl 2.10, 31.
2. Mt 24.19–23; Mk 13. 20.

see the afflictions for the purpose of returning <back to God>, those for whom the *woe* is especially appropriate, dwelling on the earth and thinking in an earthly manner, breathing dirt instead of the Myrrh which was emptied out[3] for us. For those who have "citizenship in heaven"[4] difficulties become the starting point of unfading crowns and trophies.

CHAPTER 26

About the Fifth Angel and the Mental Locusts and the Variety of their Form

9.1–5. *And the fifth angel blew his trumpet; and I saw a star that had fallen from heaven to earth, and the key of the pit of the abyss was given to him.* [2]*And he opened the pit of the abyss, and smoke rose from the pit like the smoke* [96] *of a great furnace, and the sun and the air were darkened from the smoke of the pit.* [3]*And from out of the smoke locusts came upon the earth, and they were given power, like scorpions having power on the earth.* [4] *They were told not to harm the grass of the earth nor any greenery nor any tree, but only those people who do not have the seal upon their foreheads.* [5] *They were allowed not to kill them but to torture them for five months, and their torture was like the torture of a scorpion when it stings a man.*

Some said that the star descending upon the earth, that is, during the judgment that took place in the valley of Jehosaphat, is the divine angel in charge of the punishments.[5] The *pit of the abyss* is the Gehenna, and the *smoke* that comes from it causes the sun and the air to be invisible to the suffering ones.[6] The *locusts* <represent> the worms of which the prophet says, "their worm will never die."[7] They will torment neither the earth nor the grass, but human beings because these <other created> things will escape corruption, to which today they are in bondage because of us.[8] The *five months of torture* <indicates> some delineated period of time for those being punished intensely, after which [97] <they will suffer> less vio-

3. Cf. Phil 2.7.   4. Phil 3.20.
5. Oik. 5.17.2.   6. Oik. 5.17.4.
7. Oik. 5.17.5. The quotation is from Is 66.24.
8. Rom 8.21.

lently, but eternally. I agree that *the star* is the divine angel.[9] By divine allowance he <the angel> leads up the evil demons who had been condemned in the abyss, those whom Christ bound when he became man, so that they might do their uncompleted tormenting work before the end. The *smoke* is the gloom which precedes the evil deeds out of their encounters; those will receive authority given to them to torment people. The *darkness* of the sun and air means the spiritual blindness of the people who cut off their light, or the ill-tempered attitude <shown> by them because darkness is considered light to those in pain. And the mental *locusts*, who sting people like scorpions, show the death which is the harm of the soul hiding at the end of evil deeds, to which <death> those are subjected who had not been sealed with the divine seal on their foreheads and <who do not> shine round about with the enlightenment of the Life-giving Cross through the Holy Spirit, so that according to the saying of the Master, they "shine their light before men for the glory of the divine name."[10] The *five months* of their *torture* we believe to mean either the shortness of time—"if those days were not shortened, no flesh would have been saved," according to the statement of the Lord[11]—or <it means> some fivefold <period of> time on account of the five senses, through which <senses> sin goes into people, or it means a defined <period of> time known only to God. [98]

9.6. *And in those days people will seek death and will not find it; and they will long to die, and death will flee from them.*

By these is signified the extreme extent of the sufferings. For it is customary to ask for death when in pain. That this <death> without pain does not come to those who ask is due to the di-

9. This is the only detail of Oikoumenios's interpretation of this passage with which Andrew agrees. Note that Andrew reported the opinion of Oikoumenios first, even though he did not agree with it. This is typical of Andrew. The reader, therefore, is strongly advised to exercise caution through a careful reading of the commentary in order to distinguish the opinion of Andrew from that of Oikoumenios. A hasty reading or sloppy citation of this commentary will result in a misunderstanding of Andrew's opinion.

10. Cf. Mt 5.16.

11. Mt 24.22; Mk 13.20.

vine judgments; it is judged advantageous to them, by the bitterness of pains being brought upon them to make sin hateful to the people, since sin is the mother and cause of these <pains>.

9.7–9a. ⁷*And the likeness of the locusts was like horses prepared for war, and on their heads were crowns like gold, and their faces like human faces;* ⁸*and they had hair like hair of women, and their teeth were like lions' teeth,* ⁹ᵃ*and they had thoraxes like iron breastplates.*

Through all these and the things which will be said immediately afterwards, some understood the *locusts* mentioned parabolically to be the punishing divine angels, figuratively interpreting each of the things said,[12] either because of the fearful and astonishing <quality>, or because of their speed, or because of the chastisement upon those deserving to be led to the punishment in Gehenna. I think that by these *locusts* are to be understood, rather, the evil demons who have been prepared for the war against us. [99] And *the crowns upon their heads* like gold bearing their victory over us, by which, we think, they are to be crowned as conquerors in evil victory when we are defeated by pleasure. The *hair of women* is to imply the demons' love of pleasure and the arousal to fornication. The *teeth of lions* <indicate their> murderous and poisonous <quality>, and the *thoraxes* hardheartedness.

9.9b–12. ⁹ᵇ*And the sound of their wings was like the sound of many chariots with horses rushing into war,* ¹⁰*having tails like scorpions, and stingers in their tails, and their authority to harm people for five months.* ¹¹*They have over them, as a king, the angel of the abyss; his name in Hebrew is Abaddon, and in Greek he has the name Apollyon. The one woe has passed; behold, two woes come after these.*

The *sound of the wings* of the mental locusts we believe is compared to the sound of military chariots because of their exalted appearance and swiftness. For [100] "they fight" us "from above,"[13] as the blessed David says. Their *tails,* which are *like scorpions,* imply the outcome of sins giving birth to spiritual

12. Oik. 5.21.1–2.
13. Ps 56(55).2.

death. In this manner it is taken by us, for "sin, having been accomplished, produces death,"[14] through which the five-month torture comes upon people, both through the five senses and through the shortness of time compared to the future age, as it is written. It follows that their king is understood <to be> the devil,[15] the one destroying those who are truly persuaded by him. Thus, with our assurance that two more woes will come after these, let us take up the battle against <the devil> without a truce.

CHAPTER 27

*About the Sixth Angel and the Angels Released
upon the Euphrates*

9.13–16. [13]*And the sixth angel blew the trumpet, and I heard a voice from the four horns of the golden altar before God,*[14] *saying to the sixth angel who has the trumpet, "Release upon the great river Euphrates the four angels who have been bound up."* [15]*And the four angels were released, who had been held ready for the hour, the day, the month, and the year, in order to kill* [101] *a third of humankind.* [16]*The number of the troops of cavalry was twice ten thousand times ten thousand. I heard their number.*

Some say that the *four angels* are Michael, Gabriel, Uriel, and Raphael who had been bound by the gladness of the divine vision, to be untied on the day of judgment with innumerable angels for the condemnation of the impious, of whom one third is to be destroyed.[16] I myself think, however, that these *four angels* are the most cunning demons who were bound upon the coming of Christ[17] who, by the divine command coming out of the heavenly altar, which was an image of the ancient tabernacle, were released by the divine angel so as to rouse the nations, not only against Christians, but also against one another, so that those tested might be revealed as the faithful ones and shown

14. Jas 1.15.
15. Since he is described in verse 11 as the "angel of the abyss," and as *Apollyon,* which means Destroyer.
16. Oik. 5.23.9.
17. The first coming, the Incarnation of the Logos.

to be worthy of greater rewards and of the heavenly mansions,[18] or rather <worthy of> barns, like ripe wheat.[19] But those who are like chaff, the impious and the exceedingly [102] great sinners and the unrepentant, are to be punished justly here, by these receiving a milder sentence at the judgment. And if they are *bound at the Euphrates,* it is nothing strange. For they have been sentenced by God until the time, some in the abyss,[20] some among the swine then,[21] some in other places according to the position, bound to be eternally tormented after the completion of their war against human beings. And perhaps by the mention of the *Euphrates* it is shown that Antichrist will come out of those parts. And it is not necessary to doubt the great number of demons, for all the saints say that they fill the air.[22] And what is meant by the one third of those killed has already been said.[23]

9.17–19. [17]*And this was how I saw the horses in the vision and those sitting upon them having breastplates the color of fire and of hyacinth and of sulfur, and the heads of the horses were like the heads of lions, and fire and smoke and sulfur came from their mouths.* [18]*By these three [plagues] one third of humankind was killed by the fire and the smoke and the sulfur proceeding out of their mouths.* [19]*For the authority of the horses* [103] *is in their mouths. For their tails are like serpents having heads, and by them they injure.*

I think *the horses,* it is said, are either men who lust after women and behave like beasts, or those who had been subject to and ruled by the demons, and those that are mounted on them are their leaders. For it is customary with them, not only to help one another but also to attack by means of evil people <as> instruments for the harm of the same kind of people. The *breastplates of fire and hyacinth and sulfur* we think are indicative of the aerial nature and burning activity of evil spirits. The *heads of lions* imply their murderousness and animalistic behavior, and the *fire, smoke, and sulfur coming out of their mouths,* by which a

18. Jn 14.2.
20. Lk 8.31.
22. Eph 2.2.
19. Mt 13.30.
21. Mt 8.31; Mk 5.13; Lk 8.32–33.
23. *Chp.* 22, *Text* 90, page 115; *Chp.* 24 *Text* 93, page 117.

third is threatened with killing, either implies sins inflaming the fruit of the heart by poisonous strikes and instigations, or the setting fire to cities led by barbarian hands and the shedding of blood by divine permission, through which, as we see, not less than one third of people has been destroyed. He says correctly that their *tails* are like snakes, for poisonous sin and spiritual death are at the end of the evil suggestions of the demons. [104]

9.20–21. ²⁰*The rest of the people, those who were not killed in those plagues, neither repented of the works of their hands so as not to worship demons and idols of gold and silver and bronze and stone and wood, which are able neither to see nor to hear nor to walk;* ²¹*and they did not repent of their murders nor of their sorceries nor of their fornication nor of their thefts.*

And this has been discussed among the previous <passages>. For he said above that by these three plagues one third of the people is to be destroyed, and then after this time passed, some people continued <to sin>. And the rest of the people, who were deemed worthy to be spared, and who, not having been convinced by these things, have remained unrepentant, will submit to them, having renounced neither idolatries nor murders nor acts of fornication nor their thefts, nor the sorceries. It shows that because of these <sins>, the wrath will be brought down[24] on a global scale. For the varied deceptions inspire frenzy in nations which do not "know the truth,"[25] on the one hand those who worship idols and on the other hand those who <worship> "the creation instead of the Creator,"[26] and even above all, "those who profess to know God, but deny him," first "through deeds"[27] and [105] then by "wearing the appearance of piety but denying its power,"[28] and those who are enslaved by "mammon,"[29] which the Apostle calls idolatry, saying, "and the love of money which is idolatry."[30] May we show the sincerity and genuineness of the faith in Christ in deeds, so that we may

24. Cf. Rom 1.18.
26. Rom 1.25.
28. 2 Tm 3.5.
30. Col 3.5.

25. 1 Tm 4.3.
27. Ti 1.16.
29. Mt 6.24; Lk 16.13.

not hear that fearful voice, the "Amen, amen, I tell you that I do not know you. Go away from me, you workers of iniquity,"[31] but may we hear the blessed and desirable voice, "Come, all you blessed of my Father, inherit the Kingdom which has been prepared for you before the beginning of the world,"[32] by the grace and mercies of Christ our God, who voluntarily endured the cross for our sake, who with the Father is <worthy of> glory, together with the Holy Spirit, now and ever and unto the ages of ages. Amen.

31. Mt 7.23.
32. Mt 25.34.

SECTION TEN

CHAPTER 28
About the Angel Wrapped in a Cloud and a Rainbow, Who is Foretelling the End of the World

10.1. *And I saw another mighty angel coming down from* [106] *heaven, wrapped in a cloud, and a rainbow over his head, and his face was like the sun, and his legs like pillars of fire.*

HE CLOUD and the *rainbow* and the *sun*-like light are seemingly to be understood as <referring to> this holy angel. For through these are shown the heavenly <quality> and variety of virtues and the brightness of the angelic substance and intelligence.[1] The *pillars of fire* mean the fear and punishments against the wicked who have been robbers on the earth and pirates on the sea. For this reason, he placed *the right* <on the sea> and *the left* foot <on the land> in order to imply the judgment of each of the two <types of> criminals.[2]

10.2–3. [2]*And he had a tiny scroll open in his hand. And he set his right foot on the sea, and his left foot on the land,* [3]*and called out with a loud voice, as a lion roars. And when he called out, the seven thunders sounded with their own voices.*

The *tiny scroll*, it seems to me, even though small and called diminutive, contains the names and deeds of the very worst evil people,[3] those who are thieves on earth, or otherwise wicked people, and those who are pirates on the sea, about whom the angel hints of the punishment by [107] stretching out the legs

1. Oik. 6.3.3–4.
2. Oik. 6.3.7.
3. Oik. 6.3.6.

of fire upon both *the land and the sea*. And the voice of the angel being compared to a devouring *lion* shows the fearful and irresistible <nature> of his threats. And Daniel is a witness, being unable to behold either the gentle or the threatening appearance of the angel without pain.[4] The *seven thunders* we believe are to be understood as either seven voices coming from the one angel being described, or seven other holy angels addressing the future, since from here is shown those of the previous angel to be secondary and from there receiving the instigation to prophesy, according to the appointed angelic good order <explained> by the blessed Dionysios.[5]

10.4. *And when the seven thunders had sounded, I was about to write; and I heard a voice from heaven saying, "Seal the things which the seven thunders have said, and after these write."*

And by these <details> it is shown that now the things which are to be interpreted through the experience itself and through the outcome of these matters are unclear, of which the Evangelist learned from the heavenly voice, on the one hand that the voices are to be impressed in the mind, and on the other hand that the perfect understanding and the clear explanation of these things are to be stored up [108] until the end time. For words such as these are sealed and confined, as Daniel was also taught.[6]

10.5–6. [5]*And the angel whom I saw standing on sea and land lifted up his hand to heaven* [6]*and swore by the One who lives for ever and ever, who created heaven and the things in it, the earth and the things in it, and the sea and the things in it, that there will no longer be time.*

"God, having no one greater <than himself> by whom to swear an oath, swears by himself."[7] But the angels, as creatures, <swear> by the Creator, guaranteeing the things being said by them on account of our own unbelief. They swear an oath that there would *no longer be time*, <meaning> either in the future when time is not to be measured by the sun but eternal life, which is beyond the measurement of time, or <meaning>

---

4. Dn 10.5–11.
6. Dn 8.26; 9.24; 12.4, 9.

5. Pseudo-Dionysios, *Cel. Hier.* 6.
7. Heb 6.13.

that there will not be a long time after the six voices when the things prophesied by the angel will be fulfilled. Wherefore it leads into:

10.7. *But in the days of the voice of the seventh angel when he is about to sound the trumpet, the mystery of God will be fulfilled, as he announced to his servants the prophets.* [109]

From these is signified, I think, that after the passage of the six ages during the days of the seventh age, meaning the time of the seventh trumpet, the things said by the holy prophets to happen before the end of time will receive their end. The good news is the fulfillment of these things by the preparation of the repose of the saints.

CHAPTER 29
How the Evangelist Took the Tiny Scroll From the Angel

10.8. *And the voice which I had heard from heaven spoke with me again and said, "Go, take the tiny open scroll in the hand of the angel who stands on the sea and on the land."*

Here there appears to be some other superior angelic power giving a command to the Evangelist to receive the knowledge of the things which are foretold by the scroll.

10.9. *And I departed for the angel, telling him, "Give me the tiny scroll," and he says to me, "Take and devour it; and it will make your stomach bitter, but in your mouth it will be sweet as honey."*

The *sweetness* to you, on the one hand, he says, refers to the knowledge of the future, but *will make your stomach bitter*, clearly <refers to> the heart containing the spiritual foods, [110] in sympathy for those who are receiving the punishments sent by God according to divine judgment. This is also to be understood otherwise: although the saint has not tasted the experience of evil deeds, he is taught, through the swallowing of the scroll containing the deeds of the wicked, that in the beginning sin is sweet, but after the deed it is bitter, on account of the recompense.

10.10. *And I took the tiny scroll from the hand of the angel and de-voured it; it was sweet like honey in my mouth, and when I ate it my stomach was made bitter.*

The *scroll* is sweet in the preliminary stages because of the joyous things but painful towards the end because of the wounds, just as also sin is sweet to the taste, but bitter in the digestion and return, as has been said. The saints, being sympathetic, "rejoice with those who are joyful and weep with those who are weeping."[8]

10.11. *And he says to me, "You must again prophesy about many peoples and nations and tongues and kings."*

Through these it shows either that <it is> not immediately after the visions of the divine Apocalypse <that> the things that were seen will receive their end, but that the blessed one through his Gospel and through the present apocalypse is to prophesy the future things to those who read it until the end of the world, or <it shows> that he has not yet tasted death[9] [111] but he will come in the end to hinder the acceptance of the Antichrist's deception.

11.1–2. [1]*And a reed, like a staff, was given to me, saying: "Rise and measure the temple of God and the altar and those who worship in it;* [2] *and exclude the outer courtyard of the temple and do not measure it, for it was given to the nations, and they will trample upon the holy city for forty-two months.*

By this *reed* is shown that all things manifested in heaven and the things inanimate to us are spiritual, just as also the altar, the throne, and some others. How did the reed which was given to him say, *Rise and measure the temple of God?* By this it is shown that the temple of God is measured with angelic intelligence. If anyone says that he received the reed from the same angel, and that he heard from him <the angel> the *Rise and measure this temple,*

8. Rom 12.15.

9. Andrew refers to a legend that the Apostle John would never die (hinted at in Jn 21.23) and that he would return at the end-times. This legend must have been quite ancient and clearly was known in both the East and the West. It is discussed extensively by Augustine in *Tractates on the Gospel of John* 124.2–3.

then we say that the reed signifies the measure of the knowledge which is proportionate to the one receiving it, of which those are deemed worthy who are known by God and the divine angels through their good deeds, "For the Lord knows his own,"[10] says the divine word. One must know nonetheless that some understood *the temple of God* to mean the Old Testament, and the *outside yard,* which is not measured, to be the New, on account of the innumerable number of those saved in it.[11] [112] The *forty-two months* they[12] took to mean the shortness of time during which the sacraments of the New Testament are to prevail until the second coming of Christ arrives. But we think that the *temple of the living God* refers to the Church,[13] in which we offer rational sacrifices to God; the outside court <is> the gathering-place of the unbelieving nations and of the Jews since the unworthiness is measured by the angel through the impiety. "For the Lord knows his own,"[14] as it has been said. It is said that he who is All-Knowing does not know the unlawful. The *trampling of the holy city* <is> either the new Jerusalem or the universal Church, and the *forty-two months* by the nations I think means that the faithful and the ones being tested will be trampled upon and persecuted in the three-and-a-half-year appearance of the Antichrist.

CHAPTER 30
About Enoch and Elijah

11.3–4. ³*And I will give my two witnesses <power>, and they will prophesy for one thousand two hundred and sixty days, clothed in sackcloth. ⁴These are the two olive trees and the two lampstands which stand before the God of the earth.* [113]

Many of the teachers understood these <to be> Enoch and Elijah, who will receive time given by God to prophesy in the end time for three-and-a-half years, numbered three hundred and sixty days <each>, and showing through the clothing in

---

10. 2 Tm 2.19.
11. Oikoumenios's opinion. 6.9.1–5.
12. Oik. 6.9.8.
13. 2 Cor 6.16.
14. 2 Tm 2.19.

sackcloth that which is appropriate for sadness and mourning, to those who are deceived at that time, and leading those who are then found away from the deception of the Antichrist. <These are the two> whom Zacharias hinted at in the form of the two olive trees and lampstands,[15] to bring forth food for the light of knowledge by the olive oil of God-pleasing deeds.

11.5–6. *⁵And if anyone would harm them, fire pours out from their mouth and devours their enemies; if anyone would harm them, thus he must be killed. ⁶ They have power to shut the sky, so that it does not rain in the days of their prophecy, and they have authority over the waters to turn them into blood, and to strike the earth with every plague, as often as they wish.*

Oh, the great goodness of God! For he brings healing equivalent to the wound. For since the pseudo-Christ will be manifested in the "many signs and false wonders"[16] [114] by all drugs and enchantments because he <the pseudo-Christ> accepts every diabolical operation, so God will equip these saints by the power of true signs and wonders, so that by the placing of truth and light they will refute falsehood and darkness; those who had been deceived will return, both because of fear of the teachings and because of the chastising blows, <namely,> drought and fire and the alteration of the elements and the like, making the Deceiver into an example, and being not at all persuaded, either by him or by another, until the completion of their own prophecy.

11.7–8. *⁷And when they will finish their testimony, the beast that ascends from the abyss will make war upon them and conquer them. ⁸And their corpses will lie in the square of the great city which is allegorically called Sodom and Egypt, where their Lord was crucified.*

After their witnessing, he says, of the escape from deception, the beast, that is, the Antichrist, who comes out from the dark and deep parts of the earth to which the devil has been condemned, will destroy them by divine permission, and will abandon their bodies unburied in Jerusalem itself, that is, the old and trampled-upon <Jerusalem>,[17] in which the Lord also

15. Zec 4.3, 11–14.
17. Rv 11.2.

16. 2 Thes 2.9.

[115] suffered. In this <city> he <Antichrist> will establish the kingdoms, so he thinks, according to an imitation of David,[18] whose son Christ <is>, our true God, who was born "according to the flesh,"[19] so as to assure by this that he <the Antichrist> is Christ, fulfilling the prophetic word, saying, "I shall restore the fallen tabernacle of David and raise up that which is trampled upon,"[20] which <is what> the Jews who are deceived understand by that appearance.

11.9–10. [9] *And for three-and-a-half days the peoples and tribes and tongues and nations see their corpses and refuse to let their corpses be placed in a tomb.* [10]*And those who dwell on the earth will rejoice over them and be glad, and they will exchange gifts among themselves, because these two prophets tormented those who dwell on the earth.*

He says those who at one time beforehand seized upon the false portents of the Antichrist and have indelibly written his hateful-to-God name on their hearts, either from among the Jews or the nations, will prevent the holy bodies from being buried. [116] They will delight at escaping from the afflictions which are brought for reform, not thinking that "the Lord disciplines the one he loves, chastising every son he receives,"[21] and "with bit and bridle he will lead them lest they come near to him,"[22] so that, even if by necessity, they might return to the straight road from which, being deceived, they had strayed. But we must pray to the Lord, saying: "It is good for me that you humbled me that I might learn your statutes."[23] "Return us, O God of our salvation,"[24] "and do not enter into judgment with your servants."[25] For "we are judged by you," the Master who loves humankind. "We are chastened in order that we may not be condemned along with the world,"[26] but with a few afflictions we might escape eternal punishment, for you are rich in mercy, O Christ our God, and to you belong all glory, honor, and worship, together with the Father and the Life-giving Spirit unto the ages. Amen.
    [117]

18. 2 Sm 5.9.

19. Rom 9.5.

20. Am 9.11.

21. Prv 3.12; Heb 12.6.

22. Ps 32(31).9.

23. Ps 119(118).71.

24. Ps 85.4(84.5).

25. Ps 143(142).2.

26. 1 Cor 11.32.

SECTION ELEVEN

CHAPTER 31
How Those Who Were Destroyed by the Antichrist Will Be Raised

11.11–12a,b. [11] *But after the three-and-a-half days a breath of life from God entered them, and they stood up on their feet, and great fear fell on those who saw them.* [12]*Then I heard a loud voice from heaven saying to them, "Come up here!" And they went up to heaven in the cloud.*

AVING BEEN dead for as many days as the years of their prophecy, it says, they will be raised and taken up into heaven in the Master's chariot, the cloud,[1] causing fear and trembling to those who see it.

11.12c–13. [12c] *And their enemies saw them.* [13] *And at that hour there was a great earthquake, and a tenth of the city fell, and seven thousand people were killed in the earthquake.*

Perhaps, on the one hand, these things will take place physically at that time. On the other hand, the *earthquake* we think spiritually means movement of the things that are shaking from the solid and certain <state>. [118] The one *tenth of the city to fall* is the error of impiety, and not even one of them became prudent because of the rapture <of the two prophets> like the rest who will be saved. For *the seven thousand* who were destroyed appears to mean those who were given up to the weekly time of the present life, and who were not awaiting the eighth day of the resurrection, those also for whom it was necessary to die the *second death*[2] in Gehenna, the eternal punishment. Or,

---

1. Cf. Acts 1.9; Mt 24.30, 26.64; Mk 13.26, 14.62; Lk 21.27.
2. Rv 2.11, 20.6, 20.14, 21.8.

perhaps the seven thousand will be those among the Jews who were persuaded by the Antichrist.

11.13d–14. *¹³ᵈ And the rest were terrified and gave glory to the God of heaven. ¹⁴The second woe has passed; behold, the third woe is soon to come.*

When the unbelieving are castigated and the martyrs of Christ are glorified, it says those worthy of salvation will glorify God. After the two *woes*, it says, comes the *third* through the seventh trumpet.

CHAPTER 32

About the Seventh Trumpet and the Saints Praising God at the Future Judgment

11.15–18a. *Then the seventh angel blew his trumpet, and there were loud voices in heaven, saying, "The kingdom of the world has* [119] *become the kingdom of our Lord and of his Christ, and he shall reign for ever and ever." ¹⁶And the twenty-four elders who sit on their thrones before God fell on their faces and worshiped God, ¹⁷ saying, "We give thanks to you, Lord God Almighty, who is and who was, that you have taken your great power and begun to reign. ¹⁸The nations raged, and your wrath came, and the time of the dead.*

And here again, it says, both the holy angels and those living an angelic life send up thanksgiving to God, for the kingdom which as God he possessed from the beginning, he deigned to receive it for our sake as a man. After being long-suffering, finally he inaugurates the judgment against the unbelieving nations, which are angry at this as if it were a recent and strange teaching; wherefore, he says:

11.18b. *And your wrath came, and the time of the dead to be judged, and to give the wages to your servants, the prophets and the saints, and those who fear your name, both small and great, and to destroy those who harm the earth."*

The time of the dead, it says, <is> the time of the resurrection of the dead [120] in which each one appropriately is to be given the wages. By *the prophets and saints and those who fear*

God of course are to be understood the three levels of the orders of the apostles, those "bearing fruit one hundredfold and sixtyfold and thirtyfold,"[3] admittedly <occupying> the first appointed place and established upon twelve thrones.[4] By s*mall and great,* we think are meant either the lesser saints and those who greatly surpass them, or the *small* as the scorned sinners whereas the *great* are the righteous.

CHAPTER 33

About the Prior Persecutions of the Church and About Those at <the Time> of the Antichrist

11.19. *And the temple of God was opened in heaven, and the ark of his covenant was seen inside his temple; and there were flashes of lightning, voices and thunders and an earthquake, and large hail.*

By the opening of heaven and the vision of the ark is meant the revelation of the "good things prepared"[5] for the saints, just as all things are "concealed"[6] in Christ, "in whom all the fullness of divinity dwelt bodily," according to the Apostle.[7] At that time they will be revealed, when the awesome voices and lightning and thunder, the punishments of Gehenna, will come upon the lawless and impious, like hail raining upon them [121] in the transposition of the present things during the earthquake.

12.1. *And a great sign was seen in heaven, a woman who had been wrapped in the sun, and [the] moon under her feet, and on her head a crown of twelve stars.*

Some,[8] on the one hand, had understood this woman entirely to be the Theotokos[9] before her divine birth-giving was made known to her, <before she> experienced the things to happen. But the great Methodios took <her> to be the holy Church,[10]

---

3. Mt 13.23; Mk 4.20.
4. Mt 19.28; Lk 22.30.
5. 1 Cor 2.9.
6. Col 3.3.
7. Col 2.9.
8. Oik. 6.19.1.
9. The "Mother of God," i.e., the Virgin Mary.
10. Methodios, *Symp.* 8.5–8.

considering these things concerning her <the woman> to be incongruous with the begetting of the Master for the reason that already the Lord had been born long before. It is good to remember also the very words of the blessed Methodios, who says in his so-called *Symposium* through the person of the virgin Procle[11] thus: "The woman wrapped in the sun is the Church. That which to us is our garment, to her is light. And that which gold is for us, or glowing gemstones, for her are the stars, the superior and more brilliant stars."[12] And the following: "*She stood upon the moon.* The moon I regard figuratively <to be> the faith of those who are cleansed of corruption by the washing <of baptism>, for [122] the condition of liquid substance is regulated by the moon. She labored and gave birth anew to those 'carnal-minded into spiritually minded'[13] and formed and fashioned them according to the likeness of Christ."[14] And again he says: "We must not think that Christ is he who is to be born. For formerly, before the Apocalypse, the mystery of the Incarnation of the Logos had been fulfilled. John speaks with authority about the present and future things."[15] And afterwards <he mentions> other things, <and then says>, "Therefore, it is necessary to confess that the Church must be the one in labor and gives birth to those redeemed, as the Spirit said in Isaiah: 'Before she labored to give birth, she escaped and gave birth to a male.'[16] Whom did she escape? Either the dragon, certainly, in order for the spiritual Zion to give birth to virile people."[17] And in continuation, "so that in each one Christ is to be born in the *nous*.[18] Because of this the Church is swollen and in 'great pain'

---

11. Andrew may have had a manuscript variation that attributed this statement to Procle, or else he is mistaken. This should read "Thecla." At the beginning of *Symposium* Book 8 it states that Procle had finished speaking. The comments which follow are those of Thecla.

12. *Symp.* 8.5.

13. 1 Cor 2.14.

14. *Symp.* 8.6.

15. *Symp.* 8.7.

16. Is 66.7.

17. *Symp.* 8.7.

18. The word *nous* (νοῦς) means the "mind" or "intellect," as opposed to that which is perceived by the senses. It is difficult to translate the underlying concept especially when used as it is here, as an adjective. Sometimes translated as "spiritual" or "intellectual" or "mental," it must be understood that this does not mean a faculty in opposition to or apart from the mind. Likewise,

until Christ, having been born, might be 'formed in us,'[19] so that each one by partaking of Christ becomes Christ."[20] Moreover, the Church has been clothed in the "Sun of Righteousness."[21] And the legalistic light of the [123] moon, which shines by night, and the secular life, alterable like the moon, has been mastered under the feet, and round about upon her head <is> the crown of the apostolic precepts and virtues. Since <it is> from the moon that liquid substance depends, the same one <Methodios>[22] also says that by *the moon* is meant baptism, figuratively called "sea,"[23] which, on the one hand, <is> the salvation for those who are reborn and, on the other hand, ruination for the demons.

12.2. *And being with child, she cried out in labor and in anguish to give birth.*

Labor pains, as we say, the Church suffers for each of "those being reborn by water and the Spirit"[24] "until Christ has been formed in them," as the Apostle says,[25] for the miscarried children are those who fell from "the true light of Christ,"[26] and, at the same time as they are living, suffer death through unbelief.

12.3. *And another sign was seen in heaven; and behold, a great fire-red dragon, having seven heads and ten horns, and seven diadems upon his heads.*

Heaven here we think is to be understood <as> the air, and the *fire-red dragon* is the one who, after he was created, "was

"intellectual" does not suggest knowledge by means of discursive reasoning, or something which can be completely comprehended. The *nous* is considered by the Fathers to be the human mind at its highest level of operation and the God-given means by which we "know" God. This capacity exists in human beings by virtue of the fact that they were created in the image and likeness of God with the intent that they would come to "know" God. "Knowledge" of God in the Eastern tradition, however, does not consist of that which can be learned by study, or acquired by human reason, but only that which can be learned by spiritual experience and encounter with God, through the transformation of the *nous* by prayer.

19. Gal 4.19.
20. *Symp.* 8.8.
21. Mal 3.20 LXX (4.2 RSV).
22. Methodios, *Symp.* 8.6.
23. 1 Cor 10.1–2.
24. Jn 3.5.
25. Gal 4.19.
26. Jn 1.4–9, 8.12, 9.5, 12.46.

mocked by the angels" of God, as it has been written in Job.[27] He is *fire-red* either because of his murderous nature and delight in bloodshed or because of the fiery angelic nature,[28] even [124] though he fell from <among the> angels. The *seven heads* <are> his seven most evil powers and hostile spiritual activities, or the seven spirits as Christ said in the Gospel, settling in to dwell in a man whose heart, having been swept clean, was empty of good thoughts and deeds,[29] or seven evils which Solomon says are in the heart of the enemy who in a loud voice entreats through deceits those who are persuaded[30] <by him>. The *horns* signify either those ten offenses which are the opposite of the Ten Commandments of the Law,[31] or the divisiveness of the kingdom, adorning him because he delights in dissensions. *Seven diadems* <are> on his heads, because those victorious over demonic activities acquire the crowns for themselves from there;[32] wherefore, victory is gained by pain and toil. Concerning these things, Methodios also says these words: "The great fiery dragon with the seven heads who is pulling down one third of the stars and who stood watching in order to devour the child of the woman in labor, he is the devil."[33] Also the following: "But he misses the prey and is unsuccessful <because> those who are reborn are snatched and carried upwards to the heights."[34] And after a few words, <he writes>, "*A third of the stars* [125] is called the portion of those utterly wrong regarding one of the Trinity.[35] The desert, into which the Church came to be nourished, is destitute of evils and barren of decay."[36] "The *one thousand*," he says, "is the perfect and complete number encompassing in it one hundred multiplied by ten."[37] And the following he says concerning his crowns: "She who had

---

27. Jb 40.14 and 41.24 (LXX).
28. Heb 1.7.
29. Mt 12.43–45; Lk 11.24–26.
30. Prv 26.25.
31. *Symp.* 8.13.
32. Ibid.
33. *Symp.* 8.10.
34. Ibid.
35. Ibid. Methodios considers the fallen stars to be heretics because "they, too, wish to be acquainted with the heavenly ones, and to have believed in Christ, and to have the seat of their soul in heaven, and to come near to the stars as children of light. But they are dragged down" by their false beliefs, says Methodios, naming among them Sabellius, Marcion, Valentinus, and the Ebionites.
36. *Symp.* 8.11.
37. Ibid.

struggled before against the devil and had deadened the seven heads of the seven crowns becomes self-disciplined <with respect to> virtue."[38]

12.4. *And his tail dragged a third of the stars from the sky, and cast them to the earth.*

By these things we believe two things are meant: either his prior fall from heaven, pulling down the angels who rebelled with him through the worst initiative of envy—for first was the pride—or after the crushing of his head,[39] the tail movement which brought down, out of a heavenly mindset, those non-steadfast ones who were figuratively called *stars* [126] on account of the great brightness from baptism. For thus Daniel prophesied about Antiochus as being a type of the coming of the Antichrist.[40]

12.4b. *And the dragon stood before the woman who was about to give birth, so that when she gave birth to her child, he would devour it.*

For the Apostate <devil> is always preparing himself <to stand> in opposition to the Church, grasping to make those reborn from her his own food in due season, moreover, even persecuting, through the Church, Christ himself as her head and as taking upon himself the matters of the faithful. Wherefore he also said to Saul, "Why are you persecuting me?"[41]

12.5a. *She brought forth a male child, one who will shepherd all the nations with a rod of iron,*

Continuously the Church gives birth to Christ through those who are baptized, as if he is being fashioned in them[42] until the completion of <their> spiritual age,[43] according to the Apostle. *A male child* is the people of the Church who are not feminized by pleasures, through whom Christ God shepherded the nations, even already by the powerful iron-like hands of the strong Romans. And he will shepherd also after the resurrection of the dead when he appoints judges [127] who are strong in faith like

38. *Symp.* 8.13.
40. Dn 8.10.
42. Gal 4.19.

39. Gn 3.15.
41. Acts 9.4.
43. Eph 4.13.

iron over the fragile and weak vessels of the nations, which did not contain the mystical "new wine"[44] because of unbelief.

12.5b. *And her child was snatched up to God and to his throne,*

For even here the saints *are snatched up* in trials < by death> so that they not be overwhelmed by troubles beyond their power. "They will be snatched up in the clouds in order to meet the Lord in the air,"[45] and they will be with God at his throne with the supreme angelic powers.

12.6. *And the woman fled into the wilderness, where she has a place prepared by God there, so that there they will nourish her for one thousand two hundred and sixty days.*

When, it says, the devil, acting through the Antichrist, has arrayed himself against the Church, her chosen and supreme ones, who have spit upon the noisy public approbations and the pleasures of the world, will flee to a manner of life devoid of every evil and abundant in every virtue, according to Methodios.[46] And there they will avoid the assaults from both the hostile demons and people. [128] Of course, the actual physical desert will save those fleeing from the plot of the Apostate <devil> in the "mountains and caves and the dens of the earth,"[47] as did the martyrs previously for three-and-a-half years, that is, the *one thousand two hundred sixty days,* during which apostasy will prevail. The Great Official, "who does not allow anyone to be tested beyond his strength,"[48] will deliver us from this, granting us steadfast disposition and manly strength in the assaults against us, so that "legitimately contending"[49] "against the principalities and powers of darkness"[50] we might be adorned with the "crown of righteousness"[51] and receive the rewards of victory. For to him are due victory and power through the weak ones, <him> who routs the strong "aerial powers,"[52] together with the Father and the Life-giving Spirit unto the ages of ages. Amen.

44. Mt 9.17; Mk 2.22; Lk. 5.37.
45. 1 Thes 4.17.
46. *Symp.* 8.11.
47. Heb 11.38.
48. 1 Cor 10.13.
49. 2 Tm 2.5.
50. Eph 6.12.
51. 2 Tm 4.8.
52. Eph 2.2.

SECTION TWELVE

CHAPTER 34
About the War Between the Angels and the Demons and the Fall of Satan

12.7–8. ⁷*And there was a war in heaven. Michael and his angels fought against the dragon. And the* [129] *dragon and his angels fought,* ⁸*and they did not prevail, and there was no longer any place to be found for them in heaven.*

ND THESE things can fit both the first fall of the devil from the angelic order because of arrogance and envy, and his degradation by means of the cross of the Lord, when, as the Lord said, "The ruler of this world is judged,"[1] and of the ancient tyranny he said, "It is cast out."[2] Not bearing the arrogance <of the devil>, it is likely that the divine angels together with the commander Michael previously rejected him from their own association, just as Ezekiel said, "He had been cast out by the cherubim from the midst of the fiery stones"[3]—I think <he means> the angelic orders—on account of the wrongs found in him, and during the appearance of Christ, <the angels> ministering to him after the temptation[4] detested him <the devil> again as a dishonored servant. One must know that, as it has been given to the Fathers, after the creation of the perceptible world, this one had been cast down on account of his pride and envy, he to whom had first been entrusted the aerial authority, just as the Apostle said.[5] And Papias says in these words: "To some of them, that is, the

1. Jn 16.11. 2. Jn 12.31.
3. Ezek 28.16. 4. Mt 4.11; Mk 1.13.
5. Eph 2.2 and 6.12.

divine angels of old, [130] he gave <authority> to rule over the earth and commanded <them> to rule well." And then he says the following: "And it happened that their arrangement came to nothing."[6]

12.9. And the great dragon was thrown <down>, the ancient serpent, who is called the Devil and Satan, the deceiver of the whole world, he was thrown to the earth, and his angels were thrown.

Naturally. For heaven does not bear an earthly mentality, because "darkness has nothing in common with light."[7] If it is placed with the article, "*the satan*," it is not as <though> another is being placed alongside the devil—and if it is placed as an overstatement, such as "*the devil and the satan*"—rather he is called by two <names>: the one <the devil> because he slanders[8] virtues and those who desire them and <he slanders> God himself to human beings, as he represented him <God> slanderously to Adam;[9] and the other <Satan>, as he is opposed[10] to both the Master[11] and his servants.[12] One must know that the fall of the devil that happened after the cross is not that <of> place, <but> as <a fall to> inefficacy from those former <powers>; just as he also confessed to Anthony,[13] the verse of the Psalm had been fulfilled in him. "The swords of the enemy I utterly destroyed to the end."[14] Therefore, his fall is the annulment of his evil [131] machinations, with the complete rejection of him from heaven and the rule belonging to him, as it is said. It has been said by the blessed Justin the martyr <that>

6. Andrew is quoting Papias, one of the earliest Fathers, from a work now lost. This fragment was preserved by Andrew in this commentary.

7. 2 Cor 6.14.

8. "Devil" or in Greek διάβολος, comes from the verb διαβάλλω, "I slander" or "I accuse falsely."

9. Gn 3.5.

10. Andrew demonstrates that he knows the meaning of "Satan," which derives from a Hebrew word for "the adversary," hence one who opposes.

11. Mt 4.1–11; Mk 1.13; Lk 4.1–13.

12. Lk 22.31; Jb 1.8–12, 2.3–6; 2 Cor 12.7; 1 Pt 5.8.

13. *The Life of Antony,* by Athanasius the Great, relates an incident in which Satan himself visited St. Anthony in his cell and complained to the monk that he had been weakened. *Life of Antony* 41.

14. Ps 9.6 (LXX text).

after the coming of Christ and the decree against him <to send him> to Gehenna, the devil is to become a greater blasphemer even <to the extent that> he had never before so shamelessly blasphemed God.[15] Wherefore, correctly has it been said about him: "His heart was made solid like a stone"[16] on account of his ceaseless evil. And if the expectation of punishment makes him even more evil, then how if being punished, either himself or his workers, how are they to be cleansed of the filth of sin in Gehenna through the fire? Since they have not attained this <cessation from wickedness>, how will they have an end of the punishment against those who have vain thoughts?[17]

12.10. *And I heard a loud voice in heaven, saying, "Now the salvation and the power and the kingdom of our God and the authority of his Christ have come, for the accuser of our brethren has been thrown down, who accuses them day and night before our God.*

Accusation and Slander against human beings [132] are the names the devil had been called, as had been said, which he is. The angels are delighted about his ejection "for there is nothing in common between a believer and an unbeliever."[18]

12.11–12. [11]*And they conquered him by the blood of the Lamb and by the word of their testimony, for they did not love their lives even unto death.* [12]*Wherefore rejoice, Heaven and you that dwell therein! Woe to you, Earth and Sea, for the devil has come down to you with great anger, because he knows that he has little time <remaining>!"*

Those accused by him, it says, the saints and those slandered as <was> Job,[19] in comparison to all the people persuaded by him, have been victorious over him nonetheless by suffering for

---

15. This quotation of Justin is taken from his lost writings. This exact statement is also quoted by Irenaeus (*Heres.* 5.26.2) and by Eusebius of Caesarea (*E. H.* 4.18.9).

16. Jb 41.15 (LXX).

17. Here Andrew refers to those who teach that in the end God will save everyone, even the devil. This belief, known as "the restoration of all things," was denounced as heretical at the Fifth Ecumenical Council in 553, a few decades before the composition of this commentary.

18. 2 Cor 6.15.

19. Jb 1.9–11, 2.4–5.

Christ. The powers above, following an imitation of God, *rejoice* at his fall and grieve over those who had cleaved to his earthly plot. *Woe to those* who dwell on the *earth*, that is, to those who do not have <dwelling> "in heaven,"[20] but have their citizenship on earth. For many of them on the earth are victorious over the enemy and will be victorious, even though he is now more angered by those who are struggling because of the nearness of his punishment. Wherefore, it is necessary to deplore those who have their "minds on earthly things"[21] and who are tossed by the waves in the sea of life here.

CHAPTER 35

How the Dragon Does Not Cease Persecuting the Church

12.13–14. [13] *And when the dragon saw that he had been thrown down to the earth, he pursued* [133] *the woman who had borne the male child.* [14] *And the two wings of the great eagle were given to the woman in order to fly from the person of the serpent into the wilderness to her place, where she will be nourished for a time, and times, and half a time.*

When, it says, the devil after struggling against Christ after the baptism was defeated,[22] he armed himself against the holy apostles and was put to shame seeing <that> they found life through death,[23] and as he <on the contrary> was condemned as a serpent to crawl on the earth and to eat dirt,[24] the earthly thoughts, then he began again to persecute the Church, the brave manly people of God who had been born and who are being born, those not emasculated by pleasures. But from the beginning the love towards God and neighbor and the helpful providential care of the Crucified One has been given to her <the Church> for our sake, and on account of all these things the two Testaments[25] are symbolized by the *two wings of the eagle,* so that, flying away on high into the desert way of life devoid

---

20. Phil 3.20.   21. Phil 3.19.
22. Mt 4.1–11; Mk 1.12–13; Lk 4.1–13.
23. Mt 10.39; Lk 17.33.   24. Gn 3.14.
25. Cf. *Chp.* 2, *Text* 20, page 61, on Rv 1.13.

of every dew of pleasure, she is to be fed with them <the Testaments> always and especially in the coming of the Antichrist, who <is> to rule during the aforementioned time of three-and-a-half years, which in many places has been written. During which <time> also those hiding themselves in the actual physical desert in mountains and caves at times will flee from him. [134]

12.15–16. *¹⁵The serpent poured water like a river out of his mouth after the woman, to sweep her away with the flood. ¹⁶But the earth came to the help of the woman, and the earth opened its mouth and swallowed the river which the dragon had poured from his mouth.*

When the Church was fleeing, it says, into inaccessible places <due to> the attack of the deceiver from his mouth, that is, by his command, behind her will come a river of water, that is, a multitude of ungodly men or evil demons or various temptations against her that he might enslave her <the Church>. *The earth*, it says, *helped her* on the one hand either by lengthening the way and by the drought and dryness in the places preventing the impulses of evils, and swallowing up the river of the temptations on account of this, or by the humble-mindedness of the saints who say inwardly, "I am earth and ashes,"[26] rendering impotent all the snares of the devil, as the angel had spoken to the divine Anthony.[27]

12.17. *And the dragon became angry with the woman, and went off to make war on the rest of her offspring, on those who keep the commandments of God and have the testimony of Jesus.*

When the chosen teachers of the Church and those despising the earth have withdrawn to the hardships in the desert, if he has utterly missed them, [135] the Antichrist will declare war against those drafted for Christ in the world. It says he will begin the war, so that, just as when dust thickens the smoothness of oil, finding them vulnerable in the occupations of life, he will put them to flight. But many among them will conquer him because they have genuinely loved Christ.

26. Gn 18.27.

27. It is unclear which passage Andrew has in mind here. It does not appear to refer to any event recorded in the *Life of Antony*.

CHAPTER 36
About the Beast with Ten Horns and Seven Heads

12.18–13.1. And he stood on the sand of the sea.[28] *[13.1]And I saw a beast rising out of the sea, with ten horns and seven heads, with ten diadems upon its horns and a blasphemous name upon its heads.*

Some considered this beast as some kind of secondary ruling power of Satan and of the rest of the demons, that which comes out from the earth after this as the Antichrist.[29] And with Saints Methodios and Hippolytus and others [136] also, the present beast has been taken as the Antichrist coming out of the trouble-prone and turbulent sea of this life.[30] The ten horns with the diadems and the seven heads hint at the union of the devil with him—for these <qualities> were also explained above[31] as belonging to him—both the division into ten of the earthly kingdom at the last days and the weekly kingdom corresponding to the order of this world, which on the one hand is counted in seven days, and on the other hand is successively divided into seven, as will be spoken about in what follows. According to which, he who works in it, Satan, has been called the "ruler of this world."[32] The *blasphemous name* on his seven heads clearly <means> his defenders.[33] For these, since the beginning, have not ceased to blaspheme Christ until the accession of Constantine the Great, after whom Julian and Valens became blasphemers of Christ.[34]

28. This verse is cited by Josef Schmid and Nestle-Aland as 12.18. In some editions of the Bible, however, it is numbered as 12.17, and in others as 13.1.

29. Oik. 7.11.1–3.

30. It is difficult to explain Andrew's mistake here. No such identification can be found in Methodios. Hippolytus actually believes that the beast of the *land* is the Antichrist, not the beast of the sea (*Chr. and Ant.*, 48–49, ANF 5.214). It is Irenaeus who believes that the beast of the sea is the Antichrist (*Heres.* 5.28.2).

31. *Chp.* 33, *Text* 124, page 139.

32. Jn 12.31.

33. Those Roman emperors who blasphemed Christ.

34. None of the Roman emperors recognized Christ as God, until the rise of Constantine the Great. After Constantine, two emperors were "blasphemers." The first, Julian, known as "the Apostate," was the nephew of Constan-

13.2a. *And the beast that I saw was like a leopard, its feet were like a bear's, and its mouth was like a lion's mouth.*

The leopard means the kingdom of the Greeks; the bear, that of the Persians; the lion is the kingdom of the Babylonians over which [137] the Antichrist will rule, coming as king of the Romans, and abolishing their rule when he sees the clay toes of the feet, through which is meant the weak and fragile division of the kingdom into ten.[35]

13.2b. *And to it the dragon gave his power and his throne and great authority.*

For Satan, the spiritual dragon, will give to the Antichrist all authority by means of false signs and wonders for the destruction of those unstable <in the faith>.

13.3a,b. *And one of its heads seemed to have a mortal wound, but its mortal wound was healed,*

A head as if *wounded,* it says, is either one of the rulers who will be put to death and who will appear to rise again by him through deceitful sorcery, as Simon Magus had done who was reproached by the leader of the apostles <Peter>,[36] or the kingdom of the Romans, which, having endured some kind of wound by the division, will seem to have been healed by the monarchy, following the model of <what occurred in the time of> Caesar Augustus.[37]

---

tine and had a brief reign (361–363). He was raised as a Christian, but he was very enamored with Greek culture and philosophy and secretly became a devotee of the Greek gods. When he ascended to the throne, he openly advocated paganism, reinstituted measures to repress Christianity, and attempted to revive the worship of the traditional Greek gods. Valens (who reigned from 364–378) was an Arian who persecuted orthodox Christians, tolerated paganism, and clashed with such notables as Basil the Great and Gregory Nazianzus. Although Valens was a Christian, Andrew considers Valens a blasphemer because Valens, being an Arian, did not recognize the divinity of the Son as equal to that of the Father.

35. There is no reference to clay toes in Revelation, but this is a detail which is found in Dn 2.41–42, which describes four separate beasts. Interpreting the animals of Daniel's vision as successive kingdoms was a well-known and common end time scenario in the patristic tradition.

36. A traditional story found in the apocryphal book, *The Acts of Peter* 25.

37. Out of the divisions and civil war, such as occurred in Octavian's time,

13.3c–4. *³cand the whole earth <followed> behind the beast with wonder, ⁴and* [138] *<people> worshiped the dragon, for he had given his
authority to the beast, saying, "Who is like the beast, and who can fight
against it?"*

The miracle by the Antichrist will have a reference to the
devil who works through him, because through him <the An-
tichrist>, the dragon will be worshiped, and it will appear to
those whose eyes of the mind are disabled that he is both raising the dead and accomplishing miracles.

13.5–6. *⁵And the beast was given a mouth uttering loud and blasphemous words, and it was allowed to exercise authority for forty-two
months. ⁶And it opened its mouth to utter blasphemies against God, to
blaspheme his name and his dwelling and those who dwell in heaven.*

According to divine allowance, it says, for three-and-a-half
years he will have license both for blasphemy against God and
the ill treatment of the saints. The *dwelling of God* and the dwelling of the Logos in the flesh[38]—that is to say, the Incarnation,
and the repose in the saints—against which he will certainly direct every blasphemy, and also <against> the holy angels. [139]

13.7–8. *⁷And authority was given over every tribe and tongue and nation, ⁸and all who dwell on earth will worship it, every one whose name
has not been written before the foundation of the world in the Book of
Life of the Lamb that was slain.*

He is to use his wicked power against *every tongue and tribe*, it
says, and he will govern those whose names are not written in
the *Book of Life*.

13.9–10. *⁹If anyone has an ear, let him hear. ¹⁰If anyone is to go into
captivity, he goes; if anyone slays by the sword, by the sword he must be
slain. Here is <a call for> the endurance and faith of the saints.*

Each one, it says, is to receive the wages befitting the labors
done. Those who are prepared to do evil to their neighbor will

---

a new Augustus will arise who will unify the Empire, just as Octavian assumed
power, changed the Republic into an Empire, and was proclaimed Augustus.
Hippolytus made a comparison to Augustus, citing this verse with regard to
his accumulation of power (*Chr. and Ant.* 49).

38. Jn 1.14.

be imprisoned by the devil and will succumb to spiritual death by the satanic dagger, and in those deeds in which "they were defeated, they are to be enslaved"[39] to him. As the great James says, those who have pure "faith and" immovable "patience"[40] in tribulations will not be blotted out of *the Book of Life,* those with whom [140] the all-merciful God will show us in fellowship, considering "worthless the sufferings of this present time compared to the future glory to be revealed"[41] to the saints and walking bravely on "the narrow way,"[42] so that at its end in the future age, finding glory, repose, and spaciousness, we might "co-reign with Christ,"[43] to whom and to the Father are due all thanks and worship together with the Holy Spirit unto the ages. Amen.

39. 2 Pt 2.19.
40. Jas 1.3–4.
41. Rom 8.18.
42. Mt 7.14.
43. 2 Tm 2.12.

SECTION THIRTEEN

CHAPTER 37
About the False Prophet

13.11. *And I saw another beast which rose out of the earth, and it had two horns like a lamb, and it was speaking like a dragon.*

 HIS BEAST some say[1] is the Antichrist, but to others his two horns seemed to hint at the Antichrist and the false prophet.[2] Since it is admitted that the false prophet also is to come in his own person, we think it is not absurd to understand that the dragon is Satan, that *the beast* [141] *rising out of the sea* is the Antichrist, and that the one present, according to the opinion of the blessed Irenaeus,[3] is to be understood as the false prophet rising out of the earth, that is, out of the earthly and groveling way of life, having *horns like a lamb*, because he completely covers with sheep's skin the hidden murderous character of the wolf,[4] and because of his appearance of piety in the beginning, concerning which Irenaeus says, speaking thus verbatim: "About the adjutant which he also calls false prophet, he speaks, it says, *like a dragon*."[5] To him, it says, will be given the power so that he makes signs and wonders, going before the Antichrist, preparing for him "the way which leads to perdition."[6] The healing of the wound of the beast, we said,[7] is the apparent union for a short time of the divided kingdom, or the restoration through the Antichrist of the destructive tyranny of Satan for a short time, or the false resurrection from

---

1. Hippolytus, *Chr. and Ant.* 49, and Oikoumenios 8.3.1–2.
2. *Chr. and Ant.* 49.
3. Irenaeus, *Heres.* 5.28.2.
4. Mt 7.15.
5. *Heres.* 5.28.2.
6. Mt 7.13.
7. *Chp.* 36, *Text* 137, page 148.

the dead of one of his close associates. This one is to *speak like a dragon*, it says, for he will both act and speak the things of the devil, the source of evil.

13.12–13. [12] *It exercises all the authority of the first beast in its presence, and causes the earth and its* [142] *inhabitants to worship the first beast, whose mortal wound was healed.* [13]*And it works great signs, even making fire come down from heaven to earth in the sight of men.*

In imitation of the Baptist, who brought believers to the Savior, the forerunner[8] of the rebellious false Christ will perform all things, it says, through sorcery for the deception of people, <for them> to consider the Antichrist to be God, <the Antichrist> witnessed to by the worker of such marvels[9] and receiving indisputable glory. For the lie, to deceive people, strives eagerly to imitate the truth. It is no wonder in the eyes of the deceived, *fire* will be seen *coming down from heaven*, since we have learned also in the story of Job[10] that this one <Satan> has slandered and has consumed his <Job's> flocks <by fire> by divine permission and satanic operation.

13.14a. *And through the signs which were given to him to work in the presence of the beast, he deceives those who dwell on earth,*

He deceives, it says, those who have hearts dwelling entirely on the earth. For those who have acquired "citizenship in heaven"[11] the perception does not deceive, because they have been made perfectly secure by the prophecy of his coming. [143]

13.14b–17. [14b] *telling those who dwell on earth to make an image for the beast who has the wound of the sword and <yet> he lived.* [15]*And it was allowed him to give breath to the image of the beast so that the image of the beast should even speak, and should cause those who would not worship the image of the beast to be slain.* [16]*Also it causes all, both small and great, both rich and poor, both free and slave, to be given a*

---

8. "John the Forerunner" is the title typically used for John the Baptist in the Eastern Christian tradition since his primary role was to prepare the way for Christ.

9. Jn 1.19, 32.   10. Jb 1.16.
11. Phil 3.20.

mark on the right hand or the forehead, [17]*so that no one can buy or sell unless he has the mark, that is, the name of the beast or the number of its name.*

It has often been learned historically, both from Apollonius[12] and others, that demons speak through wooden statuettes, animals, trees, and water by means of sorcery, I think [144] even through dead bodies just as Simon Magus showed to the Romans a dead person moving in the presence of Peter, even though the apostle refuted the deception himself to show, through those whom he himself <Peter> raised, how the dead were raised.[13] Therefore, there is nothing unreasonable for even the adjutant of the Antichrist, working through demons to make an image for the beast and show it speaking, and to prepare and to destroy those who do not worship it. And the mark of the destructive name of the Apostate he will earnestly endeavor to put on all: on the right hand in order to cut off the doing of good works, and on the forehead in order to teach the deceived ones to speak boldly in error and darkness. But the ones marked with divine light on their faces will not accept it. And he will make it his business to extend the symbol of the beast everywhere, in both buying and selling so that a violent death will be suffered from lack of necessities by those who do not receive it.

12. Apollonius of Tyana, a first-century philosopher, whose life was told by Flavius Philostratus in *Life of Apollonius of Tyana;* see *Philostratus: The Life of Apollonius of Tyana,* trans. Christopher P. Jones, 3 vols., Loeb Classical Library, vols. 16, 17, and 458 (Cambridge, MA: Harvard University Press, 2005–6) 3:157. Origen mentions the view of one "Moeragenes" that Apollonius was not only a philosopher but also a magician (*Against Celsus* 6.41). In the early fourth century, the Roman governor of Alexandria, later of Bithynia, Hierocles, compared Apollonius to Christ in a treatise entitled "To the Christians," in order to discredit Christian claims that the miracles of Jesus proved his divinity. Eusebius of Caesarea countered in the treatise *Reply to Hierocles,* specifically ridiculing accounts of talking trees (*Reply* 30 and 38), among other fantastic occurrences. He also argued that Apollonius's miraculous actions, if true, were performed with demonic assistance (*Reply* 31). Victorinus remarked that even in his times magicians were skilled in performing such feats (Vic. 13.13).

13. *Acts of Peter* 28. Peter revealed the trickery used to accomplish the deception.

CHAPTER 38
About the Name of the Antichrist

13.18. *Here is wisdom: let him who has a mind reckon the number of the beast, for it is the number of a human. And his number is six hundred and sixty-six.* [145]

The exact sense of the numerical cipher, as well as the rest of the things written regarding this, time and experience will reveal to those who live soberly. For, as some of the teachers say, if it were necessary to know clearly such a name, the one who had beheld it would have revealed it.[14] But divine grace was not well pleased to set down the name of the destroyer in the divine book. As in exercises in logic, many names are to be found contained in this number, according to the blessed Hippolytus and others, both proper nouns and common nouns. First, proper nouns, such as "Lampetis,"[15] "Teitan,"[16] through the diphthong, τενῶ forming the future of the verb,[17] according to Hippolytus, and likewise "Lateinos,"[18] just as "Benedict" is interpreted as "one who is blessed" or "blessed" perhaps in imitation of the truly blessed one, Christ our God. Then common nouns "wicked guide," "real harm," [146] "slanderer of old," "unjust lamb"—these he will be called by those opposing his deception, rendering the appropriate "opinion in shame."[19]

14. The opinion of Irenaeus (*Heres.* 5.30.3–4), which seems to have been adopted by many other "teachers."

15. The origin of this name is uncertain.

16. This possibility was suggested initially by Irenaeus, *Heres.* 5.30.3, then by Hippolytus, *Chr. and Ant.* 50.

17. The present tense is τείνω, meaning to "stretch," "strive," or "reach."

18. Hippolytus, *Chr. and Ant.* 50; also Irenaeus, *Heres.* 5.30.3.

19. Phil 3.19.

CHAPTER 39
About the Lamb and the 144,000

14.1. *Then I saw, and behold, on Mount Zion stood the Lamb, and with him a hundred and forty-four thousand having his name and his Father's name written on their foreheads.*

It is acknowledged that Christ is unambiguously the *Lamb*. Standing upon *Mount Zion,* not that of old but the new, which is the "city of the living God."[20] These thousands signify either the fruitful abundance of the apostolic seed of grace in each one being brought to perfection to twelve thousand, the perfect fruit of faith of those being saved, or those virgins of the New Testament <who are such> according to both "the inner"[21] and "outer person."[22] For among the ancients, rare is the achievement of virginity, found among very few, wherefore one must suppose therefore these others, besides those spoken of before, are assembled by name out of the tribes of Israel [147] in whom virginity had not been witnessed before. The *foreheads* of all these are sealed by the light of the divine countenance, by which venerable ones appear to the destroying angels.

14.2–3a. [2]*And I heard a voice from heaven like the sound of many waters and like the sound of loud thunder, and the voice I heard was like the sound of harpers playing on their harps.* [3a]*And they sing a new song before the throne and before the four living beings and the elders.*

The sound of many waters and *of the thunder* and *of harps* signifies the thrilling aspect of the hymns of the saints and their melodious, well-sounding, and harmonious song echoing all around the church and the "assembly of those" registered as "first born in heaven."[23] Just as in the harmony of strings, by means of the symphonic union of the saints, it <the song> is sounded forth which they achieved by "mortifying the desires"[24] of the body. And this, it says, no one else is able to learn except them. Wherefore, to each one, knowledge is given abun-

---

20. Heb 12.22.
22. 2 Cor 4.16.
24. Col 3.5.

21. Eph 3.16; Rom 7.22.
23. Heb 12.23; Lk 10.20.

dantly by the measure of the way of life, just as the manifestation of the mysteries of the Lord is given to the servants of men proportionately according to his favor.

14.3b–5. *3b No one could learn that song except the hundred and forty-four thousand who had been redeemed from the earth. 4These are the ones who have not defiled themselves with women, [148] for they are virgins; it is these who follow the Lamb wherever he goes. These have been redeemed from mankind as first fruits for God and the Lamb, 5and in their mouth no lie was found. For they are spotless.*

We believe that these, after the aforementioned twenty-four elders, are superior to the rest on account of both virginity and blamelessness in tongue and hand, after the appearance of Christ, and they possess splendor in virtues through which they are taught the new song, the song which is unknown to the many, not only in the present life but also in the future age. For if "perfect knowledge will come" at that time "abolishing the partial,"[25] according to the divine Apostle, suitably, however, there will be a manifestation of the divine mysteries in the way of life of the saints here. For <there are> "many mansions in the Father's" <house>[26] and <one> "star differs from another in glory,"[27] just as <there are> many different punishments, from which the Lord of all redeems us; he will reckon us among those who are saved on account of his goodness, not looking at the multitude of our sins, but in his compassion, because of which he had come to earth and poured out his precious blood for us, in order to wash clean our defilements and stains, to bring us to the Father, with whom to him must be, [149] as the "Leader of our Salvation,"[28] together with the All-Holy Spirit, glory, dominion, and honor, now and ever and unto the ages of ages. Amen.

25. 1 Cor 13.10.
27. 1 Cor 15.41.
26. Jn 14.2.
28. Heb 2.10.

SECTION FOURTEEN

CHAPTER 40
About the Angel Proclaiming the Imminence of the Future Judgment

14.6–7. *⁶And I saw an angel flying in mid-heaven, with an eternal Gospel to evangelize those who dwell on earth, and every nation and tribe and tongue and people, ⁷saying in a loud voice, "Fear God and give him glory, for the hour of his judgment has come; and worship him who made heaven and the earth and [the] sea and the fountains of water.*

HE *MID-HEAVEN* shows the angel, who appeared to be both high and heavenly, having been sent from above to the people below to lead <them> up into heaven through this intermediate place by his own intercession in imitation of God, so as to unite the "body of the Church to Christ, our head,"¹ and to predefine the *eternal Gospel*, as the one of eternity <coming> from God. He says this: *fear God* and do not be afraid of the Antichrist, "who does not have the power to kill the soul along with the body,"² but [150] battle against him eagerly, for he rules for a little while because of the imminence of judgment and the reward of those who are steadfast.

1. Col 1.18, 24.
2. Mt 10.28.

CHAPTER 41
About the Angel Announcing the Fall of Babylon

14.8. *And another angel, a second one, followed, saying, "Fallen, fallen is Babylon the great! She has watered all nations from the wine of desire of her fornication."*

Babylon is the name he significantly gives to the confusion of the world[3] and to the tumult of daily life, which, as much as he foretells, is not yet to end. *The wine of desire of fornication* he calls not only the Bacchanalia of idolatry and the alienation of the mind, but also the drunkenness and lack of control which derives from each sin, according to which all those who are unfaithful[4] to God, according to the saying of the Psalmist, will be utterly destroyed.[5] Such a Babylon finally falls, and is completely overthrown in the appearance of the Jerusalem above, while the workers of transgression are sent "to the eternal fire."[6] [151]

CHAPTER 42
About the Third Angel Warning the Faithful Not to Accept the Antichrist

14.9–10. [9]*And another angel, the third one, followed them, saying in a loud voice, "If anyone worships the beast and its image, and receives a mark on his forehead or on his hand, [10]he also will drink the wine of God's wrath, poured unmixed into the cup of his anger, and he will be tormented with fire and sulfur in the presence of the holy angels and in the presence of the Lamb.*

If anyone, it says, bows down to the beastly Antichrist and pursues the ungodly lifestyle modeling him, and either in word or in deed proclaims him God—for this can be clear by the mark given on the forehead and hand—he also will partake with him of the drink of the cup of vengeance, on the one hand

3. Gn 11.9, which provides the meaning of the word "Babel," derived from the confusion of tongues.
4. Greek: πορνεύοντες, literally, to fornicate against God.
5. Ps 73(72).27.
6. Mt 18.8, 25.41.

unmixed and separated from the divine mercies because of the righteous judgment, on the other hand having been *poured* with various punishments on account of the multiplicity and variety of its self-chosen wickedness. Appropriately is the punishment called *the wine of wrath*, being a consequence of the wine of impiety, making drunk those drinking from it, so that "whoever sins through them is also punished through them."[7] [152]

14.11a. *And the smoke of their torment goes up for ever and ever.*

This smoke must imply either the labored breath that comes out along with the groaning of those being punished emanating up from below,[8] or the smoke coming forth from the fire punishing those who have fallen. It is to *go up for ever and ever,* it says, that we might learn that it is endless, just as the bliss of the righteous <will be endless>, and in like manner also the torment of the sinners.

14.11b. *And they have no rest, day or night, these worshipers of the beast and its image, and whoever receives the mark of its name."*

Day and night, not to say that the condition of the future age is measured by the sun, predicting by this not that the impious are to have rest, but <this is said> either according to habit because the present time is counted as night and day, or *day* means the life of the saints and *night* the punishment of the profane,[9] which will fall upon those who commit evil deeds and pronounce the blasphemies of the apostate beast against Christ, depicting <the beast> through the deeds they commit and engraving his name on their own hearts as honorable. [153]

14.12. *Here is a call for the endurance of the saints. Here are those who keep the commandments of God and the faith of Jesus.*

The impious, it says, will be tortured throughout the age to come, and so the saints here display patient endurance in <which>, time quickly slipping away, they preserve inviolate the divine commandments and the faith in Christ.

---

7. Wis 11.16.   8. Oik. 8.13.8.

9. Greek: τῶν βεβήλων, those who are profane, impure, or defiled. The word has a nuance which implies idolatrous worship.

14.13. *And I heard a voice from heaven saying to me, "Write this: Blessed are the dead who die in the Lord henceforth." "Indeed," says the Spirit, "that they may rest from their labors. For their deeds follow them!"*

The heavenly voice does not bless all of the dead, but those *who die in the Lord,* having been put to death in the world, and who "bear in the body the death of Jesus"[10] and "suffer with Christ."[11] For those, actually, the exodus from the body is rest from toils, and the consequence of their deeds is the occasion of "unfading crowns" and "rewards of glory,"[12] <which are> the prizes for those winning the contests by a wide margin of victory, <the prizes> which the contestants of Christ our God achieved against the invisible powers. "For the sufferings of the present time cannot be compared to the future glory to be revealed"[13] [154] to those who are well-pleasing to God, as the Apostle says, for which we must also desire to pray unceasingly to God, saying, "Incline our hearts, Lord, to your testimonies, and turn our eyes away from all vanity,"[14] "and enter not into judgment with your servants, for no one living is justified before you,"[15] but visit us in your rich mercies, for yours is the dominion and the kingdom and the power and the glory of the Father, Son, and Holy Spirit, now and ever and unto ages of ages. Amen.

10. 2 Cor 4.10.
12. 1 Pt 5.4; 1 Cor 9.24–25.
14. Ps 119(118).36–37.

11. Rom 8.17.
13. Rom 8.18.
15. Ps 143(142).2.

SECTION FIFTEEN

CHAPTER 43
How the One Sitting on the Cloud Destroys by Means of the Sickle the Things Growing on Earth

14.14. Then I saw, and behold, a white cloud, and seated on the cloud one like a son of man, with a golden crown on his head, and a sharp sickle in his hand.

LOUD WE understand <is> either a cloud perceptible to the senses that took Christ up from the eyes of the apostles[1] or some angelic power by the purity [155] and loftiness, as the Psalmist says, "and he mounted upon the cherubim and flew."[2] Through these things we infer Christ to be the one like a son of man seen upon the clouds, the *crown* upon him to be indicative of the dominion of both the visible and invisible powers, and this is *golden* because this material is precious among us, and the *sickle* signifies consummation. For the Lord himself also called the consummation of the world "harvest."[3]

14.15–16. [15]And another angel came out of the sky, calling with a loud voice to him who sat upon the cloud, "Send your sickle, and reap, for your hour to reap has come, for the harvest of the earth has become dry." [16]And he who sat upon the cloud cast his sickle on the earth, and the earth was reaped.

The cry of the angel periphrastically means the supplication of all the powers of heaven, having been permitted to see on the one hand the honor of the righteous, and on the other hand

1. Acts 1.9.
3. Mt 13.30.

2. Ps 18(17).10.

the cutting-down of the lawless sinners, because of the fact that the things moving and changing cease and the immovable and abiding things are manifested. For *the harvest* to be *dry* means the end time has arrived when the seed of piety has ripened like "ripe wheat";[4] [156] it will be deemed worthy of the heavenly "storehouses,"[5] the fruitfulness being rendered to the "Husbandman"[6] "thirtyfold, sixtyfold, and one hundredfold."[7]

CHAPTER 44
About the Angel Harvesting the Vine of Bitterness

14.17. *And another angel came out of the temple in heaven, and also having a sharp sickle.*

Even if Christ is called the "Angel of the Great Counsel"[8] of the Father, nonetheless the present <angel> is shown to be from the "ministering powers"[9] from what follows. First, coming out of the heavenly temple with *a sharp sickle,* then performing the harvest of the exceedingly impious.

14.18. *And another angel [came out] from the altar, the angel having authority over fire, and he called with a loud cry to him who had the sharp sickle, saying, "Send your sharp sickle, and gather the clusters of the vineyard of the earth, for its grapes are ripe."*

And from this we learn that the angelic powers have been assigned to created things, some to water, some to fire, and some to another part of creation. So we learn that this one was assigned to the punishment by fire. It says that, being among the highest angels, with a cry he urged the one with the sickle to reap *the clusters* of the *vineyard of the earth,* [157] through which the impious and lawless are depicted, filling the "cup of wrath of the Lord,"[10] bearing <fruit of> "wrath of serpents and wrath

4. Ibid..
5. Ibid.
6. Jn 15.1.
7. Mt 13.23; Mk 4.20.
8. Is 9.6, the "Angel" or "Messenger" of the Great Counsel.
9. Heb 1.14.
10. Rv 14.10; Jer 25.15; Is 51.17.

of asps"[11] instead of the wine of gladness to the Good "Husbandman."[12]

14.19. *So the angel cast his sickle on the earth and gathered the vintage of the earth, and threw it into the great wine press of the wrath of God.*

Wine press of God is the place of torment which has been "prepared for the devil and his angels,"[13] *great* because of the multitude of those tormented in it. "For the road to destruction is wide and spacious."[14]

14.20. *And the wine press was trodden outside the city, and blood flowed from the wine press, as high as the bridles of horses, for one thousand six hundred stadia.*

For the place of torment of those deserving this is outside the heavenly city Jerusalem. And their blood reached *as high as the bridles of horses* to *one thousand six hundred stadia* probably means the magnitude of the punishments through the angels, who customarily are figuratively called *horses* in the divine Scripture; *to reach* to their *bridles* <means> the lamentations of those being tormented. The holy powers [158] possess as bridles the divine command by which they hold reins for those things being commanded, as Habakkuk says, "You will mount on your horses,"[15] and the Canticles, "I likened you to my horse in the chariots of Pharaoh."[16] And it is possible to think otherwise. Since the lawbreakers have become <like> horses, mad for women, devoted to pleasure, they will be seized by torments up to the height of the bridles, for they knew no bridle in their pleasures. By the great expanse of *one thousand six hundred stadia* we are taught the "great chasm,"[17] the separation <of> the righteous from the sinners, because of the perfection in evil and abomination in deeds, ten times one hundred signifying the perfect magnitude of wickedness, and the six of them are the anxious toil of sin due to the abuse of creation, which had been made in six days, and the flooding of all the land in Noah's six hundredth year.[18]

11. Dt 32.33.
13. Mt 25.41.
15. Hab 3.8.
17. Lk 16.26.

12. Jn 15.1.
14. Mt 7.13.
16. Song 1.9.
18. Gn 7.11.

[The *wine press* will be trampled on *outside the city* of the righteous. For in no way is "the rod of these sinners to be near the inheritance,"[19] according to the prophetic saying. For their habitation will be unmingled <with the righteous>, just as their way of life has become. The *blood* being shed from those trodden who are brought to justice is the fair and impartial judgment of God that he has pronounced. [159] For the "blood" of the grape is "wine."[20] Unmixed *wine* fills the cup of divine wrath, through which it shows the punishment to be received by those deserving it. Reaching *up to the bridles,* like lust-driven horses, because they did not know a bridle in pleasures and wickedness. *To one thousand and six hundred stadia* giving themselves up to the perfection of their evil. For the one thousand is the most perfect of the numbers. And by *six hundred* we understood the years of Noah, the sin deluged in the water. *Six* because they insulted creation, which had come into existence in six days, by means of their evil practices. The number six, a symbol of toil, is the number of days in which the world was put together.]

CHAPTER 45
About the Seven Angels Bringing the Plagues
Upon People Before the End of the World, and
About the Sea of Glass

15.1. *Then I saw another portent in heaven, great and wonderful, seven angels with seven plagues, which are the last, for with them the wrath of God is ended.*

Everywhere he refers to the number seven, showing that those offenses undertaken in the seven days of the present age are to be restrained by means of the seven plagues and seven angels, after which is the future way of life of the saints, implied by the sea of glass.

15.2. *And I saw <something> like a sea of glass mingled with fire, and those who had conquered the beast and its image and its mark and the*

19. Ps 125(124).3.
20. Gn 49.11; Dt 32.14; Wis 39.26.

number of its name, [160] *standing upon the sea of glass having harps of God.*

The *sea of glass* signifies, we think, both the multitude of those being saved and the purity of the future condition and the great brilliance of the saints who will shine by means of their sparkling virtue. That which had been written by the Apostle, "the fire will test the type of work of each one,"[21] makes it possible to understand *the fire* mingled there, even if this is not inflicted on the pure and undefiled, being bifurcated un-mixed into different functions, according to the saying of the Psalm,[22] and it will be distributed both burning the sinners and illuminating the righteous, as Basil the Great had realized.[23] It is natural that by the fire both the divine knowledge and the grace of the Life-giving Spirit are meant—for in fire God was seen by Moses,[24] and the Spirit was visited upon the apostles in the form of tongues of fire[25]—and *the harps* show the "mortifica-tion of members"[26] and the harmonious life in a symphony of virtues plucked by the plectrum of the divine Spirit.

15.3–4. [3]*And they sing the song of Moses, the servant of God,* [161] *and the song of the Lamb, saying, "Great and wonderful are your deeds, O Lord God the Almighty! Just and true are your ways, O King of the nations!* [4]*Who shall not fear and glorify your name, O Lord? For you alone are holy, for all nations will come and worship before you, for your judgments have been revealed."*

From *the song of Moses* we learn the hymnody sent up to God of those justified in the Law before grace, and from the *song of the Lamb* <we learn the hymnody> of those who conducted their lives piously after the coming of Christ, the unceasing thanks-giving for his benevolence and grace coming upon our race, when all the nations were summoned to awareness of him by the divine apostles.[27]

---

21. 1 Cor 3.13.

22. Ps 29(28).7. In the LXX it reads, "The voice of the Lord divides a flame of fire."

23. *On the Six Days of Creation* 6.3.

24. Ex 3.1–6.   25. Acts 2.3.

26. Col 3.5.   27. Cf. Mt 28.19; Mk 16.15; Acts 1.8.

15.5–6. *⁵And after these things I saw, and the temple of the tabernacle of witness in heaven was opened, ⁶and out of the temple came the seven angels with the seven plagues, robed in pure clean linen, and their chests belted around with golden belts.*

A *tabernacle,* it says here, in the heavens, is similar to that which God called upon Moses likewise to pitch as the tabernacle down <below>.[28] From out of this temple, it says, [162] the angels will come *dressed in clean linen* or *stone,* as some copies have,[29] on account of the purity of their nature and their closeness to "the Cornerstone,"[30] Christ, and the luminescence of virtues. *The chests* are *belted in gold* on account of the might of their nature and the purity and honor and limitlessness in service.

15.7. *And <one of> the four living beings gave the seven angels seven golden bowls full of the wrath of God, who lives for ever and ever.*

The reception <by> the angels of the *golden bowls full of the wrath* of the Lord from *the four living beings,* just as it also says in Ezekiel,[31] signifies receiving the knowledge of the works to be done in heaven, to be conveyed always from the first ones to the second ones, according to the great Dionysios.[32]

15.8a. *And the temple was filled with smoke from the glory of God and from his power.*

Through *the smoke* we learn the frightfulness, awesomeness, and chastisement of divine wrath, with which the temple is filled, and in the time of judgment it is to issue out against those deserving of this, and before this <time it issues out> [163] against those who complied with the Antichrist and those prac-

---

28. Ex 25.
29. This is a well-known variation in Revelation. In Greek, "linen" is λίνον (*linon*), and "stone" is λίθον (*lithon,* accusative case). Metzger notes that this variation was widely attested, even at a very early date; however, the preferred reading is "linen," since being dressed in "clean stone" is illogical. Bruce Metzger, *A Textual Commentary on the Greek New Testament,* 3d ed. (Stuttgart: Biblia-Druck, 1975), 754.
30. Eph 2.20; 1 Pt 2.4–6.
31. Ezek 9.8; 20.8; 13.21; 20.13; 20.21; 22.22; 22.31; 30.15; 36.18.
32. *Cel. Hier.* 8.2; 9.2; 12.2; *Eccl. Hier.* 1.2; 3.14.

ticing the deeds of apostasy. And this is to be shown by what follows. For it says:

15.8b–16.1. *8bAnd no one was able to enter the temple until the seven plagues of the angels finished. 16.1And I heard a loud voice from the temple saying to the seven angels, "Go, pour out the bowls of wrath on the earth."*

Hence, we surmise, until the divine vexation against the impious is separated from the righteous, in no way are the saints of the heavenly Jerusalem to reach their appointed lot, both worship in the temple of God and repose. For it is necessary, it says, for *the plagues* to be *finished,* by which the wages of sin are rendered to the deserving ones, and those who reached a decision chosen by them, whereupon in this way the dwelling of the heavenly capital is to be given to the saints. If anyone attaches each of *the plagues* to things to be found at the end time, he will not entirely miss what is suitable, as I think. For God, being one who loves humanity, for the diminishment of endless punishments in the future, in the present life will consent to bring on punishing afflictions to those worthy to be burdened, both by the prophets Enoch and Elijah, and by the innovations of the elements, and by the painful casualties of war, towards a moderation, at any rate, of the payment in full by those who had sinned themselves. [164] But let us pray to be educated paternally[33] rather, not to be afflicted in a chastising wrath by the Lord—"For there is no healing in our flesh before the face of his wrath"[34]—so that, by tears of repentance, "washing our garments"[35] soiled by sins, and dressed up for a "wedding,"[36] we may enter into the everlasting bridal chamber of joy of Christ our God, to whom are due all glory, honor, and worship, together with the Father and the Holy Spirit, unto the ages of ages. Amen.

33. Cf. Heb 12.6.
34. Ps 38(37).3.
35. Rv 7.15 and 22.14; Ex 19.10.
36. Mt 22.11–13.

CHAPTER 46
*How, After the First Bowl is Poured Out, Sores Come
Upon the Apostates*

16.2. *And the first angel went away and began to pour out his bowl on
the earth, and foul and evil sores came upon the men who bore the mark
of the beast and worshiped its image.*

ERE, THE BOWL, just as *the cup,* is to be understood
as a chastising activity which, it says, by its pouring out
by the angel is to become *evil sores,* implying the throb-
bing distressful penalty of a discharge in a heart, which occurs
in the hearts of the apostates, when [165] those being afflicted
by the plagues sent by God will gain not one cure by the Antichrist, whom they have deified. Probably their bodies are to be
physically wounded for the reprimand of their soul, ulcerated
by the diabolical darts of error by the Deceiver.

CHAPTER 47
The Second Plague Against Those in the Sea

16.3. *And the second angel began to pour out his bowl into the sea, and
it became as the blood of a dead man, and every living thing in the sea
died.*

It is not impressive for the divine power, for reproof of the
weakness of the pseudo-Christ and of the simplemindedness of
the deceived, through the holy prophets Enoch and Elijah[1] to
change the *sea <into> blood as of a dead man,* that is, of one who

1. Rv 11.6.

has been slain, and to cause the corruption of those things in it, just as in old times in Egypt <he> had done this through Moses,[2] for the reproof of the stubbornness of Pharaoh and for evidence of his own power,[3] so that both those steadfast in faith will be strengthened and those who are not firm will be fearful, seeing creation opposing them during the time when the Destroyer is honored. On the other hand, it is likely that what is meant by this is the slaughters in wars during his <second> coming, when Gog and Magog agitate against each other in the four parts of the earth. [166] Moreover, the rulers disobedient to him along with their entire armies will be cut to pieces, and <because of> the slaughters occurring at these various places, the sea will be contaminated by the sea battles, and the rivers will be mixed with the blood of those who perished there.

CHAPTER 48

How the Rivers are Changed to Blood
from the Third <Bowl>

16.4–6. [4]*And the third angel began to pour out his bowl into the rivers and the springs of water, and they became blood. And I heard the angel of water saying, [5]"You are just in these your judgments, You who are and who were, O Holy One. [6]For men have shed the blood of saints and prophets, and you have given them blood to drink. They are deserving!"*

And here is shown that the angels have been placed over the elements, as it had been said above.[4] And of these, it says, the one who is <placed> over the waters praises God for the deserved condemnation he brought upon those who have transgressed, for he gave *blood to drink* to the ones who stained their hands with the blood of the saints. It is shown through these things either that at that time many standing steadfast in faith are to be deemed worthy of the gift of prophecy, those who were destroyed by the adjutants of the devil, or [167] that those turning away from the preaching of the divine prophets and justifying their destruction by the hard-hearted Hebrews[5] be-

2. Ex 7.14–25.
4. *Chp.* 44, *Text* 156, page 162.

3. Ex 9.16.
5. Mt 19.8; Mk 10.5.

come intentional participants in their killing, just as the Lord said to the Jews, "Constructing the tombs of the prophets, you approved of their killing."[6]

16.7. *And I heard the altar saying, "Yes, Lord God the Almighty, your judgments are true and just."*

The altar at some times signifies Christ as in him and through him we offer to the Father our "rational" whole burnt offerings and "living sacrifices"[7] as we have been taught to offer by the Apostle. At other times it symbolizes the angelic powers, because they carry up our prayers and spiritual whole burnt offerings, which, we have heard, "are sent for service for the sake of those <who are> to inherit salvation."[8] Therefore, from this liturgical *altar*, it says, the voice is carried off, justifying all the "judgments of God, surpassing every mind and thought."[9] Since we were taught by the words in the Gospels that the spiritual powers rejoice and celebrate over those who return from repentance to salvation,[10] but grieve over those who turn aside from the straight path, and that they give thanks to God for the punishment of those transgressing against the divine commandments, so that they might make partial payment of their debts, let us make haste, granting them <the angels> joy upon our return and [168] great delight, understanding that the divine guardian angel of each of us, without saying any word, instructs us in the things we must do, as if a mind invisibly speaking to our own mind, rejoicing at those who listen to his counsels, but sorrowing in imitation of God over those who disobey. Just as also we know from narratives profitable to the soul[11] about some man, blackened by many transgressions; and when he was entering the church, an angel followed him from afar with a sad countenance. When this man was moved to compunction, and he had declared from his soul to the "One Who Desires Mercy"[12] a change for the better and a rejection of his

---

6. Mt 23.29–31; Lk 11.47–50.   7. Rom 12.1.
8. Heb 1.14.   9. Rom 11.33.
10. Lk 15.7, 10.
11. An expression for spiritual readings, especially lives of the saints.
12. Mi 7.18; Mt 9.13, 12.7.

prior life, and when he was coming out from there, the angel went before him, radiant and rejoicing; but the evil demon, distressed, followed from afar. May our way of life in God become the cause of dejection in the demons and gladness for the angels, so that, in common with them, in "a voice of gladness and a hymn of acknowledgement keeping festival,"[13] we might give thanks for the victory against the wicked demons to Christ our God, to whom, with the Father, is due glory together with the Holy Spirit, now and ever and unto the ages of ages. Amen.

[169]

13. Ps 42(41).4.

CHAPTER 49

How the People Are Burnt By the Fourth <Bowl>

16.8–9. ⁸*And the fourth angel began to pour out his bowl on the sun. And it was allowed to scorch people with fire.* ⁹*People were scorched by the fierce heat, and they cursed the name of God who had power over these plagues, and they did not repent to give him glory.*

ERHAPS people will also be physically burnt by the flames of the sun at that particular time. "With bit and bridle," God, who loves humanity, compels "the jaws of those who do not approach him"¹ in order that they might know repentance, even though those who fall into the depth of evil deeds do not turn toward repentance but turn away toward blasphemy and will be carried away by the wickedness of mind. Perhaps by *the sun* it also hints at the course of the day during which the ones deserving chastisements are to be scorched by the burning heat of temptations, it says, so that by painful afflictions they will hate sin, the mother of these <attacks>. But the fools, instead of being conscious of their own errors, "will sharpen the tongue"² against God, just as even now it is possible to see many unwilling <to repent> blaming the Divine Goodness for the unspeakable misfortunes encircling us by barbarian hands, because he had reserved such great afflictions for our generation. [170]

1. Ps 32(31).9.
2. Ps 64(63).3, 140(139).3.

CHAPTER 50

How the Kingdom of the Beast is Darkened Through the Fifth <Bowl>

16.10–11. ¹⁰*And the fifth angel began to pour out his bowl on the throne of the beast, and its kingdom became darkened.* ¹¹*<People> gnawed their tongues in anguish and cursed the God of heaven for their pain and sores, and did not repent of their deeds.*

To empty out *the bowl on the throne of the beast* means such a wrath to be poured out and portrayed as a darkening upon *the kingdom* of the Antichrist, inasmuch as it obtains no light by the "Sun of Righteousness."³ The *gnawing of tongues* shows the excess of the pain by which those misled by him, being afflicted, will be overcome by the wounds sent by God so that they might know that the one honored by them as God is deceitful, and that they might cease the error. But not even after this will they turn towards repentance, but towards cursing. If those will turn to cursing by the application of afflictions, and if those being stricken by hail as <heavy as> talents will be persuaded in the same manner—likewise, with the help of God, we interpret, as we are able, that occasion at that point⁴—and if the evil demons through human bodies, which they have used as organs, although afflicted by the holy ones <angels>, nevertheless [171] do not refrain from cursing those who plague <them>, one must ponder what, then, is necessary for us to realize about the impious being tormented in the Gehenna of fire. How then is evil so innate to the point that they completely cease from the thought of it, or are they only hindered in the carrying out of evil plans into deed, just as evildoers also are put into prison out of necessity yet <they> do not hold back the intentions to harm others? But I myself, hearing <of> eternal punishments, I cannot disbelieve what has been declared. Knowing his readiness toward compassion and goodness, I surmise that in no way would he either threaten or strike with endless condemnation those deserving it if the condemned ones had already repented

3. Mal 3.20 LXX (4.2 RSV).
4. The hail as heavy as talents will not occur until Rv 16.21.

and hated the evil which they freely chose to commit. For it is not through necessity, but voluntarily that they are punished. For if in the case of Pharaoh even though he <God> knew him to be tempered by the chastisement, but to be hardened again after their removal, nevertheless he judged him worthy of moderate treatment and spared him the chastisements although he was being asked <to do so> by Moses, how much more so <would God spare> these if he knew they put aside the filth in the fire, in accordance with the likeness of gold, which some have understood as a paradigm in this situation? But <in the case of> the gold, in as much as it is without a soul, [172] the filth is included by its nature, but it <the filth> was intentionally united <to the soul> by the reason-endowed <human beings>, rather than having been born within them. Wherefore, those who set the goodness, foreknowledge, and power of God as an impediment to eternal punishment, let them also attach righteousness to these <qualities>, as being distributive to each of them according to what is due, and in no way will they see an overturning of the divine sentence. If they are not willing to agree, let them also impute it to the kings of the earth, at least in order that they might agree with themselves; the kings make provision for not all of the contestants, wrestlers, boxers, runners, and equestrians to be victorious, but for one and only one from each of these to be crowned,[5] although the stadium is open to all for the contest. For what the stadium is indeed for the contestants, such is the passage to this life for all. For to be born or not to be born is not up to us, but to struggle and to be victorious <against> the evil demons and to gain the eternal blessings is for us. For it is necessary that those who have been defeated feel regret for these things and lament in vain, being tormented eternally, "for the one confessing will not be in Hades,"[6] according to the psalm verse; moreover, the help of the Spirit will no more accompany those who have been condemned than it does now. For "they will be cut in two," as the Lord says,[7] they will be divided by the Life-giving Spirit, who had been dishonored by them. We believe the meaning as it

5. 1 Cor 9.24.
6. Ps 6.5(6).
7. Mt 24.51; Lk 12.46.

was explained previously[8] and as the verse of the Psalm hints: "For the Lord will not allow the rod of the sinners upon the inheritance of the righteous, lest [173] the righteous stretch out their hands in wrongdoing,"[9] since their life is unmixed, not only on account of the purity of their lives and the way of life of each being incongruous <with wrongdoing> but also on account of their constancy and steadfastness in <doing> good, neither being provoked toward sin by deliberately choosing inferior interactions nor by weakness of the flesh abating the joy by changing it to fear, but certainly inheriting the incorruptible in God. And these things up to this point <suffice for now>; the discussion about other things continues at a fast pace, as was expressly promised. We will continue with the following.

CHAPTER 51
How Through the Sixth <Bowl> the Way by the Euphrates is Opened to the Kings from the East

16.12. *And the sixth angel began to pour out his bowl on the great river Euphrates. And the water was dried up, to prepare the way for the kings from the east.*

Probably by divine permission *the Euphrates* is lessened to give passage to *the kings* of the nations for the purpose of them utterly destroying one another and the rest of humanity, which <kings> we think were set into motion out of parts of Scythia recalling Gog and Magog, according to that which is brought out later in the Apocalypse. Probably the Antichrist also will come from [174] the eastern areas of the land of Persia, where the tribe of Dan originates from the root of the Hebrews, together either with other kings or with rulers designated with a royal name, to cross over the Euphrates bringing bodily or spiritual death upon people, upon some <bodily death> through faith and patient endurance, and upon others <spiritual death> through cowardice and weakness.

8. Referring to the previous angel with the sickle who reaps the earth in Rv 14.18. See *Chp.* 44, *Text* 156–57, pages 162–63.
    9. Ps 125(124).3.

16.13. *And I saw from the mouth of the dragon and from the mouth of the beast and from the mouth of the false prophet, three foul spirits like frogs.*

From these it is shown that the same person is both the devil as a dragon, and the Antichrist as the beast, and *the false prophet* as another <different> from these, as has been mentioned. From these, it says, are going out spirits similar to *frogs* through their green poison and uncleanness and sliminess and their creeping toward the wet reptilian pleasures of the evil powers which by the commands of the devil and false Christ and false prophet are manifested by mouth, which will show deceitful "signs and wonders to people,"[10] as we will become aware by what follows.

16.14. *For they are demonic spirits, performing signs, to go abroad to the kings of the whole world, to assemble them for battle on that great day of God the Almighty.* [175]

The false signs which are operated through the demons, it says, <will cause> those persuaded by them to march into war on "the great and terrible day of God,"[11] "judge of the living and dead,"[12] over which, having been entirely defeated, those fighting against God in vain will lament, bewailing their prior error.

16.15–16. [15]*"Behold, I am coming like a thief! Blessed is he who is watchful and keeps his garments that he may not walk naked and they see his shame!"* [16]*And he assembled them at the place which is called in Hebrew Armageddon.*

The *watchfulness* and guarding *the garments* mean vigilance in good deeds. For these are the garments of the saints, of which he who is deprived will need to be ashamed, since he is naked and full of indecency. <The Hebrew word> *Armageddon* is interpreted as "deep cut" or "that which is cut in two." For there, the nations, being gathered together, being minded to follow, and being commanded by the devil, who delights in the blood

10. 2 Thes 2.9.   11. Jl 2.11; Mal 4.5.
12. Acts 10.42.

of people, are to be cut down. Since we have learned from here that it is abominable to be *naked* of *the garments* of virtue, and from the gospel parable that the one being deprived of this <virtue> is cast out of the bridal chamber,[13] also from the word of the Apostle who, [176] concerning incorruption, says: "Those of us who have been clothed in this will not be found naked,"[14] that is, of good deeds, let us earnestly supplicate our Lord here to "wash out" the robes of our souls so as to be "whiter than snow"[15] according to the verse of the Psalm, never hearing, "Friend, how did you enter here without having a wedding garment?" and let us never be "bound hand and foot" and "thrown into the outer darkness."[16] But according to the wise Solomon, "garments at all times being white,"[17] and with joyful torches of the virtuous manner of life, adorned with sympathy, offering ourselves with the clean and blameless wedding garments of holy souls, let us enter together into the bridal chamber of Christ our God, to whom, with the Father, together with the Holy Spirit, belong glory, dominion, and honor, now and ever and unto the ages of ages. Amen.

13. Mt 22.11–13.   14. 2 Cor 5.3.
15. Ps 51(50).7.   16. Mt 22.12.
17. Eccl 9.8.

SECTION EIGHTEEN

CHAPTER 52
*How Through the Seventh <Bowl> Hail and Earthquake
Come Against the People*

16.17–18. *¹⁷And the seventh angel began to pour his bowl into the air.
And a voice came out of heaven, from the throne, saying, "It is done!"
¹⁸And there were flashes of lightning, voices, [177] thunders, and a
great earthquake such as never had occurred since people were on the
earth, so great was that earthquake.*

HE ANGELIC voice from heaven says, *"It is done,"* that is,
the divine command is accomplished. The *flashes of
lightning, voices, and thunders* mean the amazing nature
of these occurrences and the future coming of Christ, just as in
ancient times <they meant> the descent of God upon Mount
Sinai.¹ The earthquake <is> an alteration of all things in existence, as the Apostle had understood: "Again once and for all I
will shake not only the earth but also heaven."²

16.19a. *And the great city was split into three parts, and the cities of
the pagans fell,*

A great city we take to mean Jerusalem, not great in population nor because of great buildings, but the most ancient and
greatest in respect to reverence for God, to be exalted and
contradistinguished from the pagan cities by the sufferings of
Christ. Its division into *three* <sections> means, we think, Christians, Jews, and Samaritans in it, or the steadfast believers,
[178] and those who pollute their baptism with filthy actions,

1. Ex 19.16–19.
2. Heb 12.26, quoting Hg 2.6.

and those Jews who never accepted the apostolic preaching, all unhindered and boldly asserting the fulfillment of their own preferences, and either the sending forth <to paradise> or the disinheritance into the place appropriate to each of them. For now both Jews and Samaritans, for fear of the pious ones who reign,[3] hide their private wishes, and with us they appear to be assigned to their distinct lot, not daring to rebel. Likewise the genuine Christians find themselves mixed together with those possessing only the name <of Christian>. And when the burning of these temptations will reproach them, then the division of these into three will happen: the impious, the pious, and the sinners, joining those with the same habits and answering as is appropriate for their own fate. The *falling of pagan cities* means either their dissolution or the extinction of the pagan way of life by the coming of the divine Kingdom which the saints will take possession of, according to Daniel.[4]

16.19b. *and the great Babylon was remembered before God, to give to her the cup of the wine of the fury of his wrath.*

The populous throng, being confused, it says, by the purposeless distractions of life [179], and having been increased by wealth from wrongful acts, will drink from *the cup* of the *wrath* of God as though, forgetful through longsuffering, he comes to remembrance of the trampling upon the righteous and of the vengeance for impiety in words and deeds.

16.20. *And every island fled away, and no mountains were found.*

Islands are the churches, and *mountains* are the leaders of them, we are taught to discern from the divine Scriptures.[5] These flee at the time of attack, being foretold <as> we have heard for ourselves from the Lord, saying: "Then they will flee

3. This comment creates a clear parameter for dating the commentary. Andrew is writing while Jerusalem is still under the control of Christian emperors, prior to the conquest, destruction, and occupation of Jerusalem by the Persians in 614 (which lasted until 627 when it was retaken by Emperor Heraclius) and the Arab conquest of Jerusalem in 637 by Caliph Omar.

4. Dn 7.18, 22, 27.

5. Previously expressed in *Chp.* 18, *Text* 72, page 100, concerning his interpretation of Rv 6.14b.

from the east to the setting sun, and those from the west to the east."[6] "For there will be great tribulation of a sort which has not happened from the foundation of the world, nor ever will be."[7] Some being tormented on account of sin, others enduring these difficulties patiently in a test of virtue, not only in those difficulties will they be tormented by the Antichrist for the sake of Christ, but also in flights and in the miseries in mountains and in caves, which, in order to preserve piety, they will prefer to the way of life in the city.

16.21. *And great hailstones, heavy as a hundred-weight <talent>, fell on people from heaven. And people cursed God for the plague of the hail, so very great was this plague.*

The *hail*, in that it comes down from heaven, we had discerned to be the wrath sent by God coming down from above; its talent-sized weight <represents> its perfection [180] on account of the extreme <nature> and great weight of the sin, which is characterized as a talent, as Zechariah had seen.[8] Those being afflicted by this do not proceed toward repentance but to blasphemy, proving the hardness and obstinacy of their hearts. Therefore, they will be like Pharaoh,[9] but these will be even more stubborn than he was. When the plagues were sent by God, at least he was more pliant, even confessing his own impiety, yet they blaspheme even during the punishment.

6. Andrew offers a biblical quotation here; however, the first portion seems to be a variation of Mt 24.27. It is difficult to know whether this is a manuscript variation in Andrew's text of Matthew's Gospel, or whether Andrew was simply recalling a verse from memory and misquoted it.

7. Mt 24.21; Mk 13.19.

8. Zec 5.7.

9. Ex 4.21; 7.3; 9.12, 34–35; 14.4, 8, 17. Andrew expressed the same idea earlier in *Chp.* 50, *Text* 171, page 174.

CHAPTER 53

*About the One of the Seven Angels Showing to the Blessed
John the Destruction of the Harlot's City, and About the
Seven Heads and Ten Horns*

17.1–3. ¹*And one of the seven angels who had the seven bowls came
and spoke with me, saying to me, "Come, I will show you the judgment of the great harlot who is seated upon many waters, ²with whom
the kings of the earth have committed fornication, and the dwellers on
earth have become drunk with the wine of her fornication." And he carried me away in the Spirit into a wilderness, ³and I saw a woman
sitting on a scarlet beast which was* [181] *full of blasphemous names,
having seven heads and ten horns.*

Some understood this *harlot* to mean ancient Rome,[10] lying upon seven mountains, *the seven heads* of the beast which
bears her to be the seven most impious kings from Domitian
until Diocletian, <kings> who persecuted the Church. But we,
since we are being guided in accordance with the sequence, we
would suppose she is either the earthly kingdom in general as
<appearing> in one body or the city which is to rule until the
coming of the Antichrist. For ancient Rome from long ago lost
the power of its kingdom, unless we suppose the ancient rank
were to return to her. But if we were to give her this <rank>,
the one ruling today would be overthrown beforehand, for the
Apocalypse says, "The woman whom you see is the great city
having dominion over the kings of the earth."[11] And regarding this, in what follows, if God grants, let us express <our-
selves> accurately. It is necessary to remark what *the wilderness*
must mean into which one is carried off in the Spirit. *Wilderness*
we regard, therefore, as the spiritual deserts in every city, or a
great throng which is drunk [182] in the soul both by the fornication against God and being charged with other such recklessness. And alternatively one must realize that the Apostle

10. Oik. 9.13.1–5.

11. Rv 17.18. This verse supports Andrew's conclusion that the beast cannot
be Rome because the woman is described as having dominion over the earth,
and Rome had lost that level of worldwide supremacy.

perceives, as a mental vision in the Spirit, the desolation of the aforementioned *harlot,* whom he saw as womanish because of the luxuriant indulgence toward sin and being without a husband. And she was seated on *a scarlet beast,* because of her resting upon the murderous and blood-delighting devil through her evil deeds through which she becomes a co-worker with the apostate <devil> in the blasphemy against God. For both the beast and the scarlet color mark his savage cruelty, great ferocity, and murderous intention. About *the seven heads and ten horns* we will learn with <the help> of God from the divine angel in what follows.

17.4a. *And the woman was clothed in purple and scarlet, and adorned with gold and precious stones and pearls,*

She has been clothed in *scarlet* and *purple* as the symbols of her rule over all. Wherefore she has been adorned with *precious stones and pearls.*

17.4b. *holding in her hand a golden cup full of abominations and the impurities of her fornication.*

Through *the cup* is shown the formerly sweet-tasting drink of evil deeds, and by *the gold* <is shown> the high price <of those deeds>, as it is said about Job "drinking up scoffing like water,"[12] to show that she is not satiated, [183] but in thirsting for her own perdition she pursues wickedness. Therefore, she made her own abominations abundant, that is to say, the loathsome practices against God, by which the sin-loving multitude is given to drink, imbibing as a sweet draught the abominable strong drink of sin and the filth of *fornication* apart from God.

17.5. *And on her forehead has been written a name of mystery: "Babylon the great, mother of harlots and of earth's abominations."*

The writing *on the forehead* shows the shamelessness of the offenders filling up to the measure, and the disturbance of the heart; and the *mother,* the fact that she is the teacher of soul fornication to the leading cities, giving birth to transgressions loathsome to God.

12. Jb 34.7.

CHAPTER 54
How the Angel Explained to Him the Mystery
that was Seen

17.6–7. *⁶And I saw the woman, drunk with the blood of the saints and the blood of the martyrs [of Jesus]. ⁷When I saw her I marveled greatly. But the angel said to me, "Why did you marvel? I will tell you the mystery of the woman, and of the beast with seven heads and ten horns that carries her.*

By the literal meaning it is possible to learn much about the names of the cities applied to them in accordance with their deeds. Wherefore, the ancient Babylon was also given the name "the charming harlot, leader of sorcery,"[13] [184] and ancient Jerusalem heard, "You have the appearance of a harlot,"[14] and the older Rome was addressed as *Babylon* in the Epistle of Peter.[15] More importantly, the one having power at the time of the Persians[16] will be called both *Babylon* and *harlot,* and every other city which delighted in homicide and bloodshed. So the Evangelist, seeing one of these having been polluted with *the blood of the saints,* was amazed, and he learned from the angel the things about her, such things as to what extent it is necessary for her holding power to suffer for her offense until the end time of earthly rule, either that one chooses to understand it as the one ruling in the time of the Persians, or the Old Rome or the New, or taken generally as the kingdom in one unit, as it is said. For in each of these <cities> various sins had been born, and *blood of the saints* poured out, some more, some less, we have learned. And *the blood of the martyrs* <shed in the former Rome> until Diocletian, or the torments of those in Persia—who could enumerate them?[17] These things were endured

13. Na 3.4.   14. Jer 3.3.
15. 1 Pt 5.13.

16. The Persian kingdom in the early seventh century included the area which had been that of ancient Mesopotamia and encompassed the actual, historical city of Babylon.

17. The extensive martyrdom of Persian Christians, in which reportedly approximately 16,000 Christians were martyred in 343, is described by Sozomen in his *Ecclesiastical History* 2.9–14. Andrew may also be thinking of events

under Julian secretly,[18] and the things they dared to do in the time of the Arians against the orthodox in the New Rome,[19] the histories present to those who read.

17.8a. The beast that you saw was, and is not, and is to ascend from the abyss and goes to perdition. [185]

The *beast* is the devil, "who always seeks to devour someone."[20] This one, having been slain by the cross of Christ, it is said, will again be revived at the end of the world, performing the denial of the Savior in "signs and wonders"[21] of deception through the Antichrist. Therefore *he was* because he was exerting his power earlier than the cross. *He is not* because after the saving passion he had been enfeebled, and his power, which he had held over the nations through idolatry, had been displaced. He will come at the end of the world in the manner which we have said, *ascending out of the abyss,*[22] or from where he had been condemned—where the demons cast out had beseeched Christ not to be sent, but instead into the swine[23]—or he will come out of the present life, which is figuratively called *abyss* because of the depth of the indwelling of sin which is blown and tossed about by the winds of the passions. For thereupon, the Antichrist will come carrying Satan in himself, bringing about the ruin of human beings, going to perdition in the future age.

---

closer to his own time in which Persian Christians were martyred under the Persian Emperor Khosroe, whose own chief wife and queen was an outspoken and influential Christian. See Sebeos 13, *The Armenian History Attributed to Sebeos,* trans. R. W. Thomson, notes by James Howard-Johnston, part 1, "Translation and Notes" (Liverpool: Liverpool University Press, 1999), 29.

18. Emperor Julian, "the Apostate." See Socrates, *Ecclesiastical History* 3.12–13, 15, 19, and Sozomen, *Ecclesiastical History* 5.5, 9–11, 18. See also *Chp.* 36, *Text* 136, page 147.

19. On the persecution by Arians against the orthodox Christians, including torture, confiscation of property, martyrdom, and exile, see Socrates, *History* 2.12–16. For the persecutions of the orthodox Christians under Macedonius, the Arian Bishop of Constantinople, see Socrates, *History* 2.27 and 38. For Arian persecutions in Alexandria see 2.28, in which Socrates quotes from Athanasius's *Apology for his Flight,* describing the persecutions which occurred in that city.

20. 1 Pt 5.8.   21. 2 Thes 2.9.
22. Cf. Rv 20.1–3.   23. Mt 8.31; Mk 5.12; Lk 8.32.

17.8b. *And the inhabitants on earth whose names have not been written in the Book of Life from the foundation of the world, will marvel seeing the beast, because it was and is not and is to come.*

They *will marvel*, it says, at the coming of *the beast* on account of the wonders <caused> by trickery, [186] those who have not been written in *the Book* of those living eternally in glory and those not given elementary instruction before about the things unerringly foretold concerning Christ himself, wondering how he <the beast> regained his former sovereignty.

17.9a. *Here is the mind that has wisdom:*

Since the things being interpreted are spiritual, spiritual *wisdom* is needed to understand what is said, and not worldly <wisdom>.

17.9b. *The seven heads are seven mountains upon which the woman is seated and there are seven kings.*

Seven heads and seven mountains we think imply seven places standing out from the rest in worldly prominence and power, these upon which we know were established in due season the <ruling> kingdoms of the world. The first being the rule of the Assyrians in Nineveh,[24] the second the dynasty of the Medes in Ecbatana from the time of Arbaces,[25] which dominated the Assyrians, whose King Sardanapalos, it is narrated, Arbaces destroyed.[26] After these <came> the rule of the Chaldeans in Babylon, over whom ruled Nebuchadnezzar.[27] Thereupon, after the dissolution of these, the supremacy of the Persians in Susa under Cyrus[28] was established, [187] but after its termination by Alexander, <arose> the kingdom of the Macedonians. After them in the Old Rome, <there was> the power of the Ro-

24. The Assyrian civilization goes back to the third millennium BCE.

25. The Greek name for the sixth-century BCE Median general, also known as "Arbaku" and "Harpagus," who reportedly destroyed Nineveh.

26. Many identify this Hellenized name with the last great king of Assyria, generally known as Ashurbanipal or Assurbanipal, who reportedly reigned from 668–627 BCE.

27. Early sixth century BCE.

28. Cyrus the Great, who died in 529 BCE.

mans monarchically ruled under Augustus Caesar after the former kings and consuls and controlled by impious <emperors>
up to Constantine, after whose dissolution the imperial offices
of Christ-loving kings was transferred to the New Rome. The
same idea and *the seven kings,* we suppose to be indicated by the
alternating of genders, in no way hindering the identity of the
meaning, even though these *seven heads* are feminine and *seven
mountains* are neuter. Here *the seven kings* were signified. For
many times masculine names are found indistinguishably from
feminine in the Scripture. Also the contrary, such as "Ephraim
is a provoked heifer,"[29] and again, "Ephraim was a dove not having a heart," [30] and according to the Theologian, "These three
bear witness to Christ: the blood, the water, and the Spirit";[31]
also "They are three," according to Solomon, "a billy goat, a
rooster, and a king speaking publicly."[32] So therefore, through
seven heads femininely showing cities, and through *the seven
mountains* in neuter <showing> seven heights surpassing the
rest of the body of the earth in due season, this is not a specific place among the nations but relates to ranks of glory. And
kings we have understood, so to speak, as either the [188] places
which have been honored with royal administration, or those
who first reigned in each of the aforementioned, periphrastically defining the entire reign of each, such as that of Nino
of the Assyrians, Arbaces of the Medians, Nebuchadnezzar
of Babylon, Cyrus of the Persians, Alexander of the Macedonians, Romulus of ancient Rome, and Constantine of the New
<Rome>.

29. Hos 10.11 (LXX). Ephraim is a man, but he is described as a female
calf, δάμαλις. A male calf would be δάμαλος.

30. Hos 7.11.

31. 1 Jn 5.7–8. All three of these nouns are in the neuter in Greek; however, the word "three" which introduces them is either masculine or feminine
nominative, τρεῖς.

32. Prv 30.29, 31, in the LXX. The Hebrew Bible reads, "A strutting rooster, a he-goat, and a king striding before his people" (NRSV). Regardless of
the exact reading, Andrew's point from the LXX again remains unaffected:
all three of these nouns are masculine; however, the word "three" which introduces them is in the neuter, τρία.

17.10. There are also seven kings. Five of whom fell; one is; the other has not yet come, and when he comes he must remain a little while.

The blessed Hippolytus[33] understood these to mean ages, of which five have passed by, the sixth still stands, during which the apostle saw these things, [189] and the seventh, which is after the 6,000 years, *has not yet come,* but, coming, it *must remain a little while.* And these things, thusly <are as follows>. If, as Irenaeus says, just as seven days have been created, and in the same manner also seven heavens and seven angels ruling over the rest,[34] and it seems these things that are said by us are readily received by those hearing them, <namely> that also the seven kingdoms are the famous ones from the beginning until now, of which five already have fallen, and the sixth, during which the Revelation was seen, stood in the Old Rome, and the seventh had not yet come, the one in the New <Rome>; the statement about the worldwide Babylon would well be accomplished in the capital city until the Antichrist, reigning for a little while, as compared to the previous <kingdoms>, some of which ruled more than five hundred years, and others more than one thousand. After all, every chronological number is short compared to the future everlasting kingdom of the saints.

17.11. And the beast that was and is not, it is an eighth, but it is from the seven, and it goes to perdition.

The beast is the Antichrist; as the *eighth* he will be raised up after the seven kings for the purpose of deceiving and desolating the earth. *From the seven,* as from one of them, he will spring forth. For he will not come from another nation, along <the lines> of the things we have already said, but he will come as king of the Romans for the purpose of the dissolution and perdition of those who were persuaded by him, and after this he will go forth into the *perdition* of Gehenna.

---

33. *On Daniel* 2.4.
34. Irenaeus, *Proof of Apostolic Preaching* 9.

17.12. *And the ten horns that you saw are ten kings* [190] *who did not yet receive royal power, but they are to receive authority as kings for one hour, together with the beast.*

Daniel also previously saw these *ten horns* of the Antichrist.[35] After the accursed one has uprooted three, he will make the rest subject to him. *One hour,* it says, is either the shortness of time or the one season of the year, that is to say, a change, clearly three months, after which they will be subjected to the Antichrist as their superior.

17.13–14. [13]*These are of one mind and have given over their power and authority to the beast.* [14] *They will make war on the Lamb, and the Lamb will conquer them, for he is Lord of lords and King of kings, and those with him are called and chosen and faithful."*

Naturally. For "no one can serve two masters."[36] Therefore, those in agreement with evil and united to the Antichrist will be opposed to Christ. But he *will conquer them, the Lamb of God*[37] who was slain for us. For he was not deprived of the reign and lordship over all by becoming man, so that he might acquire his chosen participants in his own kingdom.

17.15–18. [15]*And he says to me, "The waters that you saw, where the harlot is seated, are peoples and multitudes and nations and tongues.* [16] *And the ten* [191] *horns that you saw, and the beast, they will hate the harlot; they will make her desolate, and devour her flesh and burn her up with fire.* [17]*For God has put it into their hearts to carry out his purpose by being of one mind and giving over their royal power to the beast, until the words of God will be fulfilled.* [18]*And the woman whom you saw is the great city that has dominion over the kings of the earth."*

Since the angel has explained these things clearly, a more detailed elaboration of these things is unnecessary. It is a wonder to me to read how the devil is an enemy and an avenger, because he will operate by directing those *ten horns* himself, on the one hand to put himself in place of the goodness-lov-

35. Dn 7.7–8.
36. Mt 6.24; Lk 16.13.
37. Greek: ὁ ἀμνὸς τοῦ θεοῦ, as in Jn 1.29. Rv 17.14, however, has τὸ ἀρνίον for "Lamb," as do all the passages from Revelation that mention "the Lamb."

ing and virtue-loving Christ our God, and on the other hand to devastate the densely populated *city* which has given itself over to fornication from the divine commandments and has diligently served his pleasures, and to fill up with her blood according to the nature of the bloodthirsty beast. When he will lead the burning of this city and the cutting-up of human flesh for his own food, it will be <for him> an occasion for rejoicing, and he who always rejoices at discord will grant concord to the rebellious ten horns. The fact that *the woman* being observed is understood as the greatest *city*, which has supreme power *over the kings of the earth*, makes it unambiguous that <here> is prophesied the sufferings of those holding ruling power during those times; from the trials of which <times> God, who loves humanity, redeems us for himself to enroll us in the heavenly capital, the [192] Jerusalem above, in which "he will be all things in all,"[38] according to the divine Apostle, "when he will destroy every rule"—rebellious, that is—"and authority and power,"[39] and to those who have served him here faithfully and wisely "he gives rest"[40] and "will serve them";[41] that is to say, he will appoint for them every enjoyment of the eternal blessings that have been "prepared from the foundation of the world."[42] Let us also be worthy of this, in Christ, the Savior and Redeemer of our souls, with whom is the glory and the power, with the Father together with the Holy Spirit unto the ages of ages. Amen.

38. 1 Cor 15.28.
40. Mt 11.28.
42. Mt 25.34.

39. 1 Cor 15.24.
41. Lk 12.37.

SECTION NINETEEN

CHAPTER 55
About Another Angel Declaring the Fall of Babylon and
the Heavenly Voice Commanding Flight From the City,
and About the Discarding of the Delights Which
it had Once Possessed

18.1. *And after this I saw another angel coming down from heaven,*
having great authority; and the earth was made bright with his splen-
dor.

 ERE IS shown the brightness and radiance of the holy
powers, a brilliancy surpassing the stars and luminaries by great measure. [193]

18.2–3a. [2]*And he called out [in] a great mighty voice, saying, "Fallen!*
Fallen <is> Babylon the great! And it has become a dwelling place of
demons, a habitation of every unclean and detestable spirit. [3]For all
nations have drunk of the desire of the wine of her fornication,

Also in Isaiah, concerning the seizure of the Chaldean capital of Babylon by Cyrus and the Persians, things similar to these
had been foretold,[1] inasmuch as it was destined to be filled with
wild beasts and unclean spirits on account of its complete devastation. For the custom is to banish both the beasts and the
evil demons to the deserted places,[2] both on account of the
divine Economy, which has liberated humans from the harm
<that comes> from them, and on account of their characteristic
hatred of mankind. How did the present Babylon water *the na-*
tions with the wine of her own *fornication?* By becoming altogether

1. Is 13.21, 34.13–14.
2. Mt 12.43; Mk 5.10; Lk 11.24; Tb 8.3.

the leader in all these transgressions and by her sending to the cities subject to her, through gifts, rulers who were the enemies of truth and righteousness.

18.3b. *and the kings of the earth have committed fornication with her, and the merchants of the earth have grown rich with the magnitude of her wantonness."*

On account of the excesses from unjust riches, it says, extending to that which is far above necessity and behaving insolently toward those in need, it has become a matter of profit to the merchants of the earth. [194]

18.4–5. *⁴And I heard another voice from heaven saying, "Come out [of her], my people, lest you take part in her sins, lest you receive, ⁵for her sins are heaped high as heaven, and God remembered her iniquities.*

As was declared to Lot in Sodom, "Escape, saving your own life,"³ and in Isaiah, "Come out from her and be separate, and do not touch the unclean,"⁴ likewise he speaks here. For close association with those who provoke God is shunned.

18.6–7a. *⁶Render to her as she herself has rendered to you, and repay her double according to her deeds; mix double for her in the cup she mixed. ⁷ᵃAs she glorified herself and was wanton, so give her a like measure of torment [and mourning].*

These things are either those who are blameless in her and who have suffered under the worst wickedness of those ruling in her, it says, as being the cause, through their endurance in sufferings, of the punishment of those who impose these <sufferings> on them, or it signifies the alteration from [195] roles to roles, from those who have been wronged to some holy avenging powers who through piety have appropriated the sufferings passed on from her wickedness to her co-servants. And the *double cup,* it says, is either because the sinners and transgressors are tormented very much both here and in the future, or on account of the soul and body from which the deed was common <to both> against which the punishment will be, or

3. Gn 19.17.
4. Is 52.11.

because the vastness of divine love for humankind delineated twice both her lack of pure righteousness on account of having sin <thus suffering in the body> and the torment in their conscience to be endured many times.

18.7b. *In her heart she says, 'I sit like a queen. I am no widow, and mourning I will never see,'*

For it is customary for those in abundance to say, if there is no fear of God within them, "I will not be shaken ever,"[5] which also he witnessed in her.

18.8. *On this account her plagues will come in a single day, her plagues, death, and mourning and famine, and she will be burned down with fire; for the Lord God is mighty who judges her."*

A *single day,* it says, is either the suddenness and brevity of time in which, from both the sword and famine, sorrow will come to her, and also from pestilence, [196] to be destroyed and to be *burnt down by fire,* or is the course of the day itself in which these things prophesied will prevail over her. For after the enemies have taken control of the city, even one day is sufficient for all of the evils to be brought upon the defeated ones and various manners of death. Just as the power of God saves those well-pleasing to him, in the same manner it also punishes those unrepentantly sinning.

18.9–10. [9]*And the kings of the earth, who committed fornication with her and were wanton with her, they will weep and wail over her when they see the smoke of her burning,* [10]*standing far off, on account of fear of her torment, saying, "Woe! Woe! The great city Babylon, the mighty city! In one hour your judgment came."*

Kings here, we believe, those rulers are called, as the Psalmist says concerning Jerusalem, "Behold, her kings were gathered together."[6] Those, it predicts, having committed fornication in her against the divine commandments, will weep both seeing and hearing her consumed by fire and desolation, being

5. Ps 30(29).6.
6. Ps 48(47).4, 2.2.

struck by amazement at the suddenness of the change, how it happened in such a brief time. [197]

18.11–12a. *¹¹And the merchants of the earth weep and mourn for themselves, for no one buys their cargo any more, ¹²ᵃcargo of gold, silver, precious stones and pearls, fine linen, purple, silk, and scarlet,*

For those perishing in power and luxury, the purchase and consumption of these is unnecessary.

18.12b–13a. *¹²ᵇ And all kinds of scented wood, all articles of ivory, all articles of costly wood, bronze, iron, and marble, ¹³ and cinnamon, [and spice], and incense, and myrrh, and frankincense, and wine, and oil, and fine flour and wheat, and cattle and sheep,*

In these is understood the *no one buys*. We must contemplate in which of the cities is the habitual purchasing of such things, and moreover, in which people the acquisition of superfluous things for boundless self-indulgence is obsessive. [198]

18.13b. *and horses and chariots, and bodies,*

And the use of these things, it says, will be unnecessary. By *redon* (ῥεδῶν), of course, chariots are meant, because *redium* is Latin for "chariot." The genitive plural form of this is *rediorum,* which by syncopation became *redon.*⁷

18.13c–14. *¹³ᶜand human souls. ¹⁴ "And the fruit of your soul's desire has gone from you, and all your luxury and your splendor have left you, and you will never find <them> again!"*

Neither will they trade *the souls* of human beings, it says, by enslaving free people, nor will you have enjoyment as formerly by costly and splendid items.

18.15–17a. *¹⁵The merchants of these, who gained wealth from her, will stand far off, on account of fear of her torment, weeping and mourning [and saying], ¹⁶"Woe! Woe! for the great city that was clothed in fine linen and purple and scarlet, having been adorned in gold, [199] in*

---

7. "Chariot." Since John wrote in Greek and Andrew's readership is Greek, Andrew explains the meaning of the Latin word used for "chariot" in this verse of the Apocalypse instead of a Greek word.

precious stones, and in pearls, [17a] *that in one hour such wealth was laid waste."*

He leads them by this vision to the sufferings of this Babylon, by the lamentations over her describing the magnitude of the calamity which will prevail over her, the very one who formerly boasted of her royal status.

18.17b–19. [17b] *And every shipmaster and all seafaring men, sailors and all whose trade is on the sea, stood far off,* [18] *and they cried out seeing the smoke of her burning, saying, "What city was like the great city?"* [19] *And they threw dust on their heads, as they were crying out, weeping and mourning, and saying, "Woe! Woe! The great city in which all who had ships at sea grew rich by her great distinction, that in one hour she was laid waste.*

If *the sea,* as has been said,[8] metaphorically is the present life as of many waves, and the merchants on it are those swimming like lively fish on the billows of life, yet probably also the city suffers these things by bordering on the actual physical sea; <the sea> will be the cause of sorrow for those conveyed on it [200] by the situation of her own desolation. It is necessary for those merchants of the worldwide Babylon to suffer the same, that is to say, the same disturbance, to lament inconsolably at the end of the visible things, being unwillingly deprived of the pleasures of the present life and being stabbed by their conscience for their own deeds.

18.20. *Rejoice over her, O heaven, O holy apostles and prophets, for God judged your charge against her!"*

By *heaven,* it says, either the angels or the saints who have their citizenship in it <heaven>, with whom he summons *the apostles and prophets* to be *rejoicing,* because they have been avenged for what they have been despised for by her, either as having been dishonored oftentimes through the transgression of the divine commandments, as they had uselessly called upon the inhabitants of the aforesaid city, or as having been slaugh-

---

8. *Chp.* 23, *Text* 91, page 116; *Chp.* 34, *Text* 132, page 145; and *Chp.* 36, *Text* 136, page 147.

tered on account of God by the dominion which had been dis-
turbed through the entire earth because they served his words.
Wherefore, on the one hand, *the prophets* were killed by the
Jews,[9] and, on the other hand, *the apostles* were killed by the pagans, to whom especially they preached the word; they rejoice
in the bringing-on of corrections, not as those rejoicing in misfortunes of others, but as those who have a fiery desire concerning the cutting-off of sin; perhaps they who are enslaved to it
will meet with a milder punishment in the future because they
are being afflicted in part here.

18.21–24. [21]*And one mighty angel lifted a stone like a great millstone
and threw it into the sea, saying, "Thus with violence* [201] *will Babylon the great city be thrown down, and will be found no longer.* [22]*And a
sound of harp players and musicians, of flute players and trumpeters,
will be heard in you no longer; and every craftsman of any craft will
be found in you no longer; and the sound of the millstone will be heard
in you no longer.* [23]*And the light of a lamp will shine in you no longer;
and the voice of bridegroom and bride will be heard in you no longer;
for your merchants were the great men of the earth, and all nations were
deceived by your sorcery.* [24]*And in her was found the blood of prophets
and of saints, and of all who have been slain on earth."*

It says, just as *the millstone* sinks *into the sea* by violent action,
likewise also the demolition of Babylon will be complete, so
that not even a trace of her will be preserved afterwards. For
this is what is meant by the disappearance of *the harp players
and the musicians* and the rest. The cause, it says, is that all the
nations were *deceived by her* own particular *sorcery* and she has
become the vessel of *the blood of the prophets* and the rest of the
saints. Possibly what was signified by all these is the impious
Babylon of the Persians, since it received the blood of many
saints through various times up to the present, since by both
sorceries and trickeries they rejoiced from beginning to end.
And this to us is the result of prayer: she is to receive the wages
prophesied of her arrogance against Christ and his servants.
[202] But it seems to be somehow contrary to the interpretation concerning this by the ancient teachers of the Church,

9. Mt 23.30–35.

who spoke against making an analogy of Babylon with the Romans by these things being prophesied on account of the ten horns that had been seen on the fourth beast,[10] that is, in the rule of the Romans, and from her the one sprouted uprooting the three and subjugating the rest,[11] and to come as a king of the Romans, on the one hand coming on the pretext of fostering and organizing their rule, and on the other hand in reality <coming> to work toward its complete dissolution. Wherefore, as it is said, someone who would truly take this to mean this <Roman> kingdom originally in one unit that has ruled until now, that poured out the blood of the apostles and prophets and martyrs, would not be led astray from what is appropriate. For just as also this is said about one chorus and one army and one city, even if they exchange each of those <individuals> constituting them, likewise in the same way the kingdom is one even though in many times and places it is divided.

CHAPTER 56

About the Hymnody of the Saints and the Triple Alleluia,
Which They Chanted on the Occasion of the Destruction
of Babylon

19.1–4. [1]*After these I heard what seemed to be the voice of a great multitude in heaven, saying, "Alleluia! The salvation and glory and power of our God,* [2] *for true and just are* [203] *his judgments. He has judged the great harlot who corrupted the earth in her fornication, and he has avenged the blood of his servants <shed> from her hand."* [3] *A second time they said, "Alleluia! The smoke [from her] goes up for ever and ever."* [4] *And the twenty-four elders and the four living beings fell down and worshiped God, who is seated on the throne, saying, "Amen. Alleluia!"*

The *alleluia* means "divine praise," and the *amen* "truly" or "let it be so," as is commonly sent up to God three times, it says, from both the angelic powers and people equal to the angels,

---

10. Dn 7.7, 20.

11. Dn 7.8, 19. Irenaeus and, later, other Fathers believed that Daniel and Revelation prophesied that the last kingdom would be that of the Romans, which would supplant those which had come before. *Heres.* 5.26.

on account of the tri-hypostatic, unified Divinity of Father and Son and Holy Spirit, and because *he avenged the blood of his servants <shed> from the hand of Babylon* and he benefited her inhabitants through punishment, accomplishing it by the cutting-off of sin. And *the smoke goes up for ever and ever* from the city signifies either the uninterrupted, never-to-be-forgotten <nature> of the punishments coming upon her into perpetuity, or the judgments partly rendered to her, to be tormented more fittingly but nevertheless eternally in the future.

19.5. *And from the throne came a voice, "Praise our God, all his servants, and those who fear him, small and great."* [204]

The throne of God is the cherubim and the seraphim, by whom not only *the great* but also *the small* in achievement are called upon to *praise* him, each appropriately according to his <or her> own power. I think also those presently small in age and immature children being raised as adults will praise the God who does great deeds.

19.6–7a. [6]*Then I heard a voice of a great multitude, like the sound of many waters and like the sound of mighty thunders, saying, "Alleluia! For our God the Almighty reigned.* [7]*Let us rejoice and exult and give him the glory, for the marriage of the Lamb came,*

The voice of multitudes and *of many waters* and *of thunders* signifies the thrilling <character> in hymnody of all the angels and heavenly powers who are countless, which some[12] perceived to be those waters above the heavens, with which both the entire assembly of the righteous and the fullness <of creation> glorify the Creator. Christ reigned over <creation>, of which as Creator, naturally, he was Master, having reigned over these through the Incarnation, either according to his own will, or suitably by authority both as King and as Judge. *The marriage of the Lamb* speaks of the union of the Church to Christ, [205] of which the divine apostles have been the matchmakers, through whom the *pledge of the Spirit was given*[13] to her, as having regained then the pure face-to-face union that is due.

12. The source of this interpretation is unknown.
13. 2 Cor 1.22, 5.5.

CHAPTER 57
About the Mystical Marriage and the Supper of the Lamb

19.7b–9. [7b]*And his Bride has made herself ready.* [8]*It was granted to her to be clothed with fine linen, bright and clean, for the fine linen is the righteousness of the saints.* [9]*And he <the angel> says to me, "[Write this:] Blessed are those who are invited to the supper of the Lamb." And he says to me, "These are true words of God."*

The *fine linen* that was put on the Church shows the brightness of virtues, and one will understand <it> as the refinement and loftiness in doctrines. For by these <linen threads> the acts of divine righteousness are woven together. The *supper* of Christ is the festival of those who are saved and the all-encompassing harmony in gladness, in which the blessed ones who will attain <this> will enter together into the eternal bridal chamber of the Holy Bridegroom of clean souls. For the One who promised this does not lie. Many are the blessings in the future age, and they surpass all understanding, and the participation in these is declared under many names, sometimes the "kingdom of heaven" [206] on account of its glory and honor, sometimes as "paradise"[14] because of the uninterrupted banquet of all good things, sometimes as "bosoms of Abraham"[15] because the repose of the spirits of the dead is there, sometimes as "a bridal chamber and marriage,"[16] not only because of the unceasing joy but also because of the pure and inexpressible union of God to his servants so greatly transcending the communion of bodies one with another, as much as light is separate from darkness and perfume from stench.

19.10. *And I fell down at his feet to worship him. And he says to me, "See <here>! Do not <do that>! I am a fellow servant with you and your brethren who hold the testimony of Jesus. Worship God." For the testimony of Jesus is the spirit of prophecy.*

"Do not worship me," says the divine angel because he was foretelling future events, for the confession of Christ, that is

14. Lk 23.43; 2 Cor 12.4.   15. Lk 16.22.
16. Mt 9.15, 22.1–12, 25.1–13; Mk 2.19; Lk 5.34; Rv 19.7.

to say, the testimony, is that which provides the *spirit of proph-ecy*.[17] And it should be understood in another way, because this prophecy is <given> so that the testimony of Christ might be confirmed and the faith be affirmed by the saints. Wherefore he ought not worship *a fellow servant,* but the One who holds dominion over all. And from these we learn of the humble spirit of the holy angels, how they do not usurp the glory of God, contrary to the [207] destructive demons, but rather offer this <glory> to the Master. May we also "honor one another"[18] by humble-mindedness, to fulfill the saying of the Master, "Learn from me, for I am meek and humble in heart, and you will find rest for your souls,"[19] and to obtain rest in the future where "pain, sorrow, and sighing have fled away,"[20] where "the dwelling of all those who rejoice"[21] is illumined by "the light of the countenance of Christ"[22] our God, to whom belong all glorification, honor, and worship, together with the Father and the Life-giving Spirit, unto the ages of ages. Amen.

17. Oik. 10.11.9.
18. Rom 12.10.
19. Mt 11.29.
20. Is 35.10, 51.11.
21. Ps 86.7 (LXX).
22. 2 Cor 4.6.

SECTION TWENTY

CHAPTER 58
*How the Evangelist Saw Christ on Horseback
with Angelic Powers*

19.11–12a. [11] *Then I saw heaven opened, and behold, a white horse,
and he sitting upon it is called Faithful and True, and in righteousness
he judges and makes war.* [12a] *His eyes are like a flame of fire, and on his
head are many diadems.* [208]

EAVEN opening signifies the appearance of the visible
judge to come, just as here, when the curtains of the
judges on the earth are drawn back, the judgment and
sentence come down upon those who are guilty. And the *white
horse* is the future joy of the saints, upon which he is carried
to judge the nations impartially, I think by his watchful, providential power throwing out *flames of fire,* which to the righteous
illuminate but do not burn, but to the sinners burn and do not
illumine.[1] The *many diadems* imply either his rule over all those
in heaven and on earth—for so many are the ranks of angels
and so many the royal scepters of the earth, and so many are
the congregations of the holy people—or the victory against
the sinners through forbearance in every condescension for us.
As some holy man says, "and you will be victorious in your judgment."[2]

1. This is the fourth time the dual qualities of fire have been mentioned,
also previously in *Chp.* 2, *Text* 20, page 61; *Chp.* 6, *Text* 32, page 69; and *Chp.* 45,
Text 160, page 165.

2. Ps 51(50).4.

SECTION TWENTY

19.12b. *and he has a name inscribed which no one knows but himself.*

The unknown name refers to his incomprehensible essence. For by many names is the divine condescension <known> as "good,"[3] as "shepherd,"[4] as "sun,"[5] as "light,"[6] as "life,"[7] as "righteousness,"[8] as "sanctification,"[9] as "redemption."[10] And likewise in the apophatic sense as "incorruptible,"[11] "invisible,"[12] "immortal,"[13] immutable,[14] ineffable and incomprehensible in his essence, being known only to himself together with the Father and the Spirit. [209]

19.13. *He is clad in a robe that has been dipped in blood, and the name by which he is called is the Word of God.*

Through these things is confirmed that which has been expounded before. How is he who is inexpressible and in every sense unknowable here called "*Word*"?[15] To show either the filial hypostasis and impassible begottenness from the Father, just as our word exists beforehand in the mind, or that he carries in himself the principles for all things in existence,[16] or he is "the Messenger"[17] of the Paternal wisdom and power.[18]

19.14. *And the armies of heaven followed him, many mounted upon horses and arrayed in pure white linen,*

By these are meant the heavenly ranks splendidly attired in the refinement of their nature and loftiness of their minds and the brilliance of virtues and in the perfect unity in reference to God.

---

3. Ps 34(33).8; Mk 10.18; Lk 18.9.
4. Jn 10.11–16; Heb 13.20; 1 Pt 2.25.
5. Mal 3.20 LXX (4.2 RSV).
6. Jn 1.9, 3.19, 8.12, 12.46.
7. Jn 14.6.
8. 1 Cor 1.30.
9. Ibid.
10. Ibid.
11. Rom 1.23; 1 Tm 1.17.
12. Col 1.15; 1 Tm 1.17.
13. 1 Tm 1.17.
14. Cf. Mal 3.6; Ps 102(101).26–27; Heb 1.10–12.
15. Greek: Λόγος.
16. Jn 1.1–3.
17. Is 9.6.
18. 1 Cor 1.24.

19.15. From his mouth a sharp sword comes out in order to smite the nations, and he will rule them with a rod of iron, and he will tread the wine press of the fury of the wrath of God the Almighty.

This *sword* signifies the torments that will afflict the impious and the sinners in accordance with the just judgment and the command that is proclaimed from the divine mouth, [210] through whom they will be *ruled* by the unbroken *rod* of endless torments toward <ensuring> the inactivity of manifold wickedness, about which the saints will remain inexperienced, "for the Lord will not allow the rod of the sinners to be upon them,"[19] according to the verse in the Psalm. He treads the *wine press of wrath* <meaning> that the "Father does not judge anyone, but he has given the judgment to him"[20] as a human being, which naturally he had possessed from the beginning as the Son.

19.16. On his robe and on his thigh he has a name inscribed, King of kings and Lord of lords.

This name signifies the indivisibility of the divine Incarnation, according to which, being God, he suffered in flesh, and, being human, he is <still> *King of kings and Lord of lords.* Those who have mastered the passions and acquired authority and dominion over sin as "co-workers"[21] with Christ also "will rule with him"[22] in the future.

CHAPTER 59

About the Antichrist and Those Cast with Him into Gehenna

19.17a. And I saw one angel standing in the sun. And he called [211] in a loud voice to all the birds that fly in mid-heaven,

This one we believe to be one of the superior angels who encourages cheerfulness in the rest of the angels upon the punishment of the sinners and the extermination of sin. *Birds* he called the angels, for our clarification, because they fly high and are raised aloft. Fulfillment of the divine will is food to

19. Ps 125(124).3.
21. 1 Cor 3.9.
20. Jn 5.22.
22. 2 Tm 2.12.

them, in imitation of Christ.[23] *In mid-heaven,* that the ascent also be shared by people who are equal to the angels and that the aforementioned joy come to pass, from which the intercession elevates those below, through which the saints are *taken up to meet the Lord.*[24]

19.17b–18. [17b]*"Come, to the supper of the great God,* [18]*in order to eat the flesh of kings, the flesh of captains of one thousand men, the flesh of mighty men, the flesh of horses and the riders on them, and the flesh of all men, both free and slave, and small and great."*

On the one hand, the aforementioned will of God, which is called both "well-pleasing"[25] and greatly desired *supper,* is that "people be saved and come to knowledge of the truth"[26] and that they "return and live,"[27] and on the other hand, secondly <the will of God> is the punishment of those who pursue their own punishment. Therefore, Christ suitably called the Fatherly will his *food.*[28] This [212] here is called *supper of God,* each human being receiving through his deeds that which he desired, either the Kingdom or punishment. By the *eating of flesh* is meant the abolition of all fleshy things and the disappearance of the names of all those who have authority on the earth. One is reminded of *horses,* not because they will be resurrected, but because with them he implies either men who are obsessed with women, or those who had debased themselves in fornication, or both, by which those who are mounted upon their horses <implies> those who surpassed <all others> in wickedness. And the one further down he made clear, saying *free and slave, great and small.* By *free* and *great* he means the worst ones who sin freely of their own will, and by *slaves* and *small* he means the lesser ones who offend either in accordance with advice or on account of age or weakness.

23. Jn 4.34.

24. 1 Thes 4.17.

25. Mt 11.26; Lk 10.21. See also Eph 1.5, 9; Phil 2.13.

26. 1 Tm 2.4; 2 Tm 2.25, 3.7.

27. Ezek 18.23, 32.

28. Jn 4.34.

19.19. *And I saw the beast and the kings of the earth with their armies gathered to make war against him who sits upon the horse and against his army.*

He has referred to those campaigning with the devil in the plural because of the many diverse and multifaceted forms of sin; however, there are few compared to the angelic powers and the humans who are equal to the angels, for those following Christ are expressed by the singular *army* because of the united will and unity of opinion about pleasing God the Logos.

19.20a. *And the beast was captured, and with it the false* [213] *prophet who in its presence had worked the signs by which he deceived those who had received the mark of the beast and those who worshiped its image.*

Although they, together with those kings and rulers who were obedient to them, marched against the Savior Christ, nonetheless both of them were defeated; the Antichrist and the false prophet who had performed signs and wonders, the well-received deceptions, were overtaken by the divine wrath.

19.20b. *These two will be thrown alive into the lake of fire that burns with sulfur.*

Perhaps these will not die a common death, but in the twinkling of an eye those made immortal are condemned to a second death in the *lake of fire,* as the Apostle says concerning other people: "They will not sleep but they will be changed in a moment, in the twinkling of an eye."[29] These likely will go to judgment, but those <two> who presented themselves as impious and anti-gods, not into judgment but <directly> to condemnation. If this does not appear <to be so> to some,[30] on account of the statement of the Apostle that the Antichrist is to be "destroyed by the breath"[31] of the divine command, also it is to be found in a saying of a certain one of the teachers[32] that some are to be living after the destruction of the Antichrist, those blessed by Daniel;[33] we will say that the two living in incorrupt-

---

29. 1 Cor 15.51–52.
30. Oik. 10.15.5–6.
31. 2 Thes 2.8.
32. The identity of this particular "teacher" is unknown.
33. Dn 12.12.

ible bodies, after their tyranny had been abolished by God, will be delivered to the fire [214] of Gehenna, which to them will be death and destruction by the divine command of Christ.

19.21. And the rest were slain by the sword of him who sits upon the horse, the sword which comes from his mouth, and all the birds were gorged with their flesh.

There are two deaths; the first is the separation of the soul and the body, the second is being cast into Gehenna. If \<this is applied to\> those \<who are\> together with the Antichrist, it is said they will be led to the first death in the flesh *by the sword* of God, that is, by his command, and thus afterward the second will follow, if this is correct. If it is not thus, they will participate in the second death, the eternal torment, with the ones who had deceived them. And the birds *gorged* on *their flesh,* \<means the same\> as was set forth previously,[34] as now we have understood. In addition to this, as God says to certain people through Isaiah, "You have become loathsome to me,"[35] so also, to the saints every fleshly activity is disgusting, grievous, and loathsome.

CHAPTER 60

How Satan Was Bound From the Crucifixion of Christ Until the End Time, and About the One Thousand Years

20.1–3. [1]And I saw an angel coming down from heaven, holding in his hand the key of the bottomless abyss and a great chain. [2]And he seized the dragon, that ancient serpent, [215] who is the Devil and Satan, and bound him for a thousand years, [3]and threw him into the abyss, and bound and placed a seal over him, so that he would not deceive the nations, until the thousand years were ended. After these he must be loosed for a short time.

Here he narrates the destruction of the devil which had taken place during the Master's passion, in which he who appeared to be strong, having bound us \<as\> his spoils,[36] one

---

34. *Chp.* 59, *Text* 212, page 203.   35. Is 1.14.
36. Mt 12.29; Mk 3.27; Lk 11.21.

stronger than he, Christ our God, redeemed us from his hands, condemning him to *the abyss*. This is shown by the demons urging him that they not be cast into the abyss.[37] The proof that he has been bound is the disappearance of idolatry, the destruction of the temples of idols, and the disappearance of the defilement[38] upon the <pagan> altars and the universal knowledge of the divine will.[39] And the great Justin says that at the coming of Christ the devil was to realize first that he had been condemned to the abyss and to the Gehenna of fire.[40] It is possible therefore, I suppose, that the sentence of Christ against the devil is understood on account of the aforementioned things that were said before. An angel administers such a sentence, [216] it says, in order to show both that <the devil> is weaker than these ministering powers in terms of power and that from the beginning it was in vain that he boldly ruled over all. He <John> called the restraint of his evil activity *chain* for our clarification. By the number *one thousand years* by no means is it reasonable to understand so many <years>. For neither concerning such things of which David said, "the word which he commanded for a thousand generations"[41] are we able to count out these things as ten times one hundred; rather <they are to mean> many <generations>. Here also, we infer the number one thousand to indicate either a great many or perfection. For these things require many years for the purpose of preaching the Gospel everywhere in the entire world[42] and for the seeds of piety to take root in it. They indicate perfection because during these <years>, being removed from a childish way of life

37. Lk 8.31.

38. Greek: λύθρων, meaning literally "filth" or "defilement," also "gore." This word was used to indicate blood sacrifices of the type that were performed for pagan gods. Such sacrifices were inherently defiling because they were idolatrous.

39. 1 Tm 2.4.

40. From a work of Justin the Martyr now lost. Justin's opinion is also known to us through Irenaeus in *Heres.* 5.26.2. Andrew already referred to this statement by Justin earlier. *Chp.* 34, *Text* 131, pages 143–44. It is conceivable that Andrew himself knew of it through Irenaeus.

41. Ps 105(104).8.

42. Mt 24.14; Mk 13.10.

under the Law, we have been called into "perfect manhood, to the measure of the stature of the fullness of Christ."[43] The *one thousand years*, therefore, is the time from <the year of> the Incarnation of the Lord until the coming of the Antichrist.[44] Thus *the one thousand years* that were referred to may be such as what we have explained, or ten times one hundred, as some have thought, or these might fall short <of one thousand years>. For it is <left> to God alone, who knows to what extent his forbearance is expedient for us, and in this way he determined the duration of life. After which <one thousand years> the Antichrist will disturb the entire world, containing in himself the activity of the Originator of Evil, and [217] pouring out the crop of his poisonous wickedness among people, since he sees the unalterability of his own punishment. From whose deeds the redeeming, all-merciful <Christ> God will rescue us, from the punishment "he has prepared for him and his angels,"[45] and he will show <us to be> partakers of eternal blessings prepared for those "who opposed" him <the devil> "unto the shedding of blood,"[46] for to him belongs mercy upon those who rely on him, and thanksgiving and adoration by all the holy powers, together with the Father and the Life-giving Spirit unto the ages of ages. Amen.

43. Eph 4.13.

44. This opinion, that the millennium represents the era of the Church rather than a specific number of years, has not been found represented in the existing Greek sources prior to Andrew. That is not to say that this opinion was not held by earlier Greek ecclesiastical writers and thinkers. Rather, the fact that this opinion does not appear in earlier Greek writings more likely reflects the disputed and uncertain canonical status of Revelation.

45. Mt 25.41.

46. Heb 12.4.

CHAPTER 61

About the Thrones Prepared for Those Who Kept the Undeniable Confession of Christ

20.4. *And I saw thrones, and they were seated on them, and judgment was given to them, and the souls of those who had been beheaded for their testimony to Jesus and for the word of God, and who had not worshiped the beast nor its image and had not received its mark on their foreheads or* [218] *on their hand, and they came to life, and reigned with Christ a thousand years.*

LREADY *thrones* for teaching have been given to the holy apostles through whom the nations have been enlightened. They will be given, according to the divine promise, also in the future for judging those who rejected the gospel preaching, as David said, "For there the tribes went up, the tribes of the Lord, to witness for Israel," and after that, "for there sat thrones for judgment."[1] And to the rest of the holy martyrs, those who suffered on behalf of Christ and did not accept *the mark* of the spiritual beast, the devil, the mark, that is, the image of his apostasy, *judgment was given,* that is to say, authority to judge, through which until now, as we see, "those who are glorified with Christ" [2] will judge the demons, until the consummation of the present age, being venerated by pious kings and faithful rulers, and manifesting God-given power against every bodily ailment and demonic activity. That the devil, the Antichrist, and the false prophet act in partnership with each other, just as by their deeds, even so by their

1. Ps 122(121).4–5.
2. Rom 8.17.

names, is clearly shown by the things through which each of them is called *beast,* and from the fact that this *dragon,* that is, Satan, manifests seven heads and ten horns with as many diadems placed on him. And the fact that *the beast coming up out of the sea,* that is, the Antichrist, appears in the same form additionally confirms <that he shares> this same will [219] and activity for the destruction of the deceived ones. Those liberated by Christ, according to the manner mentioned above, will co-reign until his second coming, afterwards enjoying these divine promises to an even greater degree.

CHAPTER 62

What is the First Resurrection and What is the Second Death

20.5–6. [5]*And the rest of the dead did not come to life until the thousand years were ended. This is the first resurrection.* [6]*Blessed and holy is he who has a share in the first resurrection! Over such ones the second death has no power, but they will be priests of God and of Christ, and they will reign with him a thousand years.*

From the divine Scriptures we are taught two lives and two types of deadness, that is to say, deaths. The first life is the transitory and fleshly one after the transgression of the commandment,[3] but the other one is eternal life promised to the saints after heeding the divine commandments of Christ. And in like manner, <there are> two deaths: the one transitory of the flesh and the other through sins leading to the full payment in the age to come, which is the Gehenna of fire. And we know there is a difference among the dead. For on the one hand, there are those to be avoided concerning whom Isaiah says, "The dead will not see life,"[4] [220] that is, those bringing stench and deadness by <their> conduct, and on the other hand, those praiseworthy ones who in Christ "mortify the activities of the body,"[5] who are crucified with Christ and are

---

3. Transgression of the command given to Adam and Eve not to eat the forbidden fruit in Gn 3.

4. Is 26.14.

5. Rom 8.13; Col 3.5.

dead to the world. Therefore, those unacceptable dead, those not "buried with and raised with Christ, through baptism,"[6] but those remaining in <a state of> death by sins, will not live with him until the completion of the one thousand years, that is, the perfect number extending from his first coming until the second in glory, as it has been said above, but, having been born "from the earth"[7] only and not "by the Spirit,"[8] they will return to the earth. Their death becomes the beginning of their future punishment. Those who have a share in the *first resurrection,* that is, in the rising out of deadening thoughts and mortifying actions, these are *blessed.* For the second death will have no power over them, that is, never-ending punishment, but instead, they will exercise priesthood and *reign with Christ,* as we see it, these things signifying to us *one thousand years* until the loosening of Satan and the deception of the nations, not as being then deprived of the kingdom, but as more certainly and very clearly they will possess it by the passage of temporal things and arrival of eternal things. For the time will be short after the loosening of the devil until the judgment against him and the punishment of Gehenna. Therefore, *they will be priests of God and of Christ* is thought to be a repetition of the [221] foregoing. For the things seen now, through the trial and the end result of things, the rewards of the saints and wonders were then destined to be when they were seen by the Evangelist, as was said. So then, since there are two deaths, it is necessary to understand that there are also likewise two resurrections. First, then, physical death, given as the penalty for humankind's disobedience; the second, eternal punishment. The *first resurrection* is being brought to life out of "dead works,"[9] the second, the transformation from bodily corruption into incorruption.

---

6. Rom 6.4; Col 2.12.
8. Jn 3.6, 8.

7. Jn 3.31.
9. Heb 6.1, 9.14.

CHAPTER 63
About Gog and Magog

20.7–8. *⁷And when the thousand years end, Satan will be loosed from his prison, ⁸and will come out to deceive the nations which are at the four corners of the earth,< that is,> Gog and Magog, and gather them for battle. The number is like the sand of the sea.*

Some, I don't know how, explain the aforementioned time of *one thousand years* as the three-and-a-half years from the baptism of Christ until his ascension into heaven,[10] after which they conjectured that the devil is to be loosed. [222] Others said that after the completion of the six thousand years, the first resurrection of the dead is granted only to the saints, so that in this earth, in which they displayed endurance, they will enjoy delight and honor for one thousand years, and after that the universal resurrection will occur, not of the just only but also of the sinners.[11] It is unnecessary to note that the Church has accepted none of these. We, therefore, listening to the Lord saying to the Sadducees that the righteous will be like "angels of God in heaven,"[12] and to the Apostle who said, "The kingdom of God is not food and drink,"[13] thus we took *the one thousand years* to be the time of the preaching of the Gospel.[14] For, as it had been written above, it is not necessary to understand *the one thousand* so much by the <literal> number. For neither what is being said in the Canticles, "a man will lay down one thousand pieces of silver for <a vineyard's> fruit," nor, "one thousand to Solomon and two hundred to those who keep his fruit,"[15] meant this number, but the great quantity and the per-

---

10. This precise opinion is not found in any previous author. Andrew appears to be reporting another ancient tradition no longer extant.

11. This is the classic justification provided for millennialism as found in the early Fathers such as Irenaeus. (See *Heres.* 5.32.1 and 5.35.1–2.) Justin Martyr, another millennialist of the early Church, defended this belief based on his reading of the prophets. See *Dialogue with Trypho* 80.

12. Mt 22.30; Mk 12.25; Lk 20.36.

13. Rom 14.17.

14. See also *Chp.* 60, *Text* 216, page 206.

15. Song 8.11–12.

fection in harvest, just as here also the harvest of the faith in perfection <is implied>, after which "the son of perdition, the man of lawlessness,"[16] will come [223] "in order that all will be judged, those who did not believe the truth but approved of injustice,"[17] according to the Apostle and according to the word of the Lord <who> said "I have come in the name of my Father, and you did not receive me. Another will come in his own name, and him you will receive."[18] So then, as it was said, when *Satan is loosed from his prison* he will *deceive* all *the nations*, and he will arouse *Gog and Magog* into war for the desolation of the entire inhabited world. Some think these are the Scythian nation,[19] the northernmost <peoples>, or, as we call them, the Huns,[20] who among all the kingdoms on earth, as we see, <are> the most populous and warlike, whom only by the hand of God we hinder from seizing the entire civilized world until the loosening of the devil. From the Hebrew language some interpret *Gog* as "one who gathers" or "gathering," and *Magog* as "proud." Through the names is to be signified either the gathering of the nations or arrogance. [224] It must be known that Ezekiel also prophesied that these nations will come in the end-times with great power to fall upon the land of Israel and that their weapons are to be burnt for seven years through a great fire,[21] which, on the one hand, some of the interpreters[22] took <to

16. 2 Thes 2.3.   17. 2 Thes 2.12.

18. Jn 5.43.

19. Josephus states that the Greeks identify Gog and Magog with the Scythians (*Ant.* 1.6.1). Theodore of Mopsuestia identified Gog with the Scythians in the prologue to his *Commentary on Joel*.

20. Theodoret also seems to equate the Scythians with the Huns (*Ecclesiastical History* 5.37.4). Theophanes equates the Avars with the Huns: *Chronicle of Theophanes Confessor* 315 (*Chronicle of Theophanes Confessor*, trans. Cyril Mango and Roger Scott [Oxford: Clarendon Press, 1997], 446). "Huns" seems to have been a generalized way to refer to various "barbarian" peoples at that time.

21. Ezek 39.9. Ezekiel 38 and 39 describe the invasion of Gog and Magog, who will be completely destroyed by the power of God.

22. Again, we cannot identify with certainty the interpreters who held this opinion, although Andrew may be referring to a comment by Theodore of Mopsuestia (*Commentary on Micah* 5, FOTC 108:229), who links the destruction of Gog's army at the time of the return from Babylon with the fate of the Assyrians at the time of Hezekiah. He describes the events of Hezekiah's time

mean> the fall of the Assyrians with Sennacherib having occurred many years previously at the time of Hezekiah <during>
the prophecy of Ezekiel,[23] but, on the other hand, some <inter-
pret it as> the destruction of the nations attacking those who
undertook to rebuild Jerusalem after her capture by the Babylonians,[24] first Cyrus the Persian, and after him Darius having
commanded so to the governors of Syria. And some <see> it
as meaning the forces of Antiochus that were defeated by the
Maccabees.[25] That the coming of these things is rather appropriate to the end-times is clear: First, nowhere has it been written that the Scythian nation is to strike war against the Jews at
this particular time but only its neighbors, begrudging[26] their
collective prosperity.[27] Second, this has been written about *Gog*:
"He will have been prepared from ancient days, and he will
come at the end of times."[28] Third, in the present Apocalypse,
which prophesies the future, [225] it has been written that *Gog
and Magog* will come at the end of this age.

20.9–10. ⁹*And they went up over the broad earth and surrounded the
camp of the saints and the beloved city. And fire from God came down
from heaven and consumed them.* ¹⁰*And the devil who deceives them
was thrown into the lake of fire and sulfur where the beast and the false
prophet were, and they will be tormented day and night for ever and
ever.*

Like wild beasts out of some lairs, thus, it says, they will
spread out upon the earth out of their own places, those commanded by the devil and the demons with him, to spread out
across the earth, since an army *encampment of the saints,* that is,

---

as a foreshadowing of the destruction that God would bring on the enemies of
Israel (Gog) after the return from Babylon at the later date.

23. 2 Kgs 19.35; 2 Chr 32.21.

24. Theodore of Mopsuestia, *Commentary on Joel* 3 (FOTC 108:121–22), and
Commentary on Zephaniah 3 (FOTC 108:302).

25. Polychronios in Ezek 38.

26. Greek: βασκαίνοντα. The word implies malicious intentions to slander
or to cause harm by means of sorcery or an evil eye.

27. Greek: εὐδαιμονία. The word can mean both "prosperity" and "happi-
ness."

28. Ezek 38.8.

the Church, is established in the four corners of the inhabited world, and they will be destroyed, not perceiving that not
only one angel but many are "encamped in a circle around
those who fear God,"[29] according to the saying in the Psalter,
and they will subdue in addition the new Jerusalem, *the beloved
city*,[30] out of which <came> the divine law, which was taken by
the apostles through the inhabited earth. There, they say, the
Antichrist will sit in the Temple of God,[31] either in the Judaic
one, the old divine Temple,[32] which was destroyed on account
of the [226] recklessness against Christ[33] and is <still> expected
by the God-fighting Jews to be rebuilt by him, or in the real
divine Temple, <that is> in the catholic Church, usurping that
which is inappropriate for him and "representing himself as being God," according to the divine word of the Apostle.[34] But
not for long; it says, *fire comes down from heaven,* either a visible
fire as <happened to> the two commanders of fifty men in the
presence of Elijah,[35] or the coming of Christ in glory will de-

29. Ps 34(33).7.

30. Had the Persian capture of Jerusalem in 614 already occurred, such a
statement by Andrew would be highly unlikely.

31. Andrew is incorporating this detail, taken from 2 Thessalonians, into
his end-times scenario. Revelation itself does not describe the Antichrist as
"sitting in the Temple," but Andrew presumes it because of 2 Thes 2.3–12.

32. The opinion of Irenaeus. *Heres.* 5.25.4.

33. The Second Temple in Jerusalem, so-called "Herod's Temple," was destroyed in 70 CE by the Romans after they had besieged the city for three years
in a war sparked by Jews revolting against Rome. Andrew's comment here, that
the Temple was destroyed on account of the Jews' "recklessness against Christ"
reveals a typical stance among early Christians that the Temple was destroyed
because the Jews had rejected the Messiah. Furthermore, Christians were convinced that the destruction of the Temple signified that the Old Covenant,
along with its bloody rituals, had been superseded and replaced by the New
Covenant and its bloodless, spiritual worship. (See Justin Martyr, *Dialogue with
Trypho* 11.) Christ's prediction to the disciples that the Temple would be physically destroyed, not one stone remaining on top of the other (Mt 24.2; Mk
13.2; Lk 19.44 and 21.6), was remembered along with his statements to the
Samaritan woman, "the hour is coming when you will worship the Father neither on this mountain nor in Jerusalem" (Jn 4.21) and "the hour is coming
and now is here, when the true worshipers will worship the Father in spirit and
truth" (Jn 4.23).

34. 2 Thes 2.4.

35. 2 Kgs 1.9–12.

stroy them "by the breath of his mouth"[36] and the aforementioned nations, also devouring their general, the devil, and he
<Christ> will deliver <the devil> to the *lake of fire* together with
the Antichrist and the false prophet to be tortured forever and
ever. Having been taught by the Savior Christ to pray that we
"not be led into temptation,"[37] let us earnestly do this, knowing
well our own weakness, to deliver <ourselves> from the prophesied trials, to see neither the coming of the false Christ, nor
the movement of the aforementioned nations, nor the fatal
danger assaulting us to give up the saving faith; but guarding
unwounded, if possible, "the witness of conscience,"[38] [227] and
manifesting through good deeds the fiery ardor of love toward
Christ, who purchased us by his "precious blood,"[39] let us hope
to enjoy the blessings of eternity, being strengthened for this
by the rich mercies of God. May these things be our lot in him,
our Savior and Redeemer Christ, to whom with the Father together with the Holy Spirit <are due> glory, dominion, honor,
now and to the ages of ages. Amen.

36. Is 11.4; 2 Thes 2.8. 37. Mt 6.13; Lk 11.4.
38. 2 Cor 1.12. 39. 1 Pt 1.19.

SECTION TWENTY-TWO

CHAPTER 64

About the One Sitting on the Throne and the Common Resurrection and Judgment

20.11. And I saw a large white throne and him who sat upon it, from whose presence earth and sky fled away. And no place was found for them.

Y THE *white throne* is meant the resting-place of God, which he will make in the saints shining by their virtues, being enthroned among them. The flight of heaven and earth is their passing away and renewal into <something> better, in which a place of mutability will not be found. For "if creation is subject to corruption"[1] on account of us according to the Apostle, "it will be made anew with us in the glorious freedom of the children of God,"[2] being renewed to a more radiant <existence> and remaining, not to a complete disappearance, [228] just as the blessed Irenaeus and Antipater[3] and other saints supposed. For the blessed Irenaeus says, "neither the hypostasis nor the substance of creation utterly disappears—for he who composed it is true and certain—but the 'form of this world passes away,'[4] that is to say, in which the

1. Rom 8.20.
2. Rom 8.21.
3. Antipater was a mid-fifth century Bishop of Bostra, known for a lengthy composition known as the *Refutation,* which was a response to the *Apology for Origen* composed by Pamphilus and Eusebius of Caesarea. *Refutation* was extremely important and influential during the Origenistic controversies, which were at their height not long before Andrew's time; however, only a few fragments of it remain, preserved in the writings of John of Damascus.
4. 1 Cor 7.31.

transgression occurred and humanity became old in them, and because of this, this form became temporary, all things having been foreseen by God."[5] Methodios in the treatise *On the Resurrection* reported thusly: "It is not acceptable to say that everything is to be utterly destroyed and that there will not be any earth and air and sky. For the whole world will be consumed in a cataclysm of fire coming down for purification and renewal. It will not come for absolute destruction and ruination."[6] And going forward he says, "And Paul testifies clearly saying, 'For the earnest expectation of creation awaits the revealing of the sons of God.'[7] For creation is subject to futility, not willingly, but by the one who subjected it in hope, that even the creation itself will be freed from the bondage of corruption."[8] And <other> things following <that statement>. Before these blessed men, Saint [229] David, singing a Psalm to the Lord, was saying, "You send forth your Spirit, and they will be created, and you renew the face of the earth."[9] And Isaiah says, "Heaven will be new and the earth new, and they will not remember the former and it will not come into their mind, but they will find joy and exaltation in it."[10] Naturally. For by the excessiveness of the unceasing joy and magnitude of the prizes of the rewards in the struggles, they will also forget the pains and labors. And elsewhere the same <prophet> says, "The manner in which the new heaven and new earth, which I make, remains before me, thus will be your offspring and your name."[11] Therefore, the creation which came into being for us is to receive with us the way of life changed for the better, not proceeding to non-existence, just as neither will we <have no existence> after death.

20.12. *And I saw the dead, great and small, standing before the throne, and books were opened. And another book was opened, which is the*

---

5. *Heres.* 5.36.1.

6. Methodios, *On the Resurrection* 1.8.

7. Rom 8.19.

8. *On the Resurrection* 1.8, citing Rom 8.19.

9. Ps 104(103).30.   10. Is 65.17–18.

11. Is 66.22.

Book of Life. And the dead were judged by what was written in the books, according to their deeds.

He says *dead,* <meaning> either all people as enduring the death of the body, or those, *great and small,* who became "dead by means of transgressions,"[12] either those being such by age or those who did more or fewer deeds of deadness and accordingly will be punished for the deeds, or *great* being the righteous and *small* being [230] the worthless sinners,[13] inferior by means of the soul. The *books* having been *opened* denote the deeds of each and the consciousness of each <person>. The one book is <*the Book*> *of Life,* in which are inscribed the names of the saints.

20.13. *And the sea gave up the dead in it, and Death and Hades gave up the dead in them, and all were judged by what they had done.*

Each body, it says, from out of those <places> where it is dissolved is recomposed and given back, whether it had been surrendered to the earth or the sea. And *Death* and *Hades* are not living beings as was written by some; rather, death is a separation of soul and body. To us, *Hades* is an immaterial place, that is to say, invisible, that which receives the souls departing from here. The *dead* are the souls which have pursued deadly deeds. "For the souls of the righteous are in the hand of God," just as a certain wise man used to say, "and torment will not touch them."[14]

20.14–15. [14]*Then Death and Hades were thrown into the lake of fire.* [15]*And if someone was not found written in the Book of Life, he was thrown into the lake of fire.* [231]

That *Death and Hades are to be thrown into the lake of fire* shows either that which had been written, "Death, the last enemy is abolished,"[15] or the evil powers <as> agents of death through sin having their dwelling in Hades and sending there those whom they persuaded to be condemned to the fire. For just as these inhabitants of it are called "city," thus those responsible

12. Eph. 2.1, 5; Col. 2.13.
14. Wis 3.1.

13. Oik. 11.8.2.
15. 1 Cor 15.26.

for these are <called> *Death* and *Hades*. For everything which has come into existence by God is "very good";[16] things not of that kind, that fire will make disappear. It is written, "God did not create death."[17] Moreover, by this is meant that death or corruption will no longer exist, rather that incorruption and immortality will reign, for if all *those who have not been written in the Book of Life will be thrown into the lake of fire* one must not be amazed. For also as there are "many mansions in my Father's"[18] <house> among those saved, thus, here too, there are different places and manners of punishments, those sharper and those milder, by which those not deemed worthy of the *Book of Life* will be tried. [232]

CHAPTER 65
About the New Heaven and Earth and the Heavenly Jerusalem

21.1. *And I saw a new heaven and a new earth. For the first heaven and the first earth passed away, and the sea is no more.*

Here, too, it does not mean non-existence of creation but a renewal for the better, just as the Apostle says, "The creation itself will be freed from the bondage of corruption into the glorious freedom of the children of God,"[19] and the divine melodist, "You will turn them around and they will be changed."[20] For the renewal of that which has grown old means not a disappearance from existence, but it means the stripping-off of old age and wrinkles. It is our custom to say about people that they have become either better or worse. "One has become another." [233] One must note that, concerning heaven and earth, it says that *they passed away* instead of "changed," and, just as we <do>, he accepted death as some kind of alteration from the former condition and into a better end. About the sea it says that *the sea is no more*. For what use <is there> of a sea, when people have no need to sail on it or to provide a cargo of agricultural products

---

16. Gn 1.31.   17. Wis 1.13.
18. Jn 14.2.   19. Rom 8.21.
20. Ps 102(101).26.

found in faraway lands? After this also by *the sea* is signified the life of turbulence and many waves; then there will not be any need for it. For not even a remnant of turbulence or fear will be left behind in the saints.

21.2. *And I saw the holy city, new Jerusalem, coming down out of heaven from God, prepared as a bride adorned for her husband.*

And from this is shown the expression of newness of transformation characteristic of greater joy, which the *Jerusalem* from above will reach, descending from the bodiless powers above onto human beings on account of both sides <human and angelic> having a common head, Christ our God. This [234] city is to be held together by the saints—about whom it is written, "Holy stones are employed upon the earth"[21]—having the cornerstone Christ.[22] It is called, on the one hand, *city* as the dwelling place of the Royal Trinity—for <the Trinity> dwells in her and walks about in her as it has been promised[23]—and, on the other hand, *bride* since she is united to the Master being joined to the highest and inseparable union, *adorned,* as if within, according to the Psalmist, having glory and beauty in the varied abundance of virtues.[24]

21.3–4a. [3]*And I heard a loud voice from heaven saying, "Behold, the tabernacle of God is with men, and he will dwell with them, and they will be his people, and God himself will be with them, their God,* [4a] *and he will wipe away every tear from their eyes,*

From heaven the saint is taught that this *tabernacle* is real, of which the type was shown to Moses,[25] rather the prefiguration of the type, which happens <to be> the type of the Church today. In this "tabernacle not made by hands"[26] there will be neither weeping nor tear. For the Provider of everlasting joy will give the unceasing delight to be seen by all the saints.

---

21. Zec 9.16.
23. Lv 26.12. See also Acts 17.28.
25. Ex 25.

22. Eph 2.20; 1 Pt 2.6.
24. See Ps 45(44).10–11.
26. Heb 9.11; 2 Cor. 5.1.

21.4b. *and death will be no more, and neither mourning nor crying nor pain will be any more. The first things have passed away."* [235]

That is to say, <what> has been written: "pain, sorrow, and sighing have fled away."[27] And *the first things have passed away* means that the distress of the saints and the arrogance of the impious have met an end appropriate to each of these.

CHAPTER 66
About the Things Said By the One Sitting on the Throne

21.5–6a. *⁵ And he who sat upon the throne said, "Behold, I make all things new." And he says to me, "Write that these words are true and trustworthy." ⁶ᵃ And he said to me, "I myself am the Alpha and the Omega, the Beginning and the End.*

The words are true since they are accomplished by the Truth himself[28] and no longer through symbols, but they are known through these things themselves. Christ is *the Beginning and the End,* since he is first on account of divinity and last on account of humanity[29] and extends his own providential care from the first creation of the bodiless ones until the last of humans.

21.6b. *To the thirsty freely I will give from the fountain of the water of life.*

To him who "thirsts <for> righteousness"[30] he promises to give the grace of the Life-giving Spirit, which in the Gospels he was promising to those who believe in him.[31] *Freely* because "the sufferings of the present time are not worthy to be compared to the future glory to be revealed"[32] to the saints, [236] or *freely* because this <grace> is not acquired by money but acquired by good deeds and the love for humankind of the One who will give it.

---

27. Is 35.10, 51.11.   28. Jn 14.6.

29. Andrew gave basically the same explanation earlier. See *Chp.* 2, *Text* 21, pages 61–62.

30. Mt 5.6.   31. Jn 7.37–39.

32. Rom 8.18. This is Oikoumenios's opinion.

21.7. He who conquers will inherit these things, and I will be their God and they will be my sons.

The victor, he says, <in> the war against the invisible demons will obtain these good things, by becoming a son of God, and delighting in the blessings of the Father.

21.8. But as for the cowardly, the faithless, the polluted, as for murderers, and fornicators, and sorcerers, and idolaters, and all liars, their lot will be in the lake that burns with fire and sulfur, which is the second death."

In every way, God, who thirsts for our salvation, exhorts us for the inheritance of his blessings through both benefits and misfortunes, by leading us to see the splendor of the heavenly Jerusalem and the dark and grievous gloom of the Gehenna of fire, so that either by yearning for eternal glory or by fear of endless shame, since there is <still> time, we will work to effect the good, along with renouncing all the rest; and those cowardly and unmanly in the contest against the devil [237] he said will be condemned in *the second death.* May it be that we, propitiating the "One who desires mercy"[33] and "not the death of sinners" but their return,[34] receive of his gifts by good actions, since he exhorts us to such <good actions> not only through words, but also through bringing about sufferings. For it does not suffice for him only to use good and evil for encouragement or discouragement and after this either to punish or to honor those deserving glory or punishment. He did not refuse even to go through the Passion for our sakes, so that he neither destroyed the free exercise of our own power <of choice> nor did he appear to overlook the cure and correction for our sakes. Therefore, let us not "receive the grace of God in vain,"[35] but let us make his benefits productive through showing repentance and good deeds, that we might attain the promised blessings in Christ himself our God, with whom the Father is glorified together with the Holy Spirit unto the ages of ages. Amen.

33. Mi 7.18; Mt 9.13, 12.7.   34. Ezek 18.23, 32.
35. 2 Cor 6.1.

CHAPTER 67
About the Angel Showing him the City of the Saints and Measuring its Walls with the Gates

21.9. *Then one <angel>, of the seven angels who had the seven bowls full of the seven last plagues,* [238] *came and was speaking with me, saying, "Come, I will show you the Bride, the wife of the Lamb."*

HROUGH these it is shown that not only the angels apply distressing wounds, but they are like doctors, on one occasion cutting and on another pouring on assuaging medicines. For the one <angel>, then bringing the wound upon the ones deserving it, now shows to the saint the great blessedness of the Church. Correctly it says *the Bride of the Lamb* is *wife*, for when Christ was sacrificed as a lamb, he gave himself in marriage by his own blood. For just as the woman was formed out of the sleeping Adam,[1] by <her> removal from <his> side, thus also, Christ having voluntarily slept by death on the cross, the Church, constituted by the pouring out of blood from his side, is given in marriage, having been united to the One suffering for us.

21.10–11a. [10] *And he carried me away in spirit to a great, high mountain, and showed me the great and holy city Jerusalem* [239] *coming down out of heaven from God,* [11a]*having the glory of God,*

To be *carried away in spirit* means to raise up the mindset from the earth through the spirit toward intellectual comprehension of the heavenly things; *to a great mountain* <means> the exalted and supernatural life of the saints in which the *wife of*

---

1. Gn 2.21.

the Lamb, the heavenly Jerusalem, will be adorned and glorified by God.

21.11b. *its luminance like a most precious stone, a jasper, being clear as crystal.*

Christ, the radiance of the Church, on the one hand, being clear as *crystal,* <is described> through jasper as everlasting and life-giving and pure, and through other things he is otherwise described. For it is not possible for one type of example to illustrate his various kindnesses to us in many different ways.

21.12. *having a great, high wall, having twelve gates, and at <the gates> twelve angels, and on <the gates> the names have been inscribed, which are <those> of the twelve tribes of Israel.*

The *great wall* of the Church, high and fit for guarding those in the [240] holy city, is Christ, in which the holy apostles are *twelve gates* through "which we have had access" and entry "to the Father."[2] And collaborating with them are *twelve angels,* especially those most eminent and closer to God in proximity according to sanctity. For if we have believed that a guardian angel is to be set over each of the faithful, how much more should we realize accordingly that those preeminent among the angels are co-workers in preaching the Gospel with the founders of the Church and sowers of the word of the Gospel? The *names of the tribes of* spiritual *Israel* have been written upon the apostolic entrances, since the names of the visible <tribes> were written upon the shoulder of the high priest at times in antiquity.[3] For the writing of these names also now confirms by additional evidence the concern for the faithful by the apostles, just as Paul said he had "concern for all the churches"[4] and his "heart has been wide open"[5] to contain all "to whom" he "gave birth through the Gospel."[6]

2. Eph 2.18.
4. 2 Cor 11.28.
6. 1 Cor 4.15.

3. Ex 28.12.
5. 2 Cor 6.11.

21.13. *From the east three gates, from the north three gates, from the south three gates, and from the west three gates.*

The four-part scheme of the gates and their threefold expansion means the knowledge of the worship of the Trinity in the four quarters of the inhabited earth, which we have received through the Life-giving Cross. For the position of the gates is the shape of a cross, [241] according to the figure of the twelve oxen which were holding the sea built by Solomon[7] characterizing the triple quadruple-ness of the apostles who preached the Holy Trinity, and the sending forth of the four Gospels into the four corners of the earth, through which the mental sea of baptism is represented purifying the world from sins, established by the spiritual Solomon <Christ>.

21.14. *And the wall of the city had twelve foundations, and on them the twelve names of the twelve apostles of the Lamb.*

The *foundations* of *the wall* are the blessed *apostles,* upon whom the church of Christ has been founded, whose names have been inscribed upon them, giving public notice so they can be easily learned by those reading <them>.

21.15. *And he who was speaking with me had a rod of gold in order to measure the city and its gates and walls.*

The *gold rod* signifies the dignity both of the measuring angel,[8] whom he saw in human form, and of the measured city, whose walls we take to be Christ, which is not measured by humans but by angels through their pure, wise, and celestial natures, by which of course both the grandeur and the well-ordered beauty of the heavenly city has been known. The *wall* there we believe implies the divine sacred enclosure and shelter in which the saints will be protected. [242]

7. 1 Kgs 7.23–25; 2 Chr 4.2–4.
8. Oik. 12.3.1.

21.16. *The city lies square, its length the same as its width. And he measured the city with his rod, twelve thousand stadia. Its length and width and height are equal.*

It is *square* because it is firm and solid. For what is equal-sided in depth, length and height, is called by some a cube but is said to mean stability.[9] The *twelve thousand stadia,* which it says the city has, in like manner signify its great size. For, as David says, its inhabitants "will be multiplied more than <grains of> sand,"[10] and perhaps in like manner also, by the number of the twelve apostles, it <shows those> through whom it was settled. And the number seven, being mysterious, through some analysis offers a question to be investigated. For the aforementioned thousands of stadia constitute signs, the so-called one thousand seven hundred and fourteen miles,[11] the one thousand signifying the perfection of the endless life, the seven hundred being the perfection in <eternal> rest, and the fourteen being the double Sabbath of soul and body, for two sevens are fourteen.

21.17. *And he measured its wall, a hundred and forty-four cubits, a measurement of a man, that is, of an angel.*

The measurement of the depth of the wall is *one hundred forty-four cubits*. The number, composed of twelve times twelve, showing that this number conveys the apostolic teaching. [243]

21.18. *The material of this wall was jasper, and the city was pure gold, clear as glass.*

The *jasper material of the wall* shows the evergreen and unfading life of the saints, as has been said often. Its *pure gold <is> like glass* because of the radiance and brightness of its inhabitants.

9. Oik. 12.3.2.
10. Ps 139(138).18.
11. Andrew refers to yet another unknown source of information: someone who converted the stadia into miles and gave an allegorical interpretation of the sum.

21.19a. *The foundations of the wall of the city were adorned with every precious stone.*

The twelve *foundations* are twelve *precious stones,* of which eight were carried on the breastplate of the high priest in antiquity,[12] but four have been altered in order to show the harmony of the new <Jerusalem> with the old and the superiority of those shining through in it. Moreover, the apostles are shown to have been adorned with every virtue through the precious stones.

21.19b. *The first foundation stone was jasper;*

Through the *jasper,* green in appearance, like smaragdon,[13] Peter the chief <apostle> is probably signified, inasmuch as he "bore in the body the death of Christ,"[14] and being shown evergreen and full of youthful spirit in his love toward him <Christ>, leading us into "green pasture"[15] through warm faith. [244]

21.19c. *the second, sapphire;*

Through this, similar to the body of heaven, from which they also say the azure <color> comes, is signified, I think, the blessed Paul, who was "taken up into the third heaven,"[16] and there attracts all those who believe him <to the place> where he had "citizenship in heaven."[17]

21.19d. *the third, chalcedony;*

This one is not carried on the priestly breastplate, but anthracite,[18] which is not found here. One must consider whether

12. Ex 28.17–21, 39.8–14.
14. 2 Cor 4.10; Jn 21.18–19.
16. 2 Cor 12.2.
13. Epiphanios, *de Gemmis* 6.
15. Ps 23(22).2.
17. Phil 3.20.

18. Andrew does not interpret the meaning of chalcedony, which he notes is not found among the precious stones on the high priest's breastplate, but instead substitutes "anthracite," which *is* on the breastplate, and from which Andrew derives his interpretation. In the Hebrew Bible it is listed as the third stone, and in the RSV it is translated as "carbuncle" (Ex 39.10). The LXX word for this stone is *anthrax,* which is also the Greek word for "coal," but the LXX lists it as the first stone in the second row (Ex 36.18). Nowadays the term "anthracite" indicates a very hard, shiny black stone that is indeed extremely

it does not symbolize the saint called "coal" in this way. The blessed Andrew the apostle is "coal" since he was inflamed with the Spirit.

21.19e. *the fourth, emerald;*

By the *emerald*,[19] which is of green color and is maintained by olive oil, from which it receives in addition splendor and beauty,[20] we think is meant the gospel proclamation of the Evangelist John, by the divine oil bringing gladness out of the despondency which comes to us from sins, and also granting us to be evergreen in faith by the very precious grace of theology.

21.20a. *the fifth, onyx;*[21] [245]

By this <stone> having the appearance of a shining human fingernail,[22] is probably meant James, the first who accepted bodily death for Christ before the others,[23] which the onyx characterizes <like a nail>, being deprived of sensation when it is cut off.

---

hard coal. In antiquity "anthracite," which literally means "a form of coal," most likely indicated a red stone. Its Latin form was *carbunculus* ("carbuncle"), which derives from "burning coal." Chalcedony is recognized today in a variety of colors; however, Andrew seems to believe that John is indicating a red stone. Identifying precisely which stones the authors of Revelation and Exodus had in mind is fraught with difficulties for a number of reasons, including confusion between the equivalent Hebrew and Greek names for stones, the fact that a Hebrew writer would list the stones from right to left, not to mention the various qualities and colors of the stones as they might be known by a translator of the LXX or as an interpreter, such as Andrew, living in a different time and place, knew them. Further complicating translation and interpretation is the fact that English terms for these stones often do not correspond to the colors that the Greek words are indicating. An example of this would be the ninth stone, topaz, which today usually indicates a yellow or blue stone, but which Andrew describes as red.

19. Epiphanios, *de Gemmis* 3.

20. Literally, hour, time, or season, it can also mean youth, grace, as well as prime of life and long life. Perhaps this is an allusion to the tradition that the Evangelist John lived for a very long time.

21. Or sardonyx, a type of onyx.　　　　22. Epiphanios, *de Gemmis* 12.

23. Acts 12.2.

21.20b. *the sixth, carnelian;*

By the *carnelian*,[24] inasmuch as the appearance is <like that> of fire and radiance, having a therapeutic property for inflammations and wounds from iron,[25] the beauty of the virtue of Philip is represented, I assume, becoming joyfully radiant by the fire of the divine spirit and healing spiritual wounds of those souls who had been deceived, as many as had been received by those hurt by the devil.

21.20c. *the seventh, chrysolite;*

By the *chrysolite,* the glitter being similar to gold, perhaps Bartholomew is represented, resplendent by his most precious virtues and divine preaching.

21.20d. *the eighth, beryl;*

By this <stone>, being <the color of> the deep sea and thin air, and closely associated with the sapphire, [246] perhaps Thomas is symbolized, going abroad far beyond the sea as far as India, having been dispatched for their salvation.

21.20e. *the ninth, topaz;*

The *topaz,* being red and similar to coal,[26] and discharging a milky substance, as they say, warding off the pain of those who have eye diseases, can signify the soul of the blessed Matthew, which has been inflamed with divine zeal and has been embellished by his own blood shed for Christ, both freeing from poison by the Gospel those who are blind in heart and giving milk to drink to those newly born by faith.[27]

21.20f. *the tenth, chrysoprase;*

By the *chrysoprase* having as its property and appearance a deeper <color> compared to gold, I think Thaddeus is signified, who preached the Good News of the Kingdom of Christ to Abgar, king of Edessa,[28] which is shown through the gold color, and means his death through its leek-green <color>.

24. Epiphanios. *de Gemmis* 12.
25. Or "sardius." Epiphanios, *de Gemmis* 1. See also *Chp.* 10, *Text* 48, page 82.
26. Epiphanios, *de Gemmis* 2.   27. 1 Cor 3.2.
28. Eusebius, *E.H.* 1.13.11–22.

21.20g. *the eleventh, sapphire;*

By the *sapphire,* having a kind of dark blue appearance, that is to say, like the upper atmosphere, probably Simon is signified, as a zealot[29] of the graces of Christ and having a heavenly mindset.[30] [247]

21.20h. *the twelfth, amethyst;*

By the *amethyst,* being somehow fiery in appearance, I surmise Matthias is signified, having been deemed worthy of the divine fire in the distribution of tongues and filling again the place of the one who had fallen,[31] with fiery yearning to be well pleasing to the One who had chosen <him>.

We have included these <interpretations> drawn from what has been said about the stones by Saint Epiphanios and elsewhere adapted to the leaders of the tribes of Israel, aiming them to serve as training for those pondering enigmas of truth, the precise understanding of which is known only to the one who has revealed <it>. The apostles are really the foundations and precious stones, one <pertaining> to this <stone> and another to that one, all in common with all, preserving the distinctive and remarkable character in the beautiful <stones>. Therefore, I pray, please dismiss the complaint about the comparison of these <stones and> thoughts arrayed here as forced. For by the distinctiveness of the virtue of each one of the apostles we did not separate <them> in their communion and solidarity, but through greater distinction of the individuality we were eager to point out their complete identity of content, closely connected to one another like a chain. [248]

21.21a. *And the twelve gates were twelve pearls. Each of the gates was made from one pearl,*

The *twelve gates,* clearly the <twelve> disciples of Christ, through whom we have come to know "the door"[32] and "the way,"[33] are *twelve pearls,* acquiring radiance from one "pearl of great price,"[34] Christ.

29. For the apostle called "Simon the Zealot," see Lk 6.15 and Acts 1.13.
30. Col 3.2.
31. That is, Judas. See Acts 1.26.
32. Jn 10.9.
33. Jn 14.6.
34. Mt 13.46.

21.21b. *and the wide street of the city was pure gold, transparent as glass.*

In one example it is not possible to present the exact <nature> of the good things of the heavenly city. Wherefore *the wide street of the city,* on the one hand, he viewed as very extravagant and beautifully colored like gold, and, on the other hand, <it is> clear as crystal, so that for us it is impossible for both <descriptions> to concur in one <image>. The saint saw all these things as he was able. Perfect comprehension of the heavenly city surpasses hearing and sight and thought.[35]

21.22. *And I saw no temple in it. For its temple is the Lord God the Almighty and the Lamb.*

For what need is there of a physical *temple* <in a city> in which God is guard and shelter "in whom we live and move and have our being"?[36] For he will be this for the saints, both temple and dweller, dwelling in them and moving about just as has been promised,[37] and *the Lamb*[38] is the Lamb[39] of God, sacrificed for us, which clearly by its essence is placed together with the Life-giving Spirit, which he <John> indicated by the river which follows.

21.23. *And the city has no need of sun or moon* [249] *to shine upon it, for the glory of God illumined it, and its lamp is the Lamb.*

For here <is> the spiritual "Sun of Righteousness."[40] <There is> no need of material luminaries. For he is her *glory* and *lamp.* And the nations of those who are saved will walk in her light.[41] About whom it says:

21.24–25. [24]*And the nations walk by its light. And the kings of the earth will bring their glory into it.* [25]*And its gates will never be shut by day. For there will not be night there.*

The nations which are saved, just as it has been said, it says, *in her light they will walk,* those who ruled over the passions on

35. 1 Cor 2.9.
37. Lv 26.12.
39. Greek: ὁ ἀμνός.
41. Is 60.3.

36. Acts 17.28.
38. Greek: τὸ ἀρνίον.
40. Mal 3.20 LXX (4.2 RSV).

the earth will gain the glory and honor of good deeds in her. That *the gates will not be shut* means either the security and immutability of her inhabitants, or that also there the divine gates of the apostolic teaching are to be open to all for the learning of more perfect things. It will be day there, and *not night*. For sinners will have been disinherited from sharing a portion in her.

21.26–27. [26]*And they will bring the glory and the honor of the nations into it.* [27]*But nothing profane will ever enter it, nor anyone who practices abomination and falsehood, <nor> those who have not been registered in the Book of Life of the Lamb.* [250]

The brilliance and the *glory of the nations,* that is to say, those in them who are well-pleasing to Christ, will bear fruit in that city. All that is *profane* and unclean will not enter there. For "what association does light have with darkness?"[42]

CHAPTER 68

About the Pure River Appearing to Flow From the Throne

22.1–2a. [1]*And he showed to me a pure river of the water of life, bright as crystal, flowing from the throne of God and of the Lamb* [2a]*through the middle of her wide street.*

The *river* flowing out from the Church in the present life hints at a baptism of regeneration being activated through the Spirit, those cleaned and washed, polished up, surpassing snow and crystal.[43] The river of God, having been filled with waters running through the heavenly Jerusalem, is the Life-giving Spirit which proceeds from God the Father and through the Lamb, through the midst of the most supreme powers which are called throne of divinity, filling the wide streets of the holy city, that is, the multitude in her being "increased more than the <grains of> sand,"[44] according to the Psalmist.

42. 2 Cor 6.14.
43. Cf. Ps 51(50).10 and Is 1.18.
44. Ps 139(138).18.

22.2b. *And on one side and the other of the river, the Tree of Life creating twelve fruits, yielding one of its fruits each month,* [251]

This *river*, it says, waters the saints planted alongside it, who are figuratively called the *Tree of Life* in accordance with the participation of and imitation of the Tree of Life. *Twelve fruit trees* are bursting forth fruits; that is, they will unceasingly burst forth a yield of fruit. For there is no winter of sin there forcing the trees of life to shed leaves as we see today, but there will be a fully measured age of fruit-bearing by the saints, which there is referred to as twelve months, perhaps both on account of our custom <to think of> the span of a year and on account of the preaching of the twelve apostles. It is possible also to interpret the present passage altogether differently. By *the river*, as has been said, the gifts of the Life-giving Spirit, those which <come> through the throne of the Father and the Son, that is, the cherubic ranks upon whom God is enthroned, go out into the *wide street of the city*, that is, the thickly populated crowd of the saints, as out from the first into the second, being derived according to the harmonious arrangement of the heavenly hierarchies. <By> *Tree of Life* is meant Christ, <whom> we apprehend in the Holy Spirit and in relation to the Spirit. For the Spirit is in him, and he is worshiped in the Spirit and is the Bestower of the Spirit, and through him the twelve fruits of the apostolic choral assembly are granted to us, the unfailing fruit of the knowledge of God through whom the "acceptable year of the Lord [252] and the day of recompense"[45] are proclaimed to us, having been foretold by the prophet.

22.2c. *and the leaves of the tree were for the healing of the nations.*

Leaves of the tree, that is, of Christ, <are> the most superficial understandings of the divine decrees, as his *fruits* <are> the more perfect knowledge being revealed in the future. These *leaves* will be *for healing*, that is, for the purging of ignorance of those pagans inferior in the activity of virtues, because "the glory of the sun is one thing, the glory of the moon is another, and the glory of the stars is something else,"[46] and "there are

45. Is 61.2.
46. 1 Cor 15.41.

many mansions in the Father's house."⁴⁷ They will be worthy, the one of a lesser brightness and the other of greater, according to the correspondence of the deeds of each. And one must also understand this differently. *The Tree of Life producing twelve fruits* is the apostolic assembly according to their participation in the true Tree of Life, who, by his communion with the flesh, bestowed upon us participation in his divinity. Their *fruits* are those which have produced a "harvest one hundredfold."⁴⁸ The *leaves* <are> those <who bore a harvest of> "sixtyfold and thirtyfold,"⁴⁹ those who will bring forth *healing of the nations,* those lesser, transmitting the radiance of the divine lights which they received through those who bore a fruit harvest one hundredfold. For whatever difference there is between the leaves and fruit, then such is the difference between those who were saved then, some being glorified less and some glorified more, as has been written. If it is written singularly *the tree* instead of *the trees,* it signifies the unitary, communal [253] way of life and the concord of the saints. It is customary in many places in Scripture, instead of many trees, to cite *tree* singly,⁵⁰ and instead of "horses,"⁵¹ similarly, and instead of other plurals <to give> singular names.

22.3a. *Everything under curse will not be there,*

The thing cursed is being understood in two ways: first, as that which is holy for the multitude being set apart for God alone, and, secondly, that which is left untouched by all of creation and the holy powers, since it belongs to the devil by his untempered estrangement from goodness. We think *under curse* is said here for emphasis.⁵² For such a nature is not to be set apart but to be put away, being subjugated by the devil and

47. Jn 14.2.   48. Mt 13.23; Mk 4.20.
49. Mt 13.23; Mk 4.20.
50. See Gn 1.11–12; 1 Chr 16.32; Eccl 2.5; and Jl 2.22.
51. Gn 14.11. The LXX passage reads literally, "They took all of the *horse* of Sodom and Gomorrah, and their provisions and departed." Similarly in Ex 14.7, in which Pharaoh took "six hundred chariots and *all the horse* of the Egyptians." See also 14.9, 23, and 15.1, 21, and Dt 11.4, 17.16, and 20.1.
52. Rv 22.3 uses κατάθεμα, an intensified expression for "curse," instead of simply ἀνάθεμα.

condemned together with <him>, since in that city there will
not be <anything accursed>.

22.3b–4. ³ᵇ *And the throne of God and of the Lamb will be in it, and
his servants will worship him.* ⁴*They will see his face, and his name will
be on their foreheads.*

They become *the throne of God,* it says, for the resting-place of
the Master is upon them. These will be the inhabitants of the
city, and they will see him "face to face,"⁵³ not in riddles but as
seen by the holy apostles on the holy mountain,⁵⁴ as the great
Dionysios said.⁵⁵ [254] Instead of the gold tablet, as the ancient
high priest was wearing,⁵⁶ they will have the divine *name* en-
graved not only on <their> *foreheads* but also on <their> hearts,
signifying steadfast, boldly confident, and unchangeable love
for him. For the writing on the forehead implies enhancement
in confidence.

22.5. *And there will not be night there, and they will not have need of a
lamp or the light of the sun, for the Lord God lights them, and they will
reign for ever and ever.*

If "the righteous," as Christ says, "will shine as the sun,"⁵⁷ how
could there be need of *a lamp or sunlight* for those who have the
"Lord of Glory"⁵⁸ as illumination and king, under whom they
will be ruled for ages of ages, <or> rather, "they will reign" with
him, according to the divine Apostle?⁵⁹

CHAPTER 69

*That Christ is the God of the Prophets and
Master of the Angels*

22.6a. *And he said to me, "These words are trustworthy and true.*

Trustworthy and true, since they are brought forth from The
Truth.⁶⁰ Up to here the vision of the angel and the interpreta-

---

53. 1 Cor 13.12.
54. Cf. Mt 17.1–8; Mk.9.2–8; Lk 9.28–36.
55. Pseudo-Dionysios, *The Divine Names* 1.4.
56. Ex 28.36–38 (Ex 28.32–34 LXX).   57. Mt 13.43.
58. 1 Cor 2.8.   59. 2 Tm 2.12.
60. Jn 14.6.

tion of the things that have been seen were presented alongside each other; the rest he says as from his own self. [255]

22.6b. *And the Lord, God of the holy prophets, has sent his angel to*
show his servants what must take place soon.

If the *God of the prophets* is Christ, who *sent his angel,* the
blessed John having seen the vision in the middle <of the
book>, in order *to show his servants* the future things to come, it
is very clear that <it is> by condescension according to the Incarnation by the Son <that> he said in the proem that the Revelation was given on account of the flesh.[61] For the God of the
prophets, also <being> the one who sends the angels as "ministering spirits"[62] for the manifestation of future things, would
not be ignorant of anything, neither the hour nor the day of
the consummation,[63] so that here through the Father, the One
who holds all "secret treasures of wisdom and knowledge,"[64] he
<John> might learn that which now the Evangelist discusses in
<his own> person, saying:

22.7. *'Behold, I am coming soon.' Blessed is he who keeps the words of*
the prophecy of this book."

For this is also customary in many places in the prophets
to utter the divine things as if from one's own person. The *I*
am coming soon means either the shortness of the present time
compared to the future,[65] or the sudden and quick end of each
<person's life>. For to each human being [256] the departure
from here is his end. Moreover, since "we do not know at which
hour the thief comes,"[66] wherefore we are commanded to be
"watchful and gird our loins and to have burning lamps"[67] in
the way of life according to God, and give light to our neigh-

---

61. Rv 1.1. See also above, *Chp.* 1, *Text* 11, page 55, where Andrew expresses
the same concept.
62. Heb 1.14.
63. Mt 24.36; Mk 13.32. Andrew makes this comment to defend Christ's
divinity against any charge of "ignorance." This statement by Christ in the
Gospels was used by Arians to argue that the Son was "ignorant" of the time of
the end, and therefore is not equal to the Father.
64. Col 2.3.   65. Oik. 12.9.2.
66. Mt 24.43; Lk 12.39.   67. Lk 12.35.

bors,[68] let us unceasingly supplicate God with a contrite heart
to "rescue us from all who persecute us,"[69] lest they defeat and
take possession of our souls, and seize them unprepared as if
there were "none redeemed and none saved,"[70] lest either, on
the one hand, the soul of each be entangled by chains of base
and earthen affairs, and, not bearing separation from these,
she <the soul> vainly turn back toward them, or, on the other
hand, urged by angelic charge and divine command to leave
these things behind, she uselessly lament the carelessness of
the time allotted her. But rather inwardly let us sing the Da-
vidic verse, "I prepared myself and was not terrified, to keep
your commandments";[71] through the observation of these let
us receive the wages, the glory from God, the "well done, good
and faithful servant; you have been faithful over a little; I will
place you over much. [257] Enter into the joy of your Lord,"[72] to
whom with the Father together with the Holy Spirit are due glory, honor, dominion, now and ever and unto the ages of ages.
Amen.

68. Mt 5.16.
70. Ps 7.2.
72. Mt 25.21, 33.

69. Ps 7.1.
71. Ps 119(118).60 (LXX text).

SECTION TWENTY-FOUR

CHAPTER 70
About the Credibility of the Things Seen by the Apostle

22.8–9. *⁸And I, John, am he seeing and hearing these things. And when I heard and saw them, I fell down to worship at the feet of the angel who showed them to me. ⁹And he says to me, "See <here>! Do not <do that>! I am a fellow servant with you and your brethren the prophets, and those who keep the words of this book. Worship God."*

ND THIS is characteristic of the apostolic soul: just as he had done in the Gospel by saying, "and the one who saw <these things> has testified, and his testimony is true,"[1] in this way here also he himself guaranteed the things seen, confessing to be an ear-witness and an eye-witness of the things prophesied. He showed the piety of the angel who stamped the vision <on his mind>, how he did not accept as proper the adoration of a fellow servant, but right-mindedly he assigned <the adoration> to the common Master. [258]

CHAPTER 71
How He was Commanded Not to Seal, but to
Preach the Apocalypse

22.10. *And he says to me, "Do not seal up the words of the prophecy of this book, for the time is near.*

Until these things here, having passed on the angelic words, then he follows in the person of Christ the Master, saying, *Do not seal up the words of the prophecy.* For the book is also worthy

1. Jn 21.24.

for reading by the faithful, for both through the punishment prepared for the sinners and by the repose promised to the saints, it guides those who read it to true life.

22.11–12. [11] *Let the evildoer still do evil, and the filthy still be filthy, and the righteous still do right, and the holy still be holy.* [12]*And behold, I am coming soon, and my recompense with me, to repay each one as his deeds will <require>.*

It is not as though urging wrongdoing and filth that he said these things presented—may it not be so!—but as <expressing> the non-compulsion, of keeping one's own will, as though he said, "Each one may do as he likes; I do not compel free choice," showing for each pursuit the corresponding end to follow "when I come to render to each the wages of the things he has done." [259]

22.13. *I am the Alpha and the Omega, the Beginning and the End, the First and the Last."*

For neither before me nor after me is there a God. For there is neither anything older than the *Beginning*, nor will there be an *end* of the divine kingdom and authority. Many times it has been said above, Christ is *First* on account of the divinity and *Last* on account of humanity.[2]

22.14. *Blessed are they who do his commandments,*[3] *that they may have the right to the Tree of Life and that they may enter the city by the gates.*

People such as these are truly worthy of blessedness. For they will have authority in the unceasing life, by the *Tree of Life*, Christ our God, to rest upon him and to delight in beholding him, in no way hindered by evil power; and by the apostolic *gates*, that is, through their instruction, they will enter into the

---

2. See Rv 2.8 and Andrew's comment on it; also 1.17.

3. A significant textual variation occurs here. This reading is found in the Majority Andreas text, as well as Sinaiticus and Alexandrinus. The preferred reading is "Blessed are they who wash their robes," which is also the reading in Oikoumenios. Metzger believes the scribal variation occurred because of the similarity in sound and because elsewhere the author writes of keeping the commandments (Rv 12.17 and 14.12). *A Textual Commentary,* 765.

heavenly city through the True "Door,"[4] not leaping over from the other side as the "hired shepherds,"[5] but they will be admitted by the Doorkeeper of Life.

22.15. *Outside are the dogs and the sorcerers and the fornicators and the murderers and the idolaters, and every one who loves and practices falsehood.*

Dogs are not only people who are shameless, faithless, and "evildoers among the circumcised"[6] [260] whom the Apostle lamented, but also those who after baptism "returned to their own vomit."[7] Wherefore, with the fornicators and the murderers and the idolaters they will be estranged from the city above.

CHAPTER 72

How the Church and the Spirit in it Are Invited to the Glorious Appearance of Christ, and About the Curse by Which Those Falsifying the Book are Thrown Down

22.16a. *"I, Jesus, have sent my angel to testify to these things to you for the churches.*

Here is shown the high status of the Master as the One who has sent the angel. The <word> *to testify*[8] has been used instead of "to bear witness solemnly."[9]

22.16b. *I am the root and the offspring of David,*

Christ is the *root of David* as God, and <is> also a descendant as having sprung forth from him <David> according to the flesh.

22.16c. *the bright morning star."*

He is *the bright morning star* who has risen in the morning on the third day for us, and who, after the night of the present life, in the morning of the [261] general resurrection will shine upon the saints and will bring the endless day.[10]

---

4. Jn 10.9.
6. Phil 3.2.
8. Greek: μαρτυρῆσαι.
10. An allusion to 2 Pt 1.19.

5. Jn 10.12.
7. Prv 26.11; 2 Pt 2.22.
9. Greek: διαμαρτύρασθαι.

22.17a. *The Spirit and the Bride say, "Come." And let him who hears say, "Come."*

For both the Church and the Spirit in her cry out in our hearts, "Abba, Father!"[11] to call for the coming of the "Only-begotten Son of God."[12] And every one of the faithful who hears prays to God the Father, just as he had been instructed: "Thy kingdom come."[13]

22.17b. *And let him who is thirsty come, let him who desires take the water of life freely.*

For thirst is necessary for the drink of life, for the firm possession of the one who has acquired it, especially because it is also granted as a gift, not to those who did not toil at all, but to those who offered not things worthy of the greatness of the gift, but only a genuine and fiery resolve instead of gold and silver and pains of the body.

22.18–19. [18]*I bear witness to everyone who hears the words of the prophecy of this book: if anyone adds to them, God will add to him the seven plagues which have been written in this book.* [19]*And if anyone takes away from the words of the book of this prophecy, God will take away his share* [262] *from the Tree of Life and from the holy city, which have been written in this book.*

Fearful is the curse against those who falsify the Holy Scripture, since their rashness and boldness is able to alienate the stubborn from the good things of the future age. Indeed, in order that we not suffer, it warns us who hear neither to add anything nor subtract, but to consider the written peculiarities <of the Apocalypse> as more trustworthy and dignified than the Attic syntax and dialectic syllogisms,[14] since also when someone discovers many things in those <writings> that do not measure

11. Rom 8.15; Gal 4.6.   12. Jn 3.18.
13. Mt 6.10; Lk 11.2.
14. This is probably a comment directed at those who rejected the Apocalypse because of its very poor Greek. Eusebius preserved the comments of Dionysios, the third-century Bishop of Alexandria, who argued that the Apocalypse could not have been written by John the Apostle because the language of the Gospel was beautiful and grammatically correct (*E.H.* 7.24–26).

up according to the rules, he is guided by the trustworthiness of the poets and authors in them. As far as <finding> a midpoint in matters of opinion between us and them, <it is> even impossible to grasp in the mind. I think there is more <difference> than the difference between light and darkness.

22.20–21. ²⁰*He who testifies to these things says, "Yes, I am coming soon." Amen. Come, Lord Jesus Christ!* ²¹*The grace of the Lord Jesus Christ be with all the saints.*

It says, "and I who say these things to you, <I who am> the Life, <say>, '*I am coming.*'" And he <John> says, "Be present, Lord." And otherwise, this has been said from the person of Christ: *The one testifying to these things,* that is, the One affirming solemnly: *I am coming soon.* From the person of the apostle, the following: the *Come, Lord Jesus Christ.* For the coming of Christ is greatly desired by the saints [263] since he will render the wages of the laborer many times over; wherefore likewise the present book <is> holy and God-inspired, guiding those who read it to a blessed end.

In order to summarize in a few words the advantageous purpose of all the things in it, let me provide: Through the seven churches we are taught perseverance in trials and the earnestness in good deeds and other such types of virtue. And from these, when one is elevated over all the things upon the earth it is possible to behold with the clear eye of the soul the divine glory in heaven, not its very essence, but the divine manifestation being formed either through a variety of precious stones or by the appearance of a multicolored rainbow or by some similar images of divine concessions, and around it the holy bodiless powers and those with a body who well pleased the Lord, both thunder and lightning conveying the divine presence, and <it is possible> to hold the incomprehensible divine judgments of the scroll signified by the seven seals of the Spirit and loosened by the Lamb of God, <judgments> of the things which have occurred and which will occur from his coming until the end of time, and about both the bravery of the martyrs and the double punishment of the faithless and about the harvest of the seed of the Gospel and also about the fall of those

who have little faith and are cowardly, so that the saints long
for the second coming of Christ, and about both the application of evils prior to <the coming of> the Antichrist and the
things that he dared to do against the Christians. In addition
to these things it is to be learned from there how the saints are
precious to God, since [264] punishment against the impious
is suspended before they become known to the punishing angels through the seal. And thereafter, we learn about the seven
plagues that will be brought upon those upon the earth in the
last <days>, so that by their magnitude, in view of the return, we
see also their supplication to God not to be tested. And it shows
the angels' love for humankind through the one holding fast
the Gospel and preaching to those upon the earth; and <the
love for humankind> of the saints who will come at the consummation to reprove the false Christ; the steadfast and cou-
rageous disposition of the soul; and the division of Jerusalem
and the disappearance of the pagan cities; and the thanksgiving for these things by the powers above; and the persecution
against the Church; and the fall of the devil and the coming
of the Antichrist and the deception of the false prophet; and
the numerous crowd of the saved; and the fall of Babylon; and
the threshing-floor reaping of the entire world and the wine
harvest of the bitter clusters <of grapes>; and the most pure
end of the saints, likened to a sea of glass; and the pouring out
of seven bowls of divine wrath bringing forth evils upon those
on the earth and the sea and the rivers and the rest of the elements on account of the wickedness of human beings, and
darkening the throne of the beast, and leading the adjutants
of the devil to the crossing of the Euphrates and reprimanding
their weakness, and bringing about to the world the general
[265] earthquake of the change of the present things, when
the harlot and beast-like city, also resting upon the devil, will
receive the destruction befitting her. After which <destruction>
God is praised by the supernatural powers, and the Church,
the Jerusalem above, is united with Christ for the most perfect
union, the wine press of wrath is trampled upon, and the angels and people equal to the angels partake of the spiritual supper of the disappearance of earthly things, delivering the An-

tichrist and his adjutant to Gehenna. Next to be learned from here is both the binding of the devil and his temporary release and the sending forth into perdition, and the blessedness of the holy martyrs co-reigning with Christ before the coming of the Antichrist, after which the devil is to be loosed for a little while and will disturb Gog and Magog, and he will be punished with them when the books of the deeds done by each and the Book of Life will be opened, and when some, on the one hand, will suffer the second death, but some, on the other hand, will be found worthy of the Jerusalem above and of marriage with Christ. From this divine book we also learn by the angel the dimension of the heavenly city, with walls and gates and foundations, as much as is possible, and from the angel we learn also the divine river of the Spirit flowing from there, that no word is able to express the well-ordered beauty of the things above or the unfading glory, into which, urging us, [266] he commands, saying: "Come," that is, the One who will grant these things, just as you have prepared <them> for the saints.

Starting from these things by the vision and the enjoyment we might, by ardent yearning through keeping the divine commandments, acquire these in long-suffering and meekness and humility and purity of heart. From which <heart> unsullied prayer is born free of distraction, and offers to God, the Overseer of all hidden things, a mind devoid of every material thought, uncorrupted by demonic deception and attacks. For the deceiving enemy is allowed, in the petitions to God in the heart, adulterously to come into contact with her, scattering corrupting seeds, tearing her away from her divine union, in order that the fire not be kindled in her ardor, <fire> destroying his machinations—"for our God is a consuming fire"[15]— and the soul conversing with him clearly and undisturbed, even if it becomes chilled by sin, is made warm and fertile by demon-burning fire. Just as the sun strongly shining on a glass vessel full of water will produce heat therein because of some exposure <to the light> and reflection <of rays>, if then we also are a clean temple of the Spirit like glass, not clay or earthenware,

15. Dt 4.24.

which does not admit the divine Ray, then we will show <this> to the [267] "Sun of Righteousness,"[16] "who wills all to be saved and come to knowledge of the truth,"[17] shining upon all the unhindered grace of his own bright beam. He is imparted to each person according to the measure of purity of the spiritual eyes. May the All-merciful One deem us worthy to acquire this pure <light>, he who suffered in the flesh for us, Christ our God, to whom belongs every doxology, honor, and adoration together with the Father and the Life-giving Spirit unto the ages of ages. Amen.

16. Mal 3.20 LXX (4.2 RSV).
17. 1 Tm 2.4.

EPILOGUE

NE MUST know that the author of the present book furnished it to those esteemed individuals who asked to study it, <and> then later, giving the book to the hesitant, he did not diligently guard some of the rough drafts but cast them aside; as it happened, again having been asked by others, he combined those of the rough drafts which had been saved; in a few places the thought of the lost <pages> naturally he restored in other words. If some small disagreement may appear in the words, it in no way will create any injurious effect upon those reading them, the meaning remaining the same, and variation of the words being very slight.

INDICES

GENERAL INDEX

Abel, 82

Abgar, king of Edessa, 229

Abraham, 97, 198

abyss, 120, 121, 122, 123n15, 124, 205–6; beast ascends from, 132, 184; of divine judgment, 85, 116

Adam, 143, 209n3, 223

adjutant(s) of the devil, 151, 153, 169, 244

affliction(s), of the end times, 13, 97, 98, 100, 112, 115, 120, 133, 168, 172, 173, 180, 202; affects creation, 103; God blamed, blasphemed for, 172, 173, 180; suffered for Christ, 66; not to be feared, 67; will not last long, 76; purpose of, 36, 107 120, 133, 167, 172, 173, 180, 195. *See also* torment, punishment

Alexander the Great, 185, 186

Alexandria, 12, 16n21, 32, 153n12, 184n19, 241n14

Alexandrinus, Codex, 239n3

allegory, 13, 14, 26, 27, 28, 33, 52n8, 132, 226n11

"alleluia," meaning of, 196

Alogoi, 5, 54n20

Alpha and Omega. *See* Christ

altar, 23, 91n4, 92, 96, 112, 113, 123, 130, 162, 170, 206

"amen," meaning of, 25, 59, 196

anagoge. See Andrew, Commentary, exegesis

Andrew of Caesarea, 3–42; life, 4; episcopal reign, 4; assigned to write commentary, 16–17, 51–52; believes Apocalypse is inspired, 53–54; end is not near, 12–15, 51; cannot know time of the end, 13, 51, 53; pastoral interests, 14, 21, 22, 29; eschatology, 12–13, 33–34, 37–39; other works, 4, 4n2; obedient to his task, 52, 53; training, 4, 24, 28; theology, 34–37; liturgical orientation, 23; sacramental orientation, 23–24; gave out drafts of commentary, 18, 246

Andrew of Caesarea, Commentary: authorship, 3, 16–17, 51; date of commentary, 9, 15–16; does not understand everything, 51–53; historical milieu, 11–12, 15–16; motivation for commentary, 9–10; purpose of commentary, 12–14, 29; recipient of commentary, 16–17; is responding to Oikoumenios, 9–10; reports many opinions, 19–20, 22; methodology, 25–28; division of commentary, 18–19, 40n120, 53; importance of commentary, 3, 4, 6, 7, 8, 18, 10, 20, 42; commentary as catena, 19; Andreas manuscripts, 3n1, 4n2, 10, 18, 41, 42; manuscript variations in Andreas text, 25, 55n3, 75, 107n50, 108n55, 137n11, 180n6; structure and style, 18–19, 53; sources, 7, 8, 9, 19, 31–32, 207n44; translations of the commentary, 39–40

Andrew of Caesarea, Commentary, exegesis: contribution to Apocalypse text, 41–42; legacy of the commentary, 42; exegesis, 18–19, 25–31; *anagoge*, anagogical sense, 28, 52, 116; context, 28, 29–30; *skopos*, 28; *theoria*, 28; *historia*, literal sense, 26; sequence, 30; *tropologia*, 27; typology, 26–27; did not allegorize, 13, 26, 27, 28; discusses figurative meaning, figurative interpretation, 37, 53, 63, 69, 90, 92, 97, 100, 116, 122, 127, 138, 140, 163, 184, 233; discusses historical sense, literal meaning, 5, 13, 18, 19, 26–27, 52–53, 85, 92, 158, 183, 211; discusses *skopos*, 28, 29; discusses symbolic language in Revelation, 6, 13, 20, 22, 24, 26, 28, 30, 31, 34, 37, 38, 53, 61, 75, 82, 85, 87, 92, 113, 145, 153, 164, 170, 182, 221, 228, 229; three levels of interpretation, 25–28, 52–53; view of prophecy and history, 13, 26, 32–34; word-association, 28, 31

angel, angels, 55, 63, 66, 67, 69, 73, 74, 75, 77, 80, 86, 90, 102, 115, 122, 123, 127, 157, 158, 161, 162, 182, 183, 190, 194, 195, 198, 202, 224, 226, 237; orderliness of, 88, 112, 128, 166; variety of, ranking of, 60n28, 82, 88, 103, 128, 129, 200, 202, 224, 233; purity of, 63, 166, 225; piety of, 112, 238; brightness, brilliance of, 63, 127, 190, 201; unity of, 201, 204; humility of, 199; virtue of, 127, 201; knowledge of, 77, 84, 86, 103, 112, 113, 130, 131; grieve over sin, 170; imitate God, 119, 145, 157, 170; refuse to be worshiped, 199, 238; responsibilities of, 143, 157, 162, 169, 205, 206, 223, 226; guard the churches, 63, 214; reveal the vision, 55, 235, 236, 238, 240;

shows or explains the harlot, 181–83, 187; shows the Bride of the Lamb, 223; their war against the devil and demons, 142; mocked the devil, 139; delight over devil's ejection, 144; their divine love, 113; guardian angel, 170, 224; love humans, 22, 119, 243; assist, serve humans, 103, 113, 157, 170, 223, 235; co-workers with the apostles, 224; appear to people, 110; are sent by God, 236; co-celebrate liturgy with people, 110; are part of the Church, 88, 110, 220, 243; participate in worship, 23, 135, 196; bring prayers to God, 112, 113, 170; worship, praise God, 88, 110, 135, 196, 197, 243; serve God, 57, 102, 166, 240; ministered to Christ, 142; rejoice at repentance, 170–71; bring plagues, 113, 115, 116, 117, 119, 120, 164, 166–69, 172, 175, 178; measure the city, 225, 226, 244; do not know time of the end, 13, 112; seal the righteous, 103, 155, 243; assist at harvest, at judgment, 161–63; seven angels, 56, 57, 60, 62, 63–64, 73, 85, 112, 113, 164, 166–69, 181, 187; will come with Christ in glory, 59n23, 200. *See also* cherubim, seraphim, bodiless powers, heavenly powers

Antichrist, 27, 34, 37, 38, 39, 54n20, 72, 76, 98, 100, 102. 103, 106, 109, 124, 130, 131, 132, 133, 134, 135, 136, 140, 141, 146, 147, 148, 149, 151–54, 157, 158, 166, 168, 173, 175, 176, 180, 181, 184, 187, 188, 202, 204, 205, 207–9, 214–15, 243, 244. *See also* Beast, of the sea; Dan, tribe of; Euphrates; Temple, name of; pseudo-Christ; false Christ

Anthony, St., 143, 146

Antioch, 8, 11, 12

Antiochene exegesis, 28, 29

Antiochus, 26, 98, 140, 213

Antipas, 67

Antipater of Bostra, 32, 216

Apocalypse, in the canon of
    Scripture, 3–4, 5–6; definition
    of, 55; Apocalypse manuscripts,
    6, 7, 40, 41; authorship of, 3–4,
    5, 32, 53–54; inspiration and
    trustworthiness, 53, 241–42, 242;
    history of interpretation, 6–10,
    19–20, 32; value of, 238–39; not
    to be altered, 241–42; can serve
    to train the mind, 21–22; spiritual
    benefit of, 21–22, 53, 54, 67,
    238–39, 242, 244

Apollonius of Tyana, 153

apostles, 39, 51n11, 53, 62, 73, 79, 82,
    90, 91, 100, 106, 107, 136, 138,
    145, 148, 155, 161, 165, 165, 195,
    196, 197, 208, 214, 224, 225, 226,
    227–30, 232, 233, 234, 235, 239;
    false apostles, 64

Arbaces, 185, 186

Arians, 184, 236n63

Armageddon, 176

Armenian Church, the canon of, 40

Armenian revolt, 15n19, 95

Armenian translation of the
    commentary, 39–40, 41

Asher, tribe of, 104, 107

Assyrians, 33, 185, 186, 212n22,
    213

Attic syntax, 241

Augustus, Caesar, 148, 186

Averky, Archbishop, 21n55

Babylon, 15n18, 38, 158, 179, 182,
    183, 185, 186, 187, 190, 192,
    194–97, 212n22, 213, 243. See also
    harlot

Babylonia, Babylonians, 33, 38, 148

Balaam, 68

Balak, 68

baptism, 24, 57, 74n5, 77, 137, 138,

140, 178, 210, 225, 232, 240; of
    Christ, 32, 90, 145, 211

barbarians, 12, 15, 16, 17, 65n51,
    115, 125, 172, 212n20

Bartholomew, St., 229

Basil, the Great, 32, 147n34, 165

beast, mark of the, 153, 154, 158,
    159, 164, 168, 204, 208

beast of the earth, false prophet, 147,
    151, 152, 209

beast of the sea, Antichrist as, 132,
    147, 148, 149, 151, 152, 153, 173,
    176, 187, 188, 204, 209, 213, 243

beast, Rome as, 196

beast, scarlet, devil, 38, 147, 181–85,
    188–89, 208, 209, 243

beast, worship of, 152, 153, 158, 159,
    164, 168, 204, 208

beast, wound of, 148, 151, 152

beasts, wild, 82, 93, 94, 95, 124, 190,
    213

Benjamin, tribe of, 106, 108

bodiless powers, 59, 220, 221, 242.
    See also angels

Book of Life, 74, 149, 150, 185, 218,
    219, 232, 244

books of judgment, 217–28, 244

bosom of Abraham. See Abraham

bridal chamber of Christ, 167, 177,
    277, 198

bubonic plague, 11, 95n4

Bulgars, 11

Caesarea, Cappadocia, 3, 4, 6, 7, 8,
    12, 16, 18, 15, 40, 41, 42, 95n4

Caesarea, Eusebius of. See Eusebius of
    Caesarea

calf, 83, 84, 91, 186n29

canon of Scripture, 3–4, 5, 40, 42,
    53n15, 207n44

Castagno, Adele Monaci, xiii, 19n26

Chalcedon, 12

Chalcedon, Council of, 34n90, 64n51

Chalcedonian, theology, churches,
    9, 34

chalcedony, 227

Chaldean, Chaldeans, 185, 190

chariot, chariots, 122, 134, 163, 193, 234n51

cherubim, 110, 113, 142, 161, 197, 233. *See also* angels

chiliasm, 3, 6, 37. *See also* millennialism, one thousand years

Chrismation, Confirmation, 24

Christ, 13, 14, 20, 21n35, 23, 29, 30, 32, 33, 54n20, 57, 62, 63, 69, 71, 73, 77, 80, 84, 86, 87, 88, 89, 91, 92, 93, 94n2, 96, 100, 103, 104, 108, 109, 111, 113, 114, 125, 126, 133, 135, 136, 137, 138, 139, 146, 152n8, 153n12, 154, 157, 159, 160, 161, 165, 166, 167, 170, 171, 177, 184, 185, 186, 189, 195, 198, 199, 202, 203, 206, 207, 209, 215, 220, 222, 223, 224, 225, 227, 228, 228, 230, 232, 238, 239, 240, 242, 244, 245; All-Merciful, 245; Alpha and Omega, 59, 60, 221, 239; Angel of the Great Counsel, 162; Apocalypse from, 55, 59; Ascension, 161; attributes of, 201; authority over life and death, 63, 75; beginningless, endless, 59, 221; blasphemed, 147; bound Satan, 205–6; Bread of life, 69; Bridegroom, 198; Cornerstone, 166, 220; Creator, 77, 79, 80, 86, 197; crucified, 96, 132, 142, 145, 209; desires mercy, 170; divinity of, 53n15, 55, 59, 65, 79; endless, 59, 60, 62; First and Last, 62, 66, 239; Holy One, 34; is God of the prophets, 236; is, was, and is to come, 30; Judge, 59, 79, 80, 99, 109, 133, 176, 197, 200, 202, 208; kernel, 106; King, 79, 84, 108, 135, 197, 200, 235; King of kings, Lord of lords, 57, 202; Lion of Judah, 72; Lord of Glory, 235; loves goodness and virtue, 188–89; Morning Star, 31; not ignorant, 236; Physician, 93, 117; One who loves humankind, 13, 65, 80, 93, 114, 133; return of, 37, 76, 99, 112, 131, 178, 200, 214, 243; Root of David, 86, 133, 240; Ruler of all, 58, 59; sends the angels, 236; spiritual Solomon, 225; suffered in the flesh, 132–33, 202, 245; Sun of Righteousness, 62, 71, 72, 111, 138, 173, 231, 245; temptation of, 142; Tree of Life, 65, 233, 239; Truth, 77, 235; two natures of, 62, 86, 202; unknown name, 201; was emptied out, 120; Word of God, 201; vision of, 26, 61; saints co-reigning with, 118, 150, 202, 208, 210, 244; saints suffering for, 59, 92, 109, 110, 144–45, 160, 180, 208. *See also* Master, Incarnation, Logos

Church, churches, 3, 6, 17, 19, 23, 24, 26, 31, 37, 56, 57, 61, 63, 88, 96, 100, 110, 131, 136, 137, 138, 139, 140, 141, 145, 146, 155, 157, 170, 179, 181, 195, 197, 198, 207n44, 211, 214, 220, 223, 224, 225, 232, 240, 241, 242, 243; seven churches, 56, 60, 61, 62, 63; of Ephesus, 63–65; of Laodicea, 77–80; of Pergamum, 67–69; of Philadelphia, 75–77; of Sardis, 73–74; of Smyrna, 66–67; of Thyatira, 69–72

Church, Eastern Orthodox, 42

Church Fathers, 19, 32

Church traditions, 54n17

Constantine, the Great, Emperor, 34, 147, 186

Constantinople, 4, 6, 11, 12, 16, 17, 38, 40, 64n51, 102n2, 184n19

consummation of the world, 12–14, 96, 97, 115, 161, 208, 236, 243. *See also* end-times, end of the world

contest, life as, 35, 109, 160, 174, 222

creation, 33, 77, 80, 83, 88, 89, 103, 110, 111, 125, 142, 162, 163, 164,

169, 197, 169, 216, 217, 219, 221, 234

Creator, 125, 128. *See also* Christ

creature, creatures, 85, 88, 115, 116, 128

cross, 24, 90, 96, 103, 121, 126, 142, 223, 225, 184, 143

crown, crowns, 14, 35, 37, 73, 76, 82, 90, 91, 136, 138, 141, 161; of life, 14, 67; of victory, 82, 85, 139; unfading, 120, 160; of demons, 122, 139. *See also* diadems

Cyril of Alexandria, 32, 53, 54n16, 98

Cyrus the Great, 28, 185, 186, 190, 213

Daniélou, 33n88

Darius, 213

David, 25, 75, 85, 86, 109, 122, 133, 206, 208, 217, 226, 237, 240

death, 15n18, 57, 58, 67, 70, 93, 94, 95n4, 121, 141, 148, 153, 175, 192, 205, 217, 218, 219; must be despised, 14, 21, 27, 67; of Christ, 66, 90n4, 223; for Christ, 91, 144, 145, 160, 175, 227, 228, 229; two kinds of death, 67, 205, 209; second death, 67, 134, 204, 210, 222, 244; spiritual death, 114, 116, 117, 121, 122, 123, 125, 138, 150, 175, 210; our time of death unknown, 14, 74. *See also* Christ, authority over death

demonic, demons, 29, 37, 65, 82, 90, 91, 108, 109, 121, 122, 123, 124, 125, 138, 139, 141, 146, 147, 153, 171, 173, 174, 176, 184, 190, 199, 206, 208, 213, 222, 244

desert, 139, 141, 145, 146, 181, 190. *See also* wilderness

devil, 6, 37, 38, 67, 68, 69, 72, 79, 116, 139, 140, 150, 169, 182, 204, 208, 213, 222, 229, 234; blasphemes God, 144; bound by Christ, 205; deceiver, 94n2, 143; destroyer, 123, 132, 184, 188;

dragon, 176; fall of, 117, 139, 140, 142, 143, 144, 243; loosened by Christ, 210, 211, 212; meaning of, 143; name of, 143, 144; originator of evil, 152, 207; persecutes the Church, 140, 141, 145–46; punishment of, 144, 163, 207, 210, 213, 215; weakened by Christ, 143, 205, 206, 244; weaker than an angel, 206; works with Antichrist, 147, 149, 176, 208. *See also* dragon, scarlet beast

diadems, of the devil, 138, 139, 147, 147, 209; of Christ, 200

Diekamp, F., 4n2, 9

Diocletian, Emperor, 181, 183

Dionysios, Bishop of Alexandria, 241n14

Dionysios, pseudo, 19, 32, 84, 128, 166, 235

Dioscurides, 82n2

divine allowance, divine permission, 92, 116, 121, 125, 132, 149, 152, 175

divine wrath, 94, 96, 98, 100, 101, 102, 125, 135, 158, 159, 162, 163, 164, 166, 167, 173, 179, 180, 202, 204, 243

dogs, 95, 240

Domitian, Emperor, 9n8, 181

dragon, 91, 137, 138, 139, 140, 142, 143, 145, 146, 148, 151; gives power to Antichrist, 148, 149, 151, 152, 209; is devil, serpent, Satan, 176, 205, 209; worship of, 149, 152

eagle, 83, 84, 94, 145

earthquake, 11, 12, 13, 13, 97, 98, 113, 134, 136, 178, 243

Ecbatana, 185

Ecumenical Council, Fourth, 34n90, 64n51; Fifth, 144n17

Edessa, 229

Egypt, 16n21, 98, 132, 169

eighth day, 33n88, 105, 134

eighth king, 187

eighth week, 108

elders, the twenty-four, 18, 22, 26, 30, 53, 81, 82, 85, 86, 87, 88, 110, 135, 155, 156, 196

end of the world, 10, 12–14, 35, 36, 39, 51, 53, 55, 57, 71, 74, 76, 96, 97, 100, 106, 112, 113, 117, 119, 121, 127, 128, 129, 130, 131, 148n35, 158, 162, 164, 167, 183, 184, 194, 205, 212, 213, 214n31, 236n63, 242. *See also* consummation

Enoch, 71n28, 131, 167, 168

Ephesus, 12, 31, 60

Ephraim, 106, 186

Epilogue, 246

Epiphanios, 32, 58, 64, 82, 227n13, 228n19, 229n24, 229n25, 229n26, 230

eternal life, eternal blessings, 36, 37, 38, 57, 65, 66, 80, 101, 107, 111, 124, 159, 174, 189, 198, 207, 209, 222, 226

eternal punishment, eternal torment, 36, 78, 100, 114, 124, 133, 134, 158, 159, 167, 173–74, 197, 202, 205, 210

eternal rest, 33, 107, 226

Euphrates River, 12, 123, 124, 175, 243

Eusebius of Caesarea, 15n19, 32, 94, 144n15, 153n12, 216n3, 229n28, 241n14

Euthymios, St. (Ekwthime), 40

Eucharist, 23

eyes, of apostles, 161; of Christ, of the Lamb, 61, 69, 87, 200; of the four living beings, 83, 84; of saints, of righteous, 76, 82, 111, 160, 220, 245; of sinners, of deceived, 78, 87, 149, 152

Ezekiel, 103, 113, 132, 166, 212, 213

false Christ, 152, 176, 215, 243. *See also* Antichrist and pseudo-Christ

false prophet, 151–52, 176, 204, 208, 213, 215, 243

false signs, 132, 133, 148, 151, 176

famine, 11, 12, 15n18, 15n19, 79, 92, 94, 95n4, 100, 192

Father, God the, 13n10, 21, 23, 29, 30, 32, 34, 57, 58, 59, 65, 71, 72, 74, 77, 79, 80, 81, 89, 93, 101, 114, 118, 126, 133, 141, 147n34, 150, 155, 156, 160, 162, 167, 170, 171, 177, 189, 197, 199, 201, 202, 203, 207, 212, 214n33, 215, 219, 222, 224, 232, 233, 234, 236, 237, 241, 245

Fathers of the Church, 8, 19, 32, 33, 40, 51n1, 54, 116n5, 137n18, 142, 143n6, 196n11, 211n11

fire, flame, 15n18, 16, 61, 62, 69, 78, 83, 113, 115, 116, 124, 125, 127, 128, 132, 152, 172, 200, 212, 214, 215, 229, 230, 244; bifurcated, 61, 69, 165, 200; eternal, 111, 158; of Gehenna, 108, 118, 144, 173, 205, 206, 209, 222; lake of, 204, 213, 215, 218, 219, 222; punishment by, 101, 144, 159, 162, 204, 213, 219, 222; of purification, 174, 217; tests works, 107, 219

first resurrection, 209, 210, 211

free will, 22, 35–36, 92, 174, 203, 222, 239

four living beings, 20, 24, 31, 34, 83–85, 87–88, 90–92, 94, 110, 155, 166, 196

Gabriel, Archangel, 123

Gad, tribe of, 104, 107

Gaius, 54n20

garment, garments, 61, 74, 78, 109, 137, 167, 176, 177; of incorruption, 74; wedding, 177; white, 30, 78, 80, 82, 109, 177. *See also* robes

gates of heavenly Jerusalem, 223–25, 230–32, 239, 244

Gehenna, 67, 108, 114, 115, 116,

117, 118, 120, 122, 134, 136, 144, 173, 187, 202, 205, 206, 209, 210, 222, 224. *See also* fire

Georgian commentary, manuscripts, 41

Georgian commentary, translation, 39, 40

Georgian, New Testament canon, 40

God, assists humanity, 132; blamed for misfortunes, 172; co-operates, co-works with humans, 35–36, 93; desires that all be saved and know truth, 36, 137n18, 203; desires, encourages repentance, 56, 117, 120, 132, 172–73, 174, 180, 222; does not compel us, 36, 239; goodness of, 36, 78, 132, 156, 172, 173, 174, 234; helps Andrew interpret, 52, 58, 99, 173, 181, 182; knowledge of, 36, 51, 53, 75, 83, 86, 99, 111, 131, 137n18, 155, 156, 165, 174, 206, 233, 236; lessens suffering, 112, 119; loves humanity, 22–23, 35, 42, 93, 101, 167, 172, 189; nature of, qualities of, 58, 59, 60, 62, 64, 65, 82, 88, 150, 174; thirsts for our salvation, 222; will of, 36, 100, 202, 206. *See also* divine allowance, divine wrath, Christ, Holy Spirit

Gog and Magog, 39, 169, 175, 211, 212–13, 244

Gomorrah, 234n51. *See also* Sodom

Gospel, 55, 58, 67, 71, 74, 84, 86, 91, 130, 139, 157, 177, 180n6, 224, 228, 229, 238, 241n14, 243; preaching of, 37, 62, 206, 208, 211, 224, 242

Great Horologion, 67n6

Greek authors, Greek sources, 5, 7, 8, 28, 31, 32, 116n5, 207n44

Greek language, 3, 5, 7, 8, 9, 10, 20, 28, 31, 32, 39, 40n117, 41, 52n7, 59, 67n6, 317n22, 105n21, 108n57, 122, 143n8, 158n4, 159n9, 166n29, 185n25, 186n31,

188n37, 193n7, 201n15, 206n38, 213n26, 213n27, 227n18, 231n38, 231n39, 240n8, 240n9, 241n14

Greek paganism, 98n13, 147n34

Greek people, 4, 6, 9, 10, 68, 98n13

Gregory, the Theologian, of Nazianzus, 32, 53, 58, 61n31, 63, 77, 148

Habakkuk, 163

Hades, 25, 38, 63, 75, 90, 94, 174, 218, 219

harlot, 38, 107, 181–83, 188, 196, 243. *See also* Babylon

harvest, 11, 161–62, 212, 234, 242, 243. *See also* judgment

heavenly powers, 85, 99, 157, 197, 201. *See also* angels

Hebrew language, 25, 59, 105n25, 108n57, 122, 143n10, 176, 186n32, 212, 227n18

Hebrews, 99, 106, 107, 169, 175. *See also* Jews

Heraclius, Emperor, 11, 12, 17, 95n4, 179n3

Hezekiah, 212n22, 213

Hierocles, 153n12

Hippolytus, 32, 54, 105n25, 147, 154, 151n1, 148n37

Holy Spirit, 21, 23, 24, 28, 40, 51, 52, 57, 58, 60, 62, 65, 67, 69, 71, 72, 73, 74, 75, 76, 77, 79, 80, 81, 83, 84, 85, 88, 89, 93, 101, 103, 107, 111, 114, 118, 121, 126, 133, 137, 141, 150, 156, 160, 165, 167, 171, 174, 177, 181, 182, 186, 189, 197, 199, 201, 207, 210, 215, 221, 222, 228, 231, 232, 233, 237, 240, 241, 242, 244, 245

horns, 87, 123, 138–39, 147, 151, 181, 182, 183, 188, 189, 196, 209

horse, horses, 36, 90–94, 122, 124, 163, 164, 193, 200, 201, 203, 204, 205, 234

hymnody, hymns, 17, 23, 32, 34, 35,

hymnody, hymns *(cont.)*
 58, 84, 155, 165, 171, 196, 197. *See also* song, singing
Huns, 11, 212

illumination, 75, 88, 165, 200; of intellect, 55; of Christ, 61, 71, 72, 78, 111, 199, 231, 235. *See also* baptism
Incarnation, 34n90, 37, 57, 58, 77, 79, 80, 84, 91, 121, 123n17, 133, 137, 144, 149, 202, 207, 236
India, 229
Irenaeus, 19, 32, 54, 60, 64, 83, 84, 99, 106n36, 108n57, 147, 151, 154n14, 187, 196n11, 206n40, 211n11, 214n32, 216
Isaiah, 58n17, 65, 71, 83, 87, 98n13, 100, 117, 137, 191, 205, 209, 217
Israel, Israelites, 68, 79, 98, 104, 106, 155, 208, 212, 212n22, 224, 230
Issachar, tribe of, 105, 108

James, Epistle of, 5n4
James, the Great, 103, 109, 150
James, son of Zebedee, 228
Jehosaphat, valley of, 120
Jerome, St., 6, 8
Jerusalem, city of, 12, 15, 16n21, 100, 103, 113, 132, 178, 179n3, 183, 192, 213, 214n30, 214n3, 243; heavenly, above, 22, 69, 76, 77, 158, 163, 167, 189, 220, 222, 223, 224, 232, 243, 244; New, 76, 131, 214, 220, 227
Jesus, 21n35, 29, 30, 55, 57n9, 58, 59, 60, 65, 93, 146, 153n12, 159, 160, 183, 198, 208, 240, 242
Jews, 39, 66, 75, 96, 98n13, 106, 107, 131, 133, 135, 170, 178, 179, 195, 213, 214
Jezebel, 70
Job, 104, 116, 139, 144, 152, 182
Joel, 115, 191, 212n19, 213n24
John, 5, 23, 26, 34. 39, 51, 53n15,

54n17, 54n20, 55, 56, 59, 62, 67n6, 84, 91, 103, 110, 112, 129, 206, 228, 241n14, 240, 242; bears witness, 235, 238, 241; called the Theologian, 51; death of, 130n9, 228n20; eats the scroll, 129–30; measures the temple, 130–31; Son of Thunder, 79; vision of, 8, 9, 33, 55, 60, 86, 98n13, 110, 127, 128, 129, 130, 137, 160, 178, 181, 183, 187, 193n7, 198, 200, 204, 210, 221, 223, 225, 231, 232, 236, 238
John, of Alexandria, 16n21
John, Apostle, 51, 53, 54n17, 54n20, 57, 62, 65, 130n9, 181, 183, 187, 193n7, 228, 238, 241n14, 242
John, Baptist and Forerunner, 71, 152n8
John Chrysostom, 58n19, 74n5
John of Damascus, 216n3
Joseph, tribe of, 106, 108
Josephus, Flavius, 32, 100, 212n19
Joshua, 62
Judah, 66, 72, 86, 104, 107
Judaizers, 76
Judeans, 100, 102
judgment, 59, 71, 79, 96, 104, 115, 120, 122, 123, 124, 127, 133, 135, 157, 159, 160, 165, 166, 169, 170, 174, 212, 216, 218; by apostles, by saints, 79, 80, 140, 208; of the devil, 142, 157, 210; of Antichrist and the false prophet, 204; of Babylon, of the harlot, 15n18, 181, 192, 194, 196, 197; divine judgments, 85, 86, 116, 122, 129, 242; self-judgment, 109, 117. *See also* harvest, Christ as Judge
Julian, Emperor, 147, 184
Justin, martyr and philosopher, 32, 54n18, 143 144n15, 206, 211n11, 214n33
Justinian, 11

king of the Romans, Antichrist as, 38, 148, 187, 196

lake of fire. *See* fire
Lamb, 24, 30, 59, 86, 87, 88, 90, 100, 109, 110, 111, 144, 149, 151, 154, 155, 156, 158, 165, 188, 197, 198, 223, 224, 225, 231, 232, 235
Lang, D. M., 40n119
Laodicea, 60, 77
Latin Apocalypse interpretation, 6–7, 8
Latin language, 7–8, 193, 227n18
Latin translation of commentary, 39, 40, 42
Laval, Université, ix
Leah, 107
lectionary, Apocalypse in, 4, 6, 41
Levi, tribe, 105, 106, 108
life, eternal. *See* eternal life
life, two kinds, 209–11
lion, lions, 72, 83, 84, 86, 90, 122, 124, 127, 128, 148; Christ as, 72, 84, 86
literal sense or meaning. *See* Andrew, Commentary, exegesis
Logos, Logos of God, 21, 29, 30, 34n90, 57, 58, 79, 90, 91, 123n17, 137, 149, 204
Lombard language, 39–40
Lombards, 11
Lot, 191
love of humankind, God's, Christ's, 61, 65, 68, 78, 80, 93, 100, 101, 106, 114, 133, 167, 172, 189, 192, 221; by angels, 119, 243
Luke, Evangelist, 25, 84, 86

Maccabees, 98n13, 213
Macedonians, 33, 185, 186
Makarios, 52n7, 10, 17n22
Maldfeld, Georg, 55n3
male child, 137, 140, 145
Manasseh, tribe of, 105, 108
Mango, Cyril, 212n20
Mark, Evangelist, 84,
mark of the beast. *See* Beast, mark of
marriage, 78, 198; of the Lamb, 197, 198, 223, 244

martyrs, 39, 67, 74, 91, 92, 96n5, 109, 113, 135, 141, 183, 184n19, 196, 208, 242, 244
martyrdom, 6, 30, 67, 113, 183n17, 184n19
Master, Christ as, 55, 73, 77, 85, 91, 96, 104, 108, 119, 133, 137, 197, 199, 220, 235, 238, 240
Matthew, Evangelist, 25, 84, 180n6, 229
Matthias, Apostle, 230
Maurice, Emperor, 11, 95n4
Maximin, Emperor, 94
Medes, 33, 185
Melchizedek, 61
merchants, 191, 193, 194, 195
Methodios, St., 19, 32, 54, 90, 91n5, 136, 137, 138, 139, 141, 147, 217
Metzger, Bruce, 166n29, 239n3
Miaphysite, Monophysite, 8, 34
Michael, Archangel, 123, 142
millennium, millennialism, 7, 32, 37, 207n44, 211n11. *See also* chiliasm, one thousand years
Monophysite. *See* Miaphysite
Montanism, 3, 5
Mother of God, 17, 136n9
moral sense of Scripture. *See* Andrew, Commentary, exegesis
Moses, 21, 24, 29, 57, 75, 113, 165, 166, 169, 174, 220

name(s), of God, Lamb, 149, 155; of beast, 147, 153; of devil, 143, 144; of the saved, 149; of Antichrist, 154; of the Lamb, 155; of Babylon, 158
Naphtali, tribe of, 104, 107
Nebuchadnezzar, 185, 186
Nerses of Lampron, 39, 40
Nestorians, Nestorianism, 34n90
new heaven and earth, 88, 217
new name, 69, 76
New Rome, 34, 38, 183, 184, 186, 187
new song, 87, 88, 155, 156

New Testament, 3, 5, 6, 7, 24, 25, 39, 40, 41, 53n15, 82, 87, 131, 155

Nicolaitans, 64, 68, 70

Nineveh, 71, 185

Nino, 186

Noah, 163, 164

non-Chalcedonian, theology, churches, 7, 10. *See also* Miaphysite and Monophysite

nous, 137

Octavian, 148n37

Oikoumenios, 5, 7–10, 19, 21, 23, 24, 29, 30, 32, 33, 34, 36, 57n7, 82n4, 90n3, 90n4, 96n5, 102n1, 106n32, 115n1, 116n4, 117n7, 120n5, 120n6, 120n7, 121n9, 122n12, 123n16, 127n1, 127n2, 127n3, 131n11, 131n12, 136n8, 247n29, 151n1, 159n8, 181n10, 199n17, 204n30, 218n13, 221n32, 225n8, 226n9, 236n65, 239n3; Oikoumenios manuscripts, 9, 10

Old Testament, 25, 27, 31, 82, 98, 131

Oller, Thomas, 40n120

one thousand four hundred forty-four saved, 104, 155

one thousand years, 187, 205, 206, 207, 210, 211. *See also* millennium, chiliasm

order, in heaven, 90, 112, 128, 227; of creation, 102

Oriental Orthodox, 34n90

Origen, 52n8, 153n12, 216n3

Ottoman Turks, 6

Papias, 32, 54, 142, 143n6

Passion, of Christ, 87, 184, 205, 222

Patmos, 59, 60

patristic exegesis and interpretation, 3, 4, 6, 18–19, 25, 29, 32, 37, 38, 40n120. *See also* Fathers

patristic tradition, 5, 6, 7, 58, 148n35

Paul, St., Apostle, 5, 51n1, 58, 103, 105, 217, 224, 227; cited as "the Apostle," 63, 76, 79, 80, 87, 93, 97, 98, 99, 106, 117, 125, 136, 138, 140, 142, 156, 160, 165, 170, 177, 178, 189, 204, 211, 212, 214, 216, 219, 235, 240

pearl, pearls, 182, 193, 194, 230

Peltanus, Theodore, 42

Pergamum, 12, 23, 60, 67

Persia, Persians, 11, 12, 15, 16, 17, 38, 95n4, 148, 175, 179n3, 183, 185, 186, 190, 195, 213, 214n30

Peter, 71, 148, 153, 183, 227

Pharaoh, 163, 169, 174, 180, 234n51

Philadelphia, church of, 60, 75–77

philanthropos, God as. *See* love of humankind

Philip, Apostle, 229

Philo of Alexandria, 106n30

Phocas, tyrant, 11, 95n4

Pilate, Pontius, 57, 90

prayer, prayers, 23, 29, 54, 58, 74n5, 87, 104, 107n50, 112, 113, 137n18, 170, 195, 244

precious stones, 22, 81, 182, 193, 194, 224, 227–30, 242; amethyst, 230; anthracite, 237–38; beryl, 228; carnelian, 81, 229; carbuncle, 227n18; chalcedony, 227; chrysolite, 229; chrysoprase, 229; emerald, 81, 82, 228; jasper, 81–82, 226, 227; onyx, 228; sapphire, 227, 229, 230; topaz, 227n18, 229

priest, priests, 31, 58, 59, 61, 64, 84, 87, 91, 105, 106, 108, 209, 210, 224, 227

prophecy, 12, 15n18, 26, 33, 53, 56, 71n25, 75, 84, 86, 96n5, 98n13, 120, 128, 129, 130, 131, 132, 133, 134, 164, 169, 189, 192, 195, 196, 198, 199, 212, 213, 215, 217, 236, 238, 241; Book of Revelation as, 5, 13, 14, 26, 32, 33, 56, 130, 140, 196n11, 189, 196, 212

prophets, 33, 39, 51, 53, 70, 87, 96, 97, 128, 129, 134, 135, 167, 169,

170, 194, 195, 196, 211n11, 212, 217, 233, 235, 236, 238, 243. *See also* false prophet

Psalter, Psalms, Book of, 55n1, 75, 83, 108, 143, 158, 161, 165, 174, 175, 177, 192, 202, 214, 217, 220

pseudo-Christ, 97, 100, 132, 168. *See also* Antichrist, false Christ, Beast of the sea

pseudo-Dionysios. *See* Dionysios

punishment, 22, 36, 78, 97, 98, 100, 103, 112, 113, 115, 116, 117, 120, 122, 127, 134, 136, 159, 162, 163, 164, 191–92, 210, 242, 243; is self-chosen, 36, 173–74, 192, 203; of devil, 144–45, 207, 210, 244; purpose of, 22, 36, 42, 94, 112, 114, 117, 119–20, 124, 133, 167, 170, 173, 180, 191–92, 197, 203, 219, 239, 243; variety and magnitude of, 156, 159, 163, 164, 191–92, 197, 218, 219, 243. *See also* afflictions, eternal punishment

Rachel, 106n30

rainbow, 81–82, 127, 242

Raphael, 123

repentance, 14, 22, 31, 36, 64, 68, 70, 73, 75, 78, 93, 107, 116, 119, 124, 125, 167, 170, 172, 173, 180, 192

repose, of the saints, 81, 112, 129, 149, 150, 198, 239; God's throne as, 81, 109. *See also* eternal rest

rest. *See* repose, eternal rest

resurrection, 57, 60, 90n4, 100, 105, 116, 134, 135, 140. 211, 216, 217, 240; false resurrection, 151, 153; first resurrection, 209, 210, 211

Reuben, 104, 107

Revelation, Book of. *See* Apocalypse

robes, white, 30, 97, 109, 110; washed, 110, 111, 177, 239n3; of Christ and angels, 60, 166, 201, 202. *See also* garments

Roman Empire, 11, 12, 16, 33, 34, 38, 94, 95n4, 102, 103, 106, 140,

147, 148, 187, 196, 196n11, 214n33

Roman torture, 67n6, 76, 181, 183, 184

Rome, city of, 38, 76, 181, 183, 185, 187. *See also* New Rome

Romulus, 186

Russian acceptance of Apocalypse, 40

Sabbath age, 60. *See also* seventh day

Sabbath rest, 33, 112, 226

saint, saints, 40, 51, 71, 72, 86, 87, 97, 103, 110, 124, 130, 132, 135, 141, 149, 156, 210, 211, 213, 242, 243; virtues of the, 97, 103, 130, 144, 146, 150, 155, 156, 159, 165, 176, 198, 199, 202, 205, 216, 226, 233, 234, 243; endurance of, 149, 159; prayers of, praises of, 87, 96, 112, 113, 155, 196, 203; rewards of, 38, 69, 76, 79, 80, 81, 97, 99, 101, 111, 112, 129, 136, 149, 150, 164, 167, 179, 187, 194, 195, 200, 209, 216, 218, 220, 221, 223, 225, 231, 239, 240, 244; persecution of, blood of, 38, 97, 149, 169, 183, 195

Samaritans, 178, 179

Sardis, 12, 60, 73–74

Satan, 31, 66, 67, 70, 75, 147, 148, 151, 152, 184, 209; binding and loosening of, 37, 205, 210, 211, 212; all of, 142, 143; meaning of word, 25, 143

Schmid, Josef, 3n1, 40n118, 41, 53n14, 55n3, 147n28

scroll, 20, 31, 85–87, 99, 127, 129–30, 242

Scythian nation, 212, 213

sea, 11, 31, 53, 83, 88, 102, 103, 116, 127–28, 129, 138, 144, 145, 147, 151, 157, 168, 169, 194, 195, 209, 211, 218, 219, 220, 225, 229; of glass, 83, 164, 165, 243. *See also* Beast of the sea

seal, sealing: sealed faithful, 24,
    103–4, 114, 121, 155, 243; scroll
    with seven seals, 85–87, 242; first
    seal, 90–91; second seal, 91–92;
    third seal, 92–93; fourth seal,
    94–95; fifth seal, 95–97; sixth
    seal, 13, 38, 97; seventh seal, 112;
    Oikoumenios's interpretation of
    the seven seals, 90n4, 96n5; sealed
    angel, 103; sealed tribes, 104–6;
    Satan sealed, 205; John told to
    seal, 128; John told not to seal, 238
Sebeos, 95n4, 183n17
Second Coming. See Christ, return of
second death. See death, second
Sennacherib, 213
seraphim, 34n91, 58, 83, 197. See also
    angels
Sergius I, Patriarch, 16–17, 18
seven angels. See angels
seven churches. See churches
seven kings, kingdoms, 33, 38, 185–
    87. See also successive kingdoms
seven, number, 56, 60, 112, 164, 226
seven spirits, 20, 21, 56, 57, 73, 83,
    87
seventh day, age, period of days, 33,
    34, 38, 56, 129, 147. See also weekly
    period
Severus of Antioch, 8, 9
Shahin, 16
Shahrbaraz, 16n21
Simeon, tribe of, 105, 107, 108
Simon Magus, 148, 153
Simon the Zealot, Apostle, 230
Sinai, Mt., 113, 178
Sinaiticus, Codex, 41, 239n3
six hundred sixty-six, meanings of,
    154
skopos. See Andrew, Commentary,
    exegesis
slavery, slaves, 100, 152, 203; by
    Persians, 12, 16n21; blessed of
    Christ, 80, 100; of the devil, 116,
    146, 150; of mammon, 125; of sin,
    100, 195, 203

Slavonic translation and manuscripts,
    39, 40, 41
Slavs, 11, 17
Smyrna, 60, 66–67
Sodom, 132, 191. See also Gomorrah
Solomon, 65, 80, 139, 177, 211;
    Christ as spiritual Solomon, 225
song, singing, 87, 88, 217, 155–56,
    165, 237
"soon," Christ's arrival, 55, 64, 68,
    236, 239; meaning of, 8n6, 55,
    236, 239, 242
Spirit. See Holy Spirit, seven spirits
spiritual sense. See Andrew,
    Commentary, exegesis
Steinhauser, Kenneth, 7n5
Stratos, Andreas, 16n21
successive kingdoms, 33, 38, 147–48,
    185–86
Suggit, John, 5n3, 8n6
Susa, 185
symbols in Revelation. See Andrew,
    Commentary, exegesis
Syria, 213

Tabernacle, 113, 123, 133, 166, 220
Tabor, Mt., 59
teachers, 91, 96, 116, 131, 146, 154,
    204; Babylon as, 182; Christ as,
    62, 63
Temple, of God, 76, 110, 111, 130,
    136, 167, 214; of Jerusalem, 39,
    100, 214; Antichrist will sit in,
    39, 214; measuring the, 130–31;
    heavenly, 162, 166–67; pagan, 206;
    God as Temple, 231; Temple of
    Spirit, 244
textual variations. See Andrew,
    Commentary, exegesis
Thaddeus, Apostle, 229
Theodore of Mopsuestia, 212n19,
    212n22, 213n24
Theodoret of Cyrus, 212n20
theoria. See Andrew, Commentary,
    exegesis
Theotokos, 136

therapeutike, 4n2
Thomas, Apostle, 229
Thomson, R. W., 40n117, 95n4, 183n17
throne, of God, 18, 20, 22, 24, 30, 31, 56, 79, 81, 82, 83, 85, 87, 88, 100, 109, 110, 111, 113, 130, 141, 155, 178, 196, 197, 216, 221, 232, 233, 235; of apostles or elders, 79, 82, 135, 136, 208; of Satan, 67, 148; of Antichrist, 173, 243; of Ephesus, archpriest, 64; of Emperor Maurice, 11, 95n4; of Emperor Julian, 147n34
Thyatira, 60, 69–72
Titus, 100
Treadgold, Warren, 95
Tree of Life, 65, 233, 234, 239, 241
Trikki, 8
Trinity, 21, 29, 32, 34, 57, 84, 116, 139, 220, 225
Trisagion, 32, 34
tropology, *tropos*. *See* Andrew, Commentary, exegesis
two witnesses, 71n28, 131–34
Tyconius, 7, 8
typology. *See* Andrew, Commentary, exegesis

Uriel, 123

Valens, 147
Vespasian, 97, 100

Victorinus, 6, 7, 8, 153n12
virgins, virginity, 78, 136m9, 137, 155, 156
virtue, 14, 27, 29, 35, 74, 78, 79, 82, 83, 97, 103, 108, 127, 138, 140, 141, 143, 156, 165, 166, 177, 180, 189, 198, 201, 220, 227, 229, 230, 233, 242
Visigoths, 11

wages, of reward or punishment, 35, 36, 52, 59 105 108, 112, 135, 149, 167, 195, 237, 239, 242
wedding, of soul, 80, 108, 167. *See also* bridal chamber of Christ
weekly period, time of present life, 108, 134, 147, 164. *See also* seventh day
Weinrich, William, 21n35
Whitby, Michael and Mary, 16n21
white garments. *See* garments
wilderness, 141, 145, 181. *See also* desert
witnesses. *See* two witnesses
word-association. *See* Andrew, Commentary, exegesis

Zebulun, tribe of, 105, 108
Zechariah, 87, 180
Zion, 137, 155

INDEX OF HOLY SCRIPTURE

Old Testament

Genesis
1.11–12: 234
1.31: 219
2.21: 223
3.5: 143
3.14: 145
3.15: 140
7.11: 163
11.9: 158
12.1: 105
14.11: 234
18.27: 146
19.17: 191
29.32: 104, 107
29.33: 105, 107, 108
29.34: 105
29.35: 66, 104
30.6: 109
30.8: 104
30.11: 104
30.13: 104
30.16: 105
30.20: 105
30.24: 106
35.18: 106, 107
41.51: 105
49.9–10: 72
49.11: 164
49.13: 105
49.19: 104

Exodus
3.1–6: 165
3.14: 57

4.21: 180
7.3: 180
7.14–25: 169
9.12: 180
9.16: 169
9.34–35: 180
14.4: 180
14.7: 234
14.8: 180
14.9: 234
14.17: 180
14.23: 234
19.10: 167
19.16–19: 113, 178
23.8: 78
25: 166, 220
25.8–22: 114
28.12: 224
28.17–21: 227
28.36–38 (28.32–34): 235
33.12: 75
33.17: 75
39.8–14: 227
39.10: 227

Leviticus
26.12: 64, 220, 231

Numbers
25: 68
25.9: 68

Deuteronomy
4.24: 244

4.34: 68
10.9: 106
11.14: 234
12.12: 106
16.19: 78
17.16: 234
20.1: 234
32.14: 164
32.33: 163
33.22: 72

Joshua
5.14: 62

Judges
5.4: 98

1 Samuel
15.22: 51

2 Samuel
5.9: 133
22.8: 98

1 Kings
7.23–25: 225
16.31–21.26: 70

2 Kings
1.9–12: 214
19.35: 213

1 Chronicles
16.32: 234

2 Chronicles
4.2–4: 225
32.21: 213

Tobit
8.3: 190

Job
1.8–12: 143
1.9–11: 144
2.3–6: 143
2.4–5: 144
34.7: 182
40.14: 139
41.15 (LXX): 144
41.24 (LXX): 139
42: 104

Psalms
2.2: 192
6.5(6): 174
7.1: 237
7.2: 237
9.6 (LXX): 143
18(17).7: 98
18(17).10: 161
19(18).4: 60
23(22).2: 227
29(28).7 (LXX):
   165
30(29).6: 192
32(31).9: 133, 172
34(33).7: 214
34(33).8: 201
36(35).6: 85
38(37).3: 167
42(41).4: 171
45(44).10: 105, 108
45(44).10–11: 220
45(44).16: 90, 107
48(47).4: 90, 192
51(50).4: 200
51(50).7: 177
51(50).10: 232
56(55).2: 122
62(61).12: 59

64(63).3: 172
65(64).4: 108
68(67).8: 98
73(72).27: 158
85.4(84.5): 133
86.7 (LXX): 199
87(86).7: 113
90(89).4: 55
94(93).13: 113
94(93).19: 106, 108
95(94).4: 64
102(101).26: 219
104(103).3: 83
104(103).30: 217
105(104).8: 206
106(105).28–30: 68
110(109).4: 61
114(113).7: 98
119(118).36–37: 160
119(118).60 (LXX):
   237
119(118).71: 133
119(118).91: 55
122(121).4–5: 208
125(124).3: 96, 164,
   175, 202
139(138).16: 85
139(138).18: 109,
   226, 232
140(139).3: 172
143(142).2: 133,
   160

Proverbs
3.12: 133
3.18: 65
24.12: 59
26.9: 53
26.11: 240
26.25: 139
30.29 (LXX): 186
30.31 (LXX): 186

Ecclesiastes
2.5: 234
9.8: 80, 177

Song of Songs
1.9: 163
2.13: 99
4.8: 62
8.11–12: 211

Wisdom
1.3: 219
3.1: 218
11.16: 159
39.26: 164

Isaiah
1.14: 205
1.18: 232
6.2: 83–84
6.3: 58
9.2–7: 71
9.6: 201
11.1–5: 71, 87
11.2: 83
11.4: 215
13.21: 190
14.12: 31, 117
14.12–15: 71
23.4: 53
26.14: 209
34.13–14: 190
35.10: 199, 221
40.3: 84
41.1: 100
50.5: 65
51.11: 199, 221
51.17: 162
52.7: 62
60.3: 231
61.2: 233
65.17–18: 217
66.7: 137
66.22: 217

Jeremiah
3.3: 183
24.1–5: 99
25.15: 162

Ezekiel
9.2–11: 103
9.8: 166
10.6: 113
13.21: 166
18.23: 36n100, 203, 222
18.32: 36n100, 203, 222
20.8: 166
20.13: 166
20.21: 166
22.22: 166
22.31: 166
28.16: 142
30.15: 166
36.18: 166
38.8: 213
39.9: 212

Daniel
7.7: 196
7.7–8: 188
7.8: 196
7.9–10: 61
7.13: 61
7.18: 179
7.19: 196
7.20: 196

7.22: 179
7.27: 179
8.10: 140
8.17: 62
8.26: 128
9.24: 128
10.5–11: 128
10.7–9: 110
10.9–12: 62
12.3: 98
12.4: 128
12.9: 128
12.12: 204

Hosea
7.11: 186
10.11: 186

Joel
2.10: 119
2.11: 176
2.22: 234
2.30: 115

Amos
8.9–11: 79
9.11: 133

Micah
7.18: 170, 222

Nahum
3.4: 183

Haggai
2.6: 98, 178

Zechariah
4.3: 132
4.10: 87
4.11–14: 132
5.7: 180
9.16: 220

Malachi
3.1: 84
3.1–2: 72
3.6: 201
3.20 (LXX): 62, 71, 72, 138, 173, 201, 231, 245
4.1: 100
4.2: 62, 71, 72, 138, 173, 201, 231, 245
4.5: 176

New Testament

Matthew
3.3: 71
4.11: 142
5.5: 88, 107
5.8: 104
5.16: 237
6.10: 241
6.13: 215
6.24: 125, 188
6.33: 106, 108
7.1: 109
7.13: 115, 151, 163
7.14: 150
7.15: 151

7.23: 126
8.31: 124, 184
9.13: 170, 222
9.17: 141
10.18: 201
10.28: 157
10.32: 74
10.34: 92
10.39: 145
11.26: 203
11.28: 189
11.29: 199
12,7: 170, 222
12.29: 205

12.41: 71
12.43: 190
12.43–45: 139
13.7: 78
13.8: 106
13.13–15: 58
13.22: 78
13.23: 136, 162, 234
13.24–30: 68
13.30: 124, 161
13.43: 74, 235
13.44: 66
13.46: 230
16.27: 59

17.1–8: 235
17.5: 59
17.10–13: 71
18.8: 158
18.10: 63
19.8: 169
19.28: 74, 79, 82, 136
20.25: 100
21.19–22: 99
22.1–10: 30n76 82, 108
22.1–13: 198
22.11–12: 80
22.11–13: 167, 177
22.12: 177
22.30: 211
23.29–31: 170
23.30: 195
24.1–44: 100
24.14: 206
24.16–22: 117
24.19–23: 119
24.21: 180
24.22: 121
24.24: 98
24.29: 76
24.30: 134
24.30–31: 134
24.36: 112, 236
24.42–43: 74
24.43: 236
24.51: 174
25.1–13: 30n76, 82, 108, 198
25.21: 237
25.31: 59
25.33: 69, 104, 237
25.34: 69, 126, 189
25.41: 158, 163, 207
28.18: 88
28.19: 165

Mark
1.2–3: 84
1.3: 143

1.12–13: 145
1.13: 142
2.19: 198
2.22: 141
3.17: 79
3.27: 205
4.7: 78
4.8: 106
4.12: 58
4.20: 136, 163, 234
5.6: 221
5.10: 190
5.12: 184
5.13: 124
8.37: 59
9.2–8: 235
10.5: 169
10.42: 100
11.13–14: 99
11.20–24: 99
12.25: 211
13.1–37: 100
13.6: 59
13.10: 206
13.14–20: 117
13.19: 180
13.20: 119, 121
13.24: 76
13.32: 112, 236
14.62: 134
16.15: 165

Luke
4.1–13: 143, 145
4.18–19: 71
4.21: 86
5.37: 141
6.15: 230
6.37: 109
7.47: 107
8.7: 78
8.8: 106
8.14: 78
8.31: 124, 206
8.32: 184
8.32–33: 124

9.26: 59
9.28–36: 235
10.20: 155
10.21: 203
10.30: 93
11.2: 241
11.4: 215
11.21: 205
11.24: 190
11.24–26: 139
11.32: 71
11.47–50: 170
12.8: 74
12.31: 106
12.35: 236
12.37: 189
12.39: 236
12.39–40: 74
12.46: 174
15.7: 170
15.10: 170
16.13: 124, 188
16.22: 198
16.26: 163
17.21–37: 100
17.33: 145
18.9: 201
19.9: 107
19.17: 71
20.36: 211
21.27: 59, 134
22.30: 79, 82, 136
22.31: 143
23.43: 107, 198

John
1.1: 57, 84
1.1–3: 201
1.4–9: 138
1.9: 63, 201
1.14: 149
1.16: 79, 152
1.19: 152
1.29: 86
1.32: 152
1.36: 86

John *(cont.)*
3.5: 138
3.6: 210
3.8: 210
3.18: 241
3.19: 201
3.31: 210
4.34: 203
5.22: 202
5.24: 57
5.35: 71
5.43: 212
6.35: 69
6.48: 69
6.50–51: 69
6.50–55: 69
7.37–39: 221
7.38: 25, 62
8.12: 138, 201
8.51: 57
9.4: 56
9.5: 138
10.9: 230, 240
10.11–16: 201
10.12: 240
10.16: 88
12.2: 106
12.31: 142
12.31–13.1: 142, 147
12.46: 138, 201
14.2: 124, 156, 219,
   234
14.6: 201, 221, 230,
   235
14.27: 89
15.1: 162, 163
16.11: 142
21.18–19: 227
21.24: 238

Acts
1.7: 53
1.8: 165
1.9: 79, 134, 161
1.13: 230
1.26: 230

2.3: 165
9.4: 140
10.42: 176
12.2: 228
16.26: 98
17.28: 231
21.18–20: 103
28.25: 58

Romans
1.18: 125
1.23: 201
1.25: 125
2.6: 59
2.28: 66, 76
5.5: 52
6.4: 88, 210
7.5: 88
7.6: 88
7.22: 155
8.13: 209
8.15: 241
8.17: 79, 110, 160,
   208
8.18: 149, 160, 221
8.19: 217
8.19–23: 103
8.20: 216
8.21: 120, 216,
   219
9.5: 133
10.15: 62
10.18: 60
11.25–26: 106
11.33: 170
12.1: 59, 170
12.10: 199
12.15: 130
14.4: 109
15.7: 108
16.20: 71
17.28: 220

1 Corinthians
1.24: 201
1.30: 201

2.8: 235
2.9: 69, 136, 231
2.10: 85
2.14: 137
3.2: 229
3.9: 93, 202
3.13: 165
3.16: 105
4.5: 224
5.10: 59
7.31: 99, 216
9.24: 174
9.24–25: 160
10.1–2: 138
10.13: 76, 141
11.31: 117
11.32: 133
13.8: 52
13.9: 51
13.10: 156
13.12: 235
14.17: 211
15.24: 189
15.26: 218
15.28: 189
15.41: 156, 233
15.51–52: 204

2 Corinthians
1.12: 215
1.21–22: 104
1.22: 197
2.15: 69, 87,
   105
4.6: 199
4.10: 160, 227
4.16: 88, 155
5.1: 220
5.3: 177
5.5: 197
5.17: 88
6.1: 222
6.11: 224
6.14: 143, 232
6.15: 144
6.16: 105, 131

11.28: 224
12.2: 227
12.4: 198
12.7: 143

Galatians
3.24: 52
4.6: 241
4.18: 138, 140
4.26: 69
6.15: 88

Ephesians
1.5: 203
1.9: 203
1.13: 103
2.1: 218
2.2: 124, 141, 142
2.5: 218
2.14: 88
2.18: 224
2.20: 220
3.16: 155
4.13: 140, 207
4.15: 77
4.30: 103
6.12: 80, 141, 142
6.17: 62

Philippians
2.7: 120
2.13: 203
2.16: 63
3.2: 240
3.13: 105
3.19: 145, 154
3.20: 37n104, 120, 145, 152
4.9: 72

Colossians
1.5: 201
1.18: 157
1.24: 157
2.3: 75, 99, 236

2.9: 136
2.12: 210
2.13: 218
3.2: 81, 230
3.3: 136
3.5: 125, 155, 165, 209
3.10: 88
3.20: 227

1 Thessalonians
4.17: 79, 141, 203
5.1: 53
5.2: 74
5.5: 104, 109
5.17: 104
5.23: 5

2 Thessalonians
2.3: 212
2.3–12: 214
2.4: 214
2.8: 204, 215
2.9: 132, 176, 184
2.12: 212
2.15: 73
3.6: 73

1 Timothy
1.17: 201
2.4: 36n99, 203, 206, 245
2.5: 113
3.15: 76
4.3: 125
5.21: 57
6.11: 54

2 Timothy
1.13–14: 73
2.5: 92, 141
2.12: 79, 150, 202, 235
2.19: 131
2.25: 36n99, 203

3.5: 125
3.7: 36n99, 203
3.16: 52
4.8: 141

Titus
1.16: 125
2.13: 51

Hebrews
1.7: 139
1.14: 162, 236
2.10: 156
4.9: 112
4.12: 62
4.15: 79
6.1: 210
6.13: 128
9.11: 220
9.14: 210
11.38: 141
11.39: 97
11.40: 97
12.4: 207
12.6: 133, 167
12.13: 93
12.22: 155
12.23: 155
12.26: 178
12.26–27: 98
13.20: 201

James
1.3–4: 150
1.15: 123
4.12: 109

1 Peter
1.7: 107
1.19: 215
2.5: 59
2.6: 220
2.9: 59
2.25: 201
4.12: 62

1 Peter (cont.)
  5.4: 67, 70
  5.8: 143, 184
  5.13: 183

2 Peter
  1.19: 71, 240
  2.19: 116, 150
  2.22: 230

1 John
  4.1: 64
  5.7–8: 186
  5.20: 65

Revelation
  1: 26
  1.1: 55, 236n61
  1.2: 33, 55
  1.3: 14, 56
  1.4: 20, 21n35, 29,
       32, 34, 56, 59,
       60n27, 84
  1.4–5: 84n16
  1.5: 58n14, 84
  1.6: 58
  1.7: 59
  1.8: 30, 53n15, 59
  1.9: 59
  1.10: 60
  1.11: 60
  1.12: 60
  1.13: 60, 145n25
  1.14: 61, 69n17
  1.15: 20, 24, 61, 62
  1.16: 62, 73n1
  1.17: 62, 239n2
  1.18: 62, 63
  1.19: 63
  1.20: 63
  2: 26
  2.1: 63
  2.2–5: 64
  2.5–6: 64
  2.7: 65
  2.8: 66, 239n2

  2.9: 66, 76n10
  2.10: 67
  2.11: 67, 134n2
  2.12: 67
  2.13: 67
  2.14: 68
  2.15: 68
  2.16: 68
  2.17: 22, 68–69
  2.18: 69
  2.19: 68–70
  2.20: 69–70
  2.21: 70
  2.22–23: 70
  2.23–25: 70
  2.26–28: 71
  2.28: 31
  2.28–29: 71
  3: 26
  3.1: 73
  3.2: 73
  3.3: 73–74
  3.4: 74
  3.5: 74
  3.6: 74
  3.7: 25, 34, 75
  3.8: 75
  3.9: 75–76
  3.10: 76
  3.11: 76
  3.12: 76–77
  3.13: 77
  3.14: 77
  3.15: 77
  3.16: 77–78
  3.16–17: 78
  3.18: 78
  3.20: 79
  3.21: 79
  4: 24–25, 26
  4.1: 81
  4.2–3: 81
  4.4: 22, 30, 82
  4.5: 82
  4.5–6: 83
  4.6: 31, 83

  4.6–8: 20
  4.7: 83–84
  4.8: 35, 84
  4.9: 85
  4.10: 85
  5.1: 85
  5.2: 86
  5.3: 86
  5.4: 86
  5.5: 86
  5.6: 86–87
  5.7–8: 87
  5.9–10: 87
  5.11–13: 88
  5.14: 88–89
  6.1: 90
  6.2: 90–91
  6.3: 91
  6.4: 91–92
  6.5: 92
  6.5–6: 92–93
  6.7: 94
  6.8: 94–95
  6.9–10: 96
  6.11: 97
  6.12: 13
  6.12–13: 31, 97–98
  6.14: 20, 99–100,
       179n5
  6.14–17: 100–101
  7.1: 102
  7.2: 103
  7.3: 24, 103–4
  7.4: 104
  7.4–8: 107–9
  7.5: 104
  7.6: 104–5
  7.7: 105
  7.8: 105–6
  7.9: 30
  7.9–10: 109
  7.11–12: 110
  7.13: 110
  7.14–15: 110
  7.15: 167n35
  7.16: 111

7.17: 24, 111
8.1–2: 112
8.3: 112–13
8.4–5: 113
8.5–6: 113–14
8.7: 115
8.7–9.21: 26
8.8–9: 116
8.10–11: 117–18
8.12: 119
8.13: 119
9.1–4: 24
9.1–5: 120
9.6: 121
9.7–9: 122
9.9–12: 122
9.13–16: 123
9.17–19: 124
9.20–21: 125–26
10.1: 127
10.2–3: 127
10.4: 128
10.5–6: 128
10.7: 129
10.8: 129
10.9: 129
10.10: 130
10.11: 130
11.1–2: 130, 132
11.2: 132n17
11.3–4: 71n28, 131
11.5–6: 132
11.6: 168n1
11.7–8: 132–33
11.9–10: 133
11.11–12: 134
11.12–13: 134
11.13–14: 135
11.15–17: 135
11.16: 168
11.18: 135–36
11.19: 136
12: 26
12.1: 24, 136–38
12.2: 138
12.3: 138–39

12.4: 140
12.5: 140–41
12.6: 141
12.7–8: 142
12.9: 143
12.10: 144
12.11–12: 144–45
12.13–14: 145
12.15–16: 146
12.17: 146, 239n3
12.18–13.1: 147
13.1: 147
13.2: 148
13.3: 148
13.3–4: 149
13.5–6: 149
13.7–8: 149
13.9–10: 149–50
13.11: 151
13.12–13: 152
13.14: 152
13.14–17: 152–53
13.18: 154
14.1: 155
14.2–3: 155
14.3–5: 156
14.6–7: 157
14.8: 158
14.9–10: 158–59
14.10: 162n10
14.11: 159
14.12: 239n3,
   159–60
14.13: 160
14.14: 161
14.15–16: 161–62
14.17: 162
14.18: 162–63,
   175n8
14.19: 163
14.20: 163–64
15.1: 164
15.2: 164–65
15.3–4: 165
15.5–6: 166
15.6: 25

15.7: 166
15.8: 166–67
15.8–16.1: 167
16.1: 167
16.2: 168
16.3: 168–69
16.4–6: 169–70
16.7: 170–71
16.8–9: 172
16.10–11: 173–75
16.12: 175
16.13: 176
16.14: 176
16.15–16: 176–77
16.17–18: 178
16.19: 178–79
16.20: 179–80
16.21: 173n4, 180
17.1–3: 181–82
17.3: 38n112
17.4: 57, 182
17.5: 182
17.6: 38n113
17.6–7: 183–84
17.8: 184–85
17.9: 38, 185–86
17.10: 33, 38n108,
   187
17.11: 187
17.12: 188
17.13–14: 188
17.14: 57n12,
   188n37
17.15–18: 188–89
17.18: 181n11
18.1: 190
18.2–3: 190–91
18.4–5: 191
18.6–7: 191–92
18.8: 15n18, 192
18.9–10: 192–93
18.11–12: 193
18.12–13: 193
18.13: 193
18.13–14: 193
18.15–17: 193–94

Revelation *(cont.)*
18.17–19: 194
18.20: 194–95
18.21–24: 195–96
19.1–4: 196–97
19.5: 197
19.6–7: 197
19.7: 198n16
19.7–9: 198
19.10: 198–99
19.11–12: 200
19.12: 201
19.13: 201
19.14: 201
19.15: 202
19.16: 202
19.17: 202–3
19.17–18: 203
19.19: 204
19.20: 204–5
19.21: 205
20: 37–38, 54n18
20.1–3: 54, 184n22, 205–7
20.4: 54, 208–9
20.5–6: 209–10

20.6: 67, 134n2
20.7–8: 211–13
20.9–10: 213–16
20.11: 216–17
20.12: 217–18
20.13: 218
20.14: 67, 134n2
20.14–15: 218–19
21: 22
21.1: 219–20
21.2: 69, 220
21.3–4: 220
21.4: 220–21
21.5–6: 221
21.7: 222
21.8: 67, 134, 222
21.9: 223
21.10–11: 223–24
21.12: 224
21.13: 225
21.14: 225
21.15: 225
21.16: 226
21.17: 226
21.18: 134n2, 226
21.19: 227–28

21.20: 228–30
21.21: 230–31
21.22: 231
21.23: 111n65, 231
21.24–25: 231–32
21.26–27: 232
22.1: 24
22.1–2: 232–33
22.2: 233–34
22.3: 234n52
22.3–4: 234–35
22.5: 111n69, 235
22.6: 236–37
22.7: 236–37
22.8–9: 238
22.10: 238–39
22.11–12: 239
22.13: 239
22.14: 167n35, 239–40
22.15: 240
22.16: 31, 240
22.17: 111n75, 241
22.18–19: 241–42
22.20–21: 242